ADVA
POVERTY AND AUSTERITY...

"Gregg Olsen brilliantly deconstructs the individualistic concep-
tions of poverty routinely rehearsed in academic studies and government reports. He shows that poverty is rooted in systemic dynamics
of contemporary capitalism and that uprooting it requires broad
change to the direction of economic democracy. Rigorously argued
and researched, clearly and elegantly written, this book is a must-
read for anyone concerned about an urgent and pressing issue of
our time."

— *Joel Bakan, University of British Columbia*

"For two decades Gregg Olsen has been one of my 'go-to' authors for
understanding the source of social and health inequalities in Canada
and elsewhere. In this book, Olsen turns his sharp eye to the poverty
situation in Canada, the UK, and the US. In addition to documenting
the sources and effects of public policies that create poverty, Olsen provides ways of transcending the problematic present."

— *Dennis Raphael, York University*

"In bringing together the issues of poverty and homelessness, this book
deals with two of the most pressing issues of our time. It combines rich
historical detail with a clear focus on the future and what might be
done to address these issues. This book is essential reading for anyone
interested in how and why poverty persists in some of the wealthiest
nations of the world."

— *Tracy Shildrick, Newcastle University*

"Gregg Olsen has written a powerful book that clearly articulates the
meanings of poverty, major theoretical accounts, and empirics across
Canada, the UK, and the US. Highly accessible, rigorous, and erudite,
this book is simply the best social science on poverty in contemporary
liberal capitalist societies in years."

— *Larry W. Isaac, Vanderbilt University*

"All countries could do better at reducing poverty if they had universal, generous, employment-supporting social programs. But Gregg Olsen shows us in this valuable book that even in nations with a modest welfare state, such as Canada, the UK, and the US, policy choices can make a big difference."

– Lane Kenworthy, University of California, San Diego

POVERTY

AND

AUSTERITY

AMID

PROSPERITY

A Comparative Introduction

Gregg M. Olsen

UNIVERSITY OF TORONTO PRESS
Toronto Buffalo London

© University of Toronto Press 2021
Toronto Buffalo London
utorontopress.com
Printed in the U.S.A.

ISBN 978-1-4875-0984-2 (cloth)   ISBN 978-1-4875-0987-3 (EPUB)
ISBN 978-1-4875-0985-9 (paper)   ISBN 978-1-4875-0986-6 (PDF)

Library and Archives Canada Cataloguing in Publication

Title: Poverty and austerity amid prosperity : a comparative introduction/
    Gregg M. Olsen.
Names: Olsen, Gregg M. (Gregg Matthew), 1956– author.
Description: Includes bibliographical references and index.
Identifiers: Canadiana (print) 2021021547X | Canadiana (ebook) 20210215526 |
    ISBN 9781487509859 (paper) | ISBN 9781487509842 (cloth) |
    ISBN 9781487509873 (EPUB) | ISBN 9781487509866 (PDF)
Subjects: LCSH: Poverty – Canada. | LCSH: Poverty – Great Britain. | LCSH:
    Poverty – United States.
Classification: LCC HC79.P6 O47 2021 | DDC 362.5 – dc23

We welcome comments and suggestions regarding any aspect of our publications – please
feel free to contact us at news@utorontopress.com or visit us at utorontopress.com.

Every effort has been made to contact copyright holders; in the event of an error or
omission, please notify the publisher.

University of Toronto Press acknowledges the financial assistance to its publishing
program of the Canada Council for the Arts and the Ontario Arts Council, an agency of
the Government of Ontario.

Canada Council   Conseil des Arts
for the Arts   du Canada

ONTARIO ARTS COUNCIL
CONSEIL DES ARTS DE L'ONTARIO
an Ontario government agency
un organisme du gouvernement de l'Ontario

Funded by the   Financé par le
Government   gouvernement
of Canada   du Canada

Canadä

To Leo Panitch

Rise like lions after slumber
In unvanquishable NUMBER!
Shake your chains to the earth, like dew
Which in sleep had fall'n on you:
YE ARE MANY — THEY ARE FEW.

– Percy Bysshe Shelley, 1819

Contents

Figures, Tables, and Boxes

Figures

Tables

Boxes

Preface and Acknowledgments

Illuminating and instructive poverty studies are continually generated by prominent, highly respected research centers in the United States and across the globe. They typically chronicle changes in the magnitude and severity of poverty within a particular nation and over relatively short time frames, often highlighting demographic groups that are disproportionately represented among the poor. They also point to crucial catalysts that have helped to aggravate and sustain high poverty levels, such as high levels of unemployment, low wages, inadequate social supports, and low levels of education and training in critical growth areas of the economy. However vital, these studies also have notable limitations. They typically assume a familiarity and common understanding of what constitutes poverty – and neglect to consider homelessness, one of the harshest and most desperate forms of destitution. As single-country "case studies," they miss the often vastly different poverty profiles across the nations of the wealthy capitalist world – and *how* and *why* these nations address poverty in such markedly different ways and with starkly different levels of success. Consequently, these studies tend, at least implicitly, to resign themselves to the Bible's bleak prediction that the poor will always be with us, and they do not directly address the apparent paradox of "poverty amid prosperity." Other poverty narratives set their sights on elucidating some of the most critical aspects and dimensions of poverty, including technical accounts of how it is defined and measured. Or they provide a somewhat abstract overview of the dominant theoretical approaches that have been advanced to explain poverty without examining its actual manifestation in any nation or providing the necessary data to illustrate and substantiate the insightful discussions and controversies these studies generate.

As an alternative, this volume provides a comprehensive but accessible "one-stop" introduction to the study of poverty from a range of comparative vantage points, highlighting the impact of poverty on individuals, families, communities, and society. It begins with the observation that scholarly attention to poverty and homelessness in wealthy nations has been overwhelmed and largely displaced by the accelerating torrent of compelling studies of surging income and wealth disparities across the advanced capitalist world over the past decade. It then explores both the inclusive and the narrow ways that poverty and homelessness have been conceptualized, and how this shapes the way they are defined, measured, and addressed across nations. Canada, the United Kingdom, and the United States, for example – the three countries spotlighted in this study – measure and track poverty and homelessness very differently than do many European nations. But the dominant central and supplemental poverty measures employed across this trio of Anglo nations also differ markedly from each other, rendering direct, meaningful contrasts of their national data sets difficult. A close examination of poverty and homelessness in each country, one based on each nation's own official or quasi-official definitions and forms of measurement, is a very useful *starting point* because it is the only way to address poverty along various axes or fault lines (such as gender, "race," and ethnicity) over time. The distribution of poverty across these groups and other poverty dynamics are typically unavailable in most standardized cross-national and cross-temporal poverty and inequality data sets, necessitating the use of country-specific measures and data.

After a close examination of poverty within Canada, the UK, and the US, this volume explores the scope and depth of poverty from a cross-national perspective utilizing "harmonized" poverty data sets. It first compares these three widely acknowledged generators of extreme inequality and distressingly high rates of poverty and homelessness with each other and then extends its purview to include several European nations that have been far more successful at keeping rates more closely in check. The social policy contrasts between the less developed and less supportive "liberal" welfare states in the Anglo nations and the considerably more generous and accessible networks of income supports, social services, and legal protections found in the Nordic nations are especially stark and provide valuable policy lessons. But this study also demonstrates that it is useful to juxtapose closely the three Anglo nations themselves because, despite their common and befitting designation as members of the same liberal social policy family and "market capitalist" model, there are striking distinctions among them that give rise to equally striking impacts. The consummate liberal welfare state and fulsome embrace of neo-liberalism in the United States has rendered it a notable and consistent outlier even *within* this family of nations. The United States has much to learn from its liberal siblings about addressing poverty and homelessness – while often furnishing dire warnings for them. And this liberal trinity could make appreciably greater headway by adopting some of the policy measures and broader approaches employed in northern and continental Europe.

Finally, this volume presents and critically contrasts the most prominent theoretical traditions or schools that have emerged to explain poverty and homelessness. The first tradition holds poor people largely accountable for their plight. From this perspective, the biological traits and/or behaviors and "cultural" disposition of poor people themselves can best explain why poverty exists and how it is sustained over time. Far from passé, this individual-centered tradition has been continuously reconstituted, recycled, and redeployed at least since the period of the early Poor Laws. Although academic terms such as "culture of poverty" may not be familiar to most people outside of academia, the sentiment they evoke is widely and often passionately held today, particularly in the Anglo nations where it has consistently informed and shaped their social policy orientation. Despite their widespread embrace in the Anglo world, these "culture of poverty" approaches have difficulty accounting for the stark variation in poverty rates across wealthy nations and over time. They are also hard-pressed to account for the considerable turnover among members of poor populations. Although "culture of poverty" explanations that castigate the poor and hold them responsible for their plight garner little empirical support, explanations that highlight the broadly different cultural orientations or "character" of nations have far greater capacity to account for cross-national variation in poverty, homelessness, and inequality. The policy approaches of the Anglo world – and especially in the United States – reflect a strikingly more pronounced confidence in markets, commitment to individualism, and belief in equal opportunity, as well as a far greater antipathy toward the state than found in many nations with stronger and long-standing communitarian and collectivist traditions. These different traditions, in turn, reflect different constellations of power, structural conditions, and historical trajectories.

The second, "society-centered" theoretical tradition, in contrast, rejects individualistic explanations in favor of systemic factors and sociopolitical forces. It acknowledges the impact of "structural" changes, including higher levels of unemployment; lower wages; outsourcing of work; the proliferation of insecure nonstandard, precarious forms of work; the development of the "gig economy"; declining levels of unionization; and measures promoting privatization and austerity, including the paring back of social supports. But it also stresses that these structural developments reflect the natural progression of capitalism – a word that rarely appears in most mainstream investigations of poverty today. Indeed, like Lord Voldemort, the psychopathic nemesis of the eponymous hero of the Harry Potter novels and films, "capitalism" has become the name that cannot be spoken, let alone critically and objectively assessed to determine how and why it generates and sustains poverty and homelessness. The failure or refusal to consider objectively its role in promoting an escalation in inequality, poverty, and homelessness – even during periods of robust and sustained economic growth and expansion – closes off avenues of change and opportunities to address the roots of poverty seriously. Another theoretical stream within the societal tradition highlights sociopolitical factors, with a particular focus upon the changing "balance of power" among classes and other axes or groups in society. Considered conjointly, these societal approaches are much better equipped to explain both the systemically driven common developments unfolding across all rich capitalist nations and the notable variation in the level and severity of poverty and homelessness across them. They also suggest that the *eradication* of poverty will only happen when the socioeconomic system has been seriously overhauled and founded upon economic democracy.

As suggested, this volume takes a somewhat unorthodox approach, combining the orientations of both a course text and a monograph. It introduces key concepts, including the ways poverty and homelessness are defined and measured across societies and how this affects the assessment of their gravity and how they are addressed. It highlights the impact of poverty on the health and daily lives of poor children and families and their communities. It closely examines the central pillars of the welfare state, citing their strengths and limitations. Also, rather than focusing on a single concern – such as the impact of an increase in unemployment rates on poverty rates (however valuable) – it evaluates the broad theoretical traditions advanced to explain the origins and persistence of poverty, and the failure of states to eradicate it. This introductory orientation is enhanced by the inclusion of a "further readings" list at the end of each chapter and an extensive reference list at the end of the book. It also draws on accounts and depictions of poverty and homelessness from the worlds of literature and music and disburses throughout the text quotations from the writers and political thinkers of the past few centuries, all of which usefully reminds us that poverty has long been a critical problem. However, taking a comparative, cross-national approach, this volume also explores the conditions under which poverty has been greatly attenuated and the possibilities for its eradication. The Anglo nations examined here have not been nearly as successful as several European counterparts in addressing poverty. However, within this Anglo group, there are also some notable differences. The possibility and chances of eradicating poverty in *any* capitalist nation are also explored. The volume ends with an overview of some proposals and existing measures to address poverty.

I am again grateful to the Institute for Social Research at the University of Stockholm, where I have been a guest researcher on several occasions over the past decades and where I began this work on poverty. I have also benefited from the assistance of numerous people from Statistics Canada, the New Policy Institute and the Department for Work and Pensions in the UK, and the US Census Bureau, including Will Drabble and Neil Sorensen, Josh Holden and Adam Tinson, and Liana Fox. I am especially thankful for the sustained assistance and generosity of Peter Kenway and Brian Murphy. I would also like to acknowledge friends and colleagues who read the manuscript, in whole or in part, providing many valuable comments and suggestions, including Bill Carroll, Jonah Durrant Olsen, John Shields, Laureen Snider, and, especially, Joan Durrant, as well as all of the anonymous reviewers for the University of Toronto Press. The completion of this volume coincided with the death of Leo Panitch, a colleague, friend, and long-standing beacon of inspiration to me and myriad others across the globe. With a heavy heart, I dedicate this book to him.

PART ONE

Understanding Poverty

CHAPTER ONE

Poverty Matters: Introduction

> There is nothing new about poverty. What is new, however, is that
> we have the resources to get rid of it.
> — *Martin Luther King Jr. (1967/2015)*

A deluge of recent scholarship has revealed stark increases in economic inequality across the globe over the past few decades. This shift
toward rising levels of income inequality – and the even more startling
spikes in wealth inequality – has accelerated rapidly since the 1980s,
dramatically reversing the trends that characterized the first decades
of the post–WWII period. This is most compellingly encapsulated by
the notoriously familiar citations indicating that the richest 1 percent
of the world's population owned as much wealth as the bottom 99 percent in 2016; and the eight wealthiest people in the world had as much
wealth as the poorest 50 percent of humanity (3.6 billion people).[1] In
the United States, an undisputed global leader in inequality for several
decades, this trend was particularly glaring in 2017; the richest 0.1 percent had as much wealth as the bottom 90 percent in the nation, and
the three wealthiest people in the United States had more wealth than
the entire bottom half of the US population combined – 160 million
people or 63 million households (Collins & Hoxie, 2017).[2] The burgeoning body of inequality research has clarified our understanding
of crucial issues such as the exploitation of offshore investments, tax

havens, and fiscal policy by the "super rich." It has underscored the role that stagnating wages, rising levels of debt, and the collapse of the value of assets have played in eroding the wealth and earnings of many middle- and lower-income families. And it focused our attention on the "social determinants of health" and the intensely adverse impact of the deepening chasms between the top and bottom on indices of social stability, social mobility, and democracy.[3] But the outpouring of these invaluable studies has often overshadowed the critical corollary of some of the very trends that they have identified – the erosion of resources and supports for poor families and the impact that this has had on their lives. This volume redresses this problem, bringing poverty back to the forefront through a comprehensive and comparative examination of its expression in Canada, the UK, and the US – three prosperous nations where poverty and homelessness have long been urgently acute. While these three nations are commonly classified within the same family of "liberal" nations, Canada and the UK have typically done notably better than the more affluent US – providing many insights and policy lessons.[4] All three Anglo nations can also learn much from the social policy approaches in many other countries, where poverty is significantly lower and less brutal, although these countries, too, face challenges in the current era of globalization, technological change, and austerity.

POVERTY AND AUSTERITY AMID PROSPERITY

> Is this a holy thing to see,
> In a rich and beautiful land,
> Babes reduced to misery,
> Fed with cold and usurous hand?
>
> – *William Blake (1794/1970)*

The degradation, misery, and social asphyxia of poverty and homelessness in the face of opulence in the UK and the lands once under its dominion are not new. These distressing conditions were highlighted in the verses of Romantic poets such as William Blake and William Wordsworth and in the novels and sharp satire of writers such as Charles Dickens and Mark Twain in the late eighteenth and nineteenth centuries. In the first decades of the twentieth century, authors such as Jack London, Upton Sinclair, and

George Orwell went beyond that moral critique to address the structural roots of poverty. Although more than 225 years have elapsed since Blake wrote "Holy Thursday" (quoted above), many people still live in deep poverty, largely untouched by the abundant resources in their countries. The modest social supports put in place for them – still falsely indicted for promoting a culture of indolence and acclaimed as the real root of their poverty – have been steadily reduced while lower corporate income taxes and wealth taxes and tax avoidance schemes and shelters have induced a rapid proliferation of decabillionaires and allowed for the emergence of centibillionaires.[5] The increasing concentration of capital and personal wealth, in turn, has allowed a tiny but economically powerful group to further augment its influence over governments, shaping governmental fiscal and social policies under the cloak of a "free market" in ways beyond the imagination of nineteenth-century "social problem" writers.

Our understanding of poverty today is often centered on distressing media depictions of desolation and misery in some of the most destitute regions of the world – places where problems such as chronic shortages of food and water, malnutrition, starvation, disease, epidemics, unemployment, and illiteracy are pervasive and grievous. "Real" poverty, it is often suggested, is not a serious concern in wealthy capitalist nations, which are routinely portrayed as lands of almost limitless opportunities where success is practically guaranteed to anyone with a little drive and ambition. Even when it is conceded that there may be *some* poverty in wealthy lands, it is often dismissed as relatively inconsequential compared to that found in places like sub-Saharan Africa, south Asia, and other less developed parts of the world, where grinding impoverishment is ubiquitous, and its impact and death toll staggering. But poverty is not only a "developing world" concern. It permeates the rich capitalist world, and its prevalence, intensity, and impacts – in ghettoes, on reserves in Canada and reservations in the United States, and across large urban centers and remote rural areas – are profound. Contrary assertions often advanced in wealthy countries only serve to obscure the poverty that exists there. They diminish a critical social problem, inhibiting public awareness and demands to address it. They mask the tightly entwined structural, institutional, and political roots of poverty across the developed and developing worlds, undermining cross-national solidarity among some of the most dispossessed and oppressed people on earth, and among others who would support them. And they are highly misleading.

While rich countries may have the economic capacity to eliminate poverty, most often, their governments have sought only to manage it and alleviate some of its symptoms for those people deemed poor enough to qualify for assistance. Poverty has proven durable across most affluent nations over the past few decades, despite long periods of strong economic growth and intermittent government promises to effect a fairer distribution of national wealth. In many of them, including Canada, the UK, and the US, income and wealth inequality have soared dramatically as most of the gains generated by economic expansion have accrued to a small group of wealthy economic elites. Stagnating or declining wages; a proliferation of precarious jobs; higher rates of long-term unemployment; slashed income supports, social services, and other public safeguards; and greatly increased debt loads have led to a significant deterioration of living standards for many families and have markedly increased the intensity of poverty. The most acutely impoverished people in these lands sustain chronic and often life-threatening deprivations; live in soul-destroying squalor and have poor health, with significantly curtailed life expectancies; endure homelessness; starve or freeze to death in abandoned buildings or on city streets, often alone and unmourned; are unable to exercise basic civil, political, and social rights; and have few opportunities to alter their situation.

Accounts of poverty that juxtapose the conditions of the poor in developed and less-developed regions of the world conceal important aspects of poverty within affluent nations. It is often cynically suggested that poor people in wealthy lands would be considered well-off if they were living in a poorer developing nation. But they are not living there. The poor living in rich nations often require much higher levels of income and access to many additional goods, amenities, and services just to reach similar levels of capability and inclusion as those of many poorer people in developing countries. Our aspirations and our sense of self-worth are shaped within the socioeconomic and sociocultural contexts in which we reside. Living "amid plenty" fosters many different needs and expectations from those found in the developing world. Families too poor to satisfy them may experience severe anxiety, degradation, marginalization, and social exclusion. Moreover, as in the most destitute regions of the globe, the desperate conditions that imprison the poor in rich nations can cultivate resignation because poverty levels have largely held steady or increased over the past few decades, and there has been little enduring public interest in addressing this issue and ever fewer social supports in place. This sense of futility is magnified and reinforced when the poor are increasingly stigmatized and held in contempt as the sole authors of their plight and unworthy of assistance or concern – charges that are often most vociferously and viciously targeted at Indigenous peoples, racialized groups, immigrants, and women.

The view that poverty is largely the result of the inadequacies and failings of individuals who are "not my problem" has not always been as widespread or entrenched as it is now in the Anglo nations. Nor has the popular kindred idea that public measures to assist people living in poverty are a largely ineffective waste of resources that undermine personal initiative and foster debilitating dependencies upon social supports. Central to the dominant neoliberal perspective on poverty today, these narratives have a lineage that predates capitalism, but they have waxed and waned in step with its relatively brief but distinctly turbulent history. Vilification of the poor over the past few decades through corporate-funded think tanks, institutes, and the media has been steadily confronted and discredited by more thoughtful critical research. Invaluable studies by leading poverty experts have usefully identified multiple triggers and circumstances that can foster and sustain poverty, including high levels of unemployment, a dearth of stable jobs that provide livable wages, deregulation, social program retrenchment, weaker unions, and poor health (e.g., Cancian & Danziger, 2009; Rainwater & Smeeding, 2003; Rank, 2005; Ross et al., 2000; Waldfogel, 2010). But these poverty catalysts are themselves activated and promoted by the unfolding and development of capitalism and the routine operation of ever-freer markets.

Sometimes, anti-poverty narratives and the media campaigns of many political and religious organizations present the magnitude and depth of poverty in rich capitalist nations as "paradoxical." In one sense, of course, this is very true; wealthy nations have the resources, knowledge, and capacity to entirely eradicate poverty within, and well beyond, the borders of the developed world. But, in another sense, the existence of "poverty amid plenty" is not such a puzzling contradiction. Capitalism routinely manufactures poverty and other inequalities as a matter of course. Indeed, although they have been greatly attenuated or exacerbated by the character of the social and economic measures that states have been pressed to install, poverty and inequality are defining attributes and endemic symptoms of *all* capitalist systems. When groups of workers, the poor, and others have organized and banded together, they have been able to pressure states to address poverty and inequality via an array of market-constraining interventions that challenge the sacred principles of capitalism. But the powerful economic elites who benefit most from it are incentivized to use their vast and varied resources to restore, increase, and legitimate their already outsized serving of the economic pie by attacking progressive tax and transfer policies, unions, minimum wage laws, labor legislation, environmental regulations, and other measures that reduce people's dependence upon employers, provide some protection from market forces, and foster a fairer distribution of resources. From this perspective, poverty is generated by structural, institutional, and political forces – and not, as commonly portrayed and accepted, by the flaws of individuals.

Despite the brutal conditions, hardships, and inequalities that it has unleashed and sustained, neoliberalism has held sway for several decades now. As the American historian and journalist Thomas Frank (2012) notes, "there is nothing really novel about the idea that free markets are the very essence of freedom. What is new is the glorification of this idea at the precise moment when free market theory has proven itself to be a philosophy of ruination and fraud" (p. 11). Fashioned from above and endorsed by most states and the popular media, neoliberalism is an amalgamation of elements of liberalism and conservatism that has become the dominant global discourse today. It combines and refashions their central tenets: (1) a liberal fundamentalist faith in individualism and the free market, an antipathy toward unions, and the demonization of the state as the ultimate source of all economic and social problems and (2) the noxious conservative notion that poverty is largely the product of biological, moral, and/or cultural deficiencies among the poor, but without the paternalistic sense of responsibility for them. Neoliberalism has taken firm root in most developed nations, helping to ensure that poverty is an intractable and growing problem around the globe. Opposing neoliberal austerity measures has been a difficult challenge over the past few decades of its ascendency. Addressing capitalism itself, despite its reliably recurrent crises and steady generation of widespread adversity and hardship, has become taboo. This, it has often been noted, is especially true in the United States, where a healthy assessment of capitalism can be interpreted as almost akin to treason. We routinely monitor and take our governments to task for their failings; critical examinations of our schools, health care systems, and most other social programs and public institutions are properly embraced as essential. But capitalism itself has become largely off-limits; it is not often explicitly interrogated in poverty research, preventing us from assessing its inherent deficiencies and considering alternatives built upon a solid foundation of economic democracy (Parenti, 1995; Wolff, 2012; Wright, 2010).

COMPARATIVE CONTRASTS: CROSS-NATIONAL AND CROSS-TEMPORAL PERSPECTIVES

Comparative contrasts, across time and space, allow us to understand the many determinants of poverty more fully. They also allow us to critically assess popular and highly influential explanations for poverty, inequality, and other social ills. The multifaceted neoliberal policy initiatives designed to extend the scope of the market – via deregulation and the removal of impediments to capital mobility, privatization, marketization, lower corporate and wealth taxes, marked cuts in social spending, and enervating social programs – have been widely embraced by most governments in the rich, developed capitalist world and advanced as the only effective means to encourage innovation and growth and promote greater prosperity for all through "trickle down" wealth distribution and the creation of new jobs. But these policies have typically culminated in far greater economic disparity with escalating concentrations of wealth for those at the top and declining living standards, greater insecurity, and fewer prospects for almost everyone else, while the prevalence and intensity of poverty has been sustained or increased.

Even apart from the dire economic, environmental, climate, and other crises it generates, unfettered economic growth cannot reduce poverty if it is associated with the proliferation of low-paying, precarious jobs and fewer and more meager social supports. But it is crucial to observe the considerable variation in intensity and form that neoliberalism has taken across nations and how its impact has been muted or magnified by the character of each nation's welfare state and social policy responses. This cross-national variation thoroughly undermines accounts of poverty that blame the poor. Tenacious explanations insisting that poverty is rooted in the inferior biological makeup or "poverty cultures" of poor families themselves, for example, cannot account for significant variation in the rates and character of poverty across nations, and over time within nations. Neither can the closely allied accounts suggesting that social supports only aggravate poverty levels by undermining people's work ethic and fostering dependence on the state. In fact, poverty is more prevalent, deeper, and more brutal in nations with the least developed and least generous social policies.

Cross-national contrasts also allow us to challenge the dominant notion that there is nothing that can be done to reduce the prevalence and severity of poverty in the short run while more far-reaching systemic change is considered or pursued. Under the right conditions, some nations have markedly reduced their rates of poverty and homelessness and significantly attenuated their harmful effects. These impressive gains should be recognized – and they often provide valuable policy directives. Finally, comparative research helps to identify the real limitations of what can be expected within the framework of global capitalism. Capitalism, especially in its most unfettered forms, systemically breeds poverty; it is an inevitable by-product of ongoing crises and restructuring, including the unrelenting introduction of new laborsaving technologies. Efforts to redress this – which have only rarely been seriously considered as a social policy goal by governments of any political stripe in recent decades – face a difficult challenge because of the overwhelming power endowed upon corporations, financial institutions, and elites, which have steadily increased with unremitting deregulation.

The most effective way to comprehend thoroughly the extent and character of poverty, assess both popular and theoretical explanations for its growth, and evaluate accurately the existing social programs and proposals designed to address it is through comparative, cross-national research. "Case studies" of poverty can provide illuminating attention to detail and context in one nation, but they do not always allow us to interpret their findings fully; we cannot determine whether the levels and conditions of poverty observed in any single country are "normal" or inevitable, nor can we be certain that any conclusions drawn are necessarily generalizable to other nations. Conversely, inclusive studies of poverty across many nations allow us to identify broad trends and patterns, but they are inherently unable to explore and contrast closely so many historical and sociopolitical contexts in sufficient detail, or to identify potentially important factors that may be unique to any one nation.

This study takes an "intermediate" approach, incorporating the strengths of both orientations.[6] It closely examines the character and development of poverty in three strategically chosen countries – Canada, the UK, and the US – which, despite their shared historical connections and many striking similarities, differ in ways that are compelling and instructive. The focus on these nations is supplemented by an examination of trends in several other wealthy, comparator countries that have been far more successful in addressing poverty and containing its harshest forms. This two-pronged cross-national approach is complemented by a cross-temporal exploration of where and how the expressions of poverty in these nations, and their social policy responses to it, have diverged markedly over time, often in step with other key historical developments, including incremental changes in their political cultures, declining rates of unionization, and shifts in the "balance of power."[7]

Why Compare Canada, the United Kingdom, and the United States?

Sociopolitical typologies that bundle nations with institutions, organizations, and/or social policy approaches that look, operate, and interact in similar ways – and have broadly similar impacts and outcomes – typically situate Canada, the UK, and the US in the same category or "family" of nations.[8] The "varieties of capitalism" approach, for example, identifies these three nations as "liberal market economies" with systems of industrial relations that starkly differentiate them from the "coordinated market economies" of northern Europe, such as Germany and the Nordic lands (Hall & Soskice, 2001; Schneider & Soskice, 2009). Alternative but analogous and largely compatible typologies based upon the institutional mechanisms that coordinate socioeconomic activity also distinguish two broad categories: (1) an Anglo-American "pluralist market model" and (2) a European "corporatist model."[9] The first family, which typically includes Canada, the UK, and the US, is characterized by low levels of taxes and regulation, flexible labor markets, limited state intervention, a weak public sector, and a high tolerance for significant inequalities of income and wealth. The second group, including continental European nations and the Nordic lands, is characterized by high taxes, regulated labor markets, relatively high levels of unionization, an institutionalized framework of commitment and compromise among three key "social actors" ("business," labor, and the state), generous social supports, and notably lower levels of economic inequality.[10] In the familiar and highly influential "welfare worlds" typology that has dominated in this research field for over three decades, Canada, the UK, and the US have been uniformly identified as steadfast members of the "liberal" welfare regime. They have "residual" or less developed welfare states that leave their residents largely reliant upon the market for their well-being and allow for markedly higher levels of various forms of social inequality. Compared to their "social democratic" regime counterparts in the Nordic nations and the "conservative" welfare states across continental Europe, they have fewer, less generous, and less inclusive income programs; fewer social services; and weaker legislative supports in place to prevent or address increases in the rates and depth of poverty (Esping-Andersen, 1990, 2015; Olsen, 2002).

Canada, the United Kingdom, and the United States certainly share some striking "family resemblances" – similar socioeconomic, cultural, political, and institutional traits that clearly warrant their inclusion in the same category. But there are also notable differences among them. Recent research has identified "varieties" of liberalism, highlighting marked differences within the liberal world and some distinctive policy approaches across the Anglo nations.[11] Moreover, "neo-liberalization" is a complex, multidimensional process that can manifest itself in varied ways and with differing impacts. The scope, contours, and character of welfare states – and their broader sociopolitical and sociocultural environments – can profoundly shape the way that neoliberalism unfurls, the form it assumes, the particular measures it features, and, consequently, its impact upon inequality and poverty across nations.

Close, comparative scrutiny reveals noteworthy "within-group" differences among the Anglo nations. While all three of them are infamous as major "inequality generators" with relatively high rates of poverty, there is substantial variation in their poverty profiles. The level and severity of poverty in the US – a steadfast outlier among wealthy capitalist nations – is considerably greater than in Canada or the UK.

A close examination of the three countries' welfare states and social policy approaches also reveals marked differences that matter. The US welfare state is the definitive representative of "liberal regime" nations, with the least developed and least effective social policies for addressing poverty. The welfare states in Canada and the UK, although members of the same "liberal" social policy family, can be more aptly designated "*social* liberal" in at least some respects. In addition to their universal healthcare programs, they provide other more generous and inclusive social programs that have gone further to mitigate poverty than policies in the United States. Poverty in the US could be markedly reduced and ameliorated if the country adopted some of the policies in place in Canada and the UK. But neither of these nations has been nearly as effective or supportive as nations with more developed social policy approaches and welfare states.

The tri-nation focus of this volume is augmented by an examination of poverty in several other European nations, including the Nordic lands, where it is much lower and considerably less severe than it is in Canada and the UK and where there are more effective provisions for people who fall into poverty. In Finland, for example, the poverty rate is much lower, there are greater supports for people who do fall into poverty, and there have been steady, enviable declines in levels of homelessness since the 1980s. Discourses and policies highlighting the alleged deficiencies of individuals and the negative impact of social supports have far greater resonance in the Anglo nations where they have informed and animated neoliberal austerity measures. When implemented in the Nordic nations, neoliberal reforms have been more commonly and vigorously promoted as a means to provide citizens with greater "choice" across forms of social services, such as healthcare, childcare, and eldercare outside the state sector, rather than as a means to redress "irresponsible" or "immoral" behavior.

The denser networks of social supports in nations with less severe and lower levels of poverty are often closely related to other sociopolitical conditions and institutions, including higher levels of unionization; the presence, and often relatively lengthy incumbency, of social democratic or labor parties; a more collectivist culture; and less antipathy toward the state. These conditions all obtain to a greater degree in Canada and the UK than they do in the US, but to a notably lesser degree than in the Nordic and several other European nations.

In the United States, much greater emphasis has been placed upon protecting individual freedoms – more sharply expressed as freedom "from" the state – and social programs are more likely to be embraced as temporary emergency measures provided only to those who deserve support, rather than promoted as rights for everyone.

ORGANIZATION OF THIS BOOK

This volume introduces central conceptual, empirical, and theoretical discussions, debates, and research on poverty. It animates this discussion by focusing on three wealthy Anglo nations, which all have the economic capacity to eliminate poverty within their borders but have sustained strikingly high, enduring, or increasing poverty rates over the past few decades. These three countries are also compared with other nations in order to assess popular accounts and theories suggesting that their high poverty levels are inevitable, as well as to explore alternative, more gainful ways of addressing this critical social problem. Chapter 2 examines how poverty has been understood, considering more inclusive and more restrictive ways of conceptualizing it. It examines the definitions behind the strikingly different poverty measures that are employed in Canada, the UK, and the US, delineating their strengths and weaknesses. It also considers the ways that homelessness – an extreme form of poverty, deprivation, and social exclusion often neglected in poverty studies – has been understood, researched, and addressed. Chapter 3 sets out both the central dimensions of poverty – its prevalence, severity, duration, and distribution – and the character of poverty, including its impact and the tightly restricted opportunities and life chances with which it is associated. It also provides a brief overview of some of the axes of poverty and of the social groups that are most vulnerable and commonly overrepresented among the poor in each of the three nations, as well as a comparison that reveals significant cross-national variation. Chapter 4 reviews the ways that poverty has been addressed, focusing on the character of national social policy approaches. It updates relevant accounts and models of welfare states, and their central pillars of support, but focuses primarily upon how they address poverty and their impact upon it. This chapter also examines the historical roots of the abiding view that the poor are largely responsible for their poverty and undeserving of public support in the three Anglo nations. These ideas, which have experienced a renascence, are clearly echoes of the Poor Laws and other poor relief reforms and legislation that attempted to address the crises of capitalism as it developed and took root in the UK and its colonies in North America.

The next two chapters critically examine the two dominant "schools" that have been advanced to explain the existence and persistence of poverty in contemporary capitalist societies. Chapter 5 examines the first broad, long-standing tradition, with a lineage that can be traced back at least as far as the seventeenth century. It focuses on the characteristics of *individuals* who are poor, emphasizing their alleged biogenetic deficiencies (low IQs or cognitive ability) or deviant "cultural" shortcomings such as a lack of motivation and ambition, inadequate work ethics and habits, impaired values and morals, and irresponsible behaviors that are said to constitute a poverty "culture." These views have regained currency over the past few decades and significantly shaped social policy in the Anglo nations under incumbent governments of varied political stripes. In the United States, this is perhaps best signified in the 1996 termination of the long-standing New Deal entitlement, Aid to Families with Dependent Children (AFDC), by the Democratic administration of President Clinton through its tellingly titled Personal Responsibility and Work Opportunity Reconciliation Act (PRWORA). In the UK, a similarly toned suite of social security reforms was set in motion through the Welfare Reform Act by the Conservative–Liberal Democrat coalition in 2012, including the introduction of Universal Credit in 2013, to simplify benefits and tax credit schemes and incentivize people into work. In Canada, this policy drift is best reflected in the Liberal government's termination of the Canada Assistance Plan (CAP) and its replacement by the Canada Health and Social Transfer (CHST) in 1996. Proponents of the biogenetic and cultural variants within this school typically maintain that most forms of social programs and supports to help poor and low-income individuals and families are ineffectual or counterproductive and detrimental to personal and societal development. But the developments in these nations are more a reflection of the broader culture of individualism, "independence," and freedom from the state than of any attributes of poor individuals and families.

The second broad school, the focus of Chapter 6, highlights the *societal* roots of poverty – the capitalist system and sociopolitical factors, including the balance of power among key social actors. If the existence of "poverty amid plenty" is an inevitable outcome of the mechanics of capitalist systems, it should not come as a surprise that poverty has been especially durable in nations where markets have been given much freer rein. This chapter also focuses on the balance of class power in society; existing laws, rules, procedures, and institutions that operate in favor of some groups at the expense of others; and the character and needs of capitalist systems. Poverty has been held in check and its impact notably attenuated in countries where labor movements have remained stronger and welfare states have endured. But these nations also face enormous challenges and have experienced rapidly rising inequality levels and higher or deeper poverty levels over the past few decades with capital flight, the introduction of new technologies, and full-scale attacks on social policy, unions, and other progressive organizations. Vibrant labor movements and comprehensive welfare states remain crucial to the creation of more egalitarian socioeconomic systems based upon economic democracy. Finally, Chapter 7 examines the strengths and limitations of some existing and proposed measures to eradicate poverty and homelessness, highlighting the distinction between "reformist" and "transformative reforms" and the importance of fostering economic democracy.

NOTES

1 Oxfam's (2017) report is based on global wealth distribution information provided by the Credit Suisse *Global Wealth Databook 2016* and the *Forbes* billionaires list published in March 2016. Critics of Oxfam's inequality reports dismiss them because they are based upon "net wealth" (subtracting debts from assets). Consequently, they argue, students with high levels of student debt may appear poorer than people who do not have debts but are having a difficult time simply getting by from day to day, as could people who maintain large debts because they have purchased homes and cars. However, university degrees and "human capital" are less likely to lead today's graduates to a good job that will allow them to clear their great debt. Houses and vehicles – especially those purchased by lower-income families – are often repossessed by financial institutions. But, more important, most of the people with these kinds of debts are in wealthy nations in Europe and North America with privileged access to credit while the great majority of the people in the bottom 50 percent have virtually no wealth at all.

2 Saez and Zucman's (2014) study examines rising wealth inequality in the United States over the past century. Their conclusions are supported by numerous other studies (e.g., Piketty, 2014; Wolff, 2017). The wealthiest people in the United States in 2018 included Jeff Bezos (Amazon, $160 billion), Bill Gates (Microsoft, $97 billion), Warren Buffet (Berkshire Hathaway, $88.3 billion), Mark Zuckerberg (Facebook, $61 billion), Larry Ellison (Oracle, $55.4 billion), Larry Page (Google/Alphabet, $53.8 billion), Charles Koch (Koch Industries, $53.5 billion), David Koch (Koch Industries, $53.5 billion), Sergey Brin (Google/Alphabet, $52.4 billion), Michael Bloomberg (Bloomberg LP, $51.8 billion), Jim Walton (Walmart, $45.2 billion), and Alice Walton (Walmart, $44.9 billion) (*Forbes*, 2018). For an overview of the relatively dismal and declining standing of the United States on a wide variety of inequality indicators and other related measures see Friedman and Hertz (2015).

3 Recent accounts of growing income and wealth inequality and its destructive impact include Atkinson (2015), Bernstein (2017), Bourguignon (2015), Brown (2017), Carroll and Sapinski (2018), Collins (2018), Dorling (2014, 2015, 2017, 2018), Facundo et al. (2018), Heisz (2016), Huber and Stephens (2014), Huber et al. (2017), Jackson (2020), Olsen (2011), Osberg (2018), Oxfam (2016, 2017), Phillips (2018), Piketty (2014, 2015), Raphael (2013), Stiglitz (2013), Wilkinson and Pickett (2010, 2019), and Wolff (2017).

4 Research on social inequality and social policy in the developed world often employs the designation "Anglo-American," "Anglo-Saxon," or "Anglo" to refer to nations that have strong historic colonial ties to the UK and are predominantly English speaking. Canada, the UK, the US, Australia, New Zealand, and the Republic of Ireland are typically included in this category.

5 Key wealth taxes include property taxes, inheritance taxes, estate taxes, and capital taxes on businesses (Stanford 2014).

6 There are several valuable "intermediate-level" comparative studies that juxtapose and closely examine welfare states across three or four capitalist nations representing different social policy categories or families (e.g., Ginsberg, 1992; Gould, 1993; Olsen, 2002). But relatively few of them highlight and explain variation *within* clusters of similar nations, such as Ruggie (1996), which juxtaposes the healthcare systems of three liberal welfare states (Britain, Canada, and the United States). Cross-national, comparative studies that examine *poverty* at the intermediate level are also relatively uncommon – and fewer still explore its varied and similar character and its handling across a few nations *within* a particular family of states or a regime grouping.

7 The present study builds upon my previous examinations of various manifestations of inequality (Olsen, 2011) and of social policy and welfare states (Olsen, 2002) from a comparative perspective.

8 *Taxonomies*, more commonly used in the natural sciences, identify and describe unambiguous and mutually exclusive classifications on the basis of empirically observable and measurable characteristics of phenomena. The social sciences often employ *typologies* with categories or "models" based on more abstract "ideal types," slotting social phenomena into these groups according to how closely they fit the ideal.

9 See, for example, Albert (1993), Schmitter and Lembruch (1980), and Whitely (1999). Some typologies set out more than two major models of capitalism across a single continuum or spectrum. Distinctive groups *within* continental Europe, or between it and the Nordic nations, and a Japanese or Asian model, for example, have been acknowledged and accommodated in some typologies (e.g., Esping-Andersen, 1990; Hollingsworth & Boyer, 1999). Piketty (2014) also acknowledges a distinction between "Rhenish capitalism" (the "stakeholder model") most notable in Germany, and Anglo-Saxon market capitalism (the "shareholder model").

10 Although the focus is typically on the UK and the US, the liberal, individualist Anglo-American market model commonly includes the other major English-speaking nations of the developed capitalist world – Australia, Canada, the Republic of Ireland, and New Zealand.

11 For example, see Mahon (2008), O'Connor et al. (1999), Olsen (2002, 2011), Peck and Theodore (2007), and White (2017).

FURTHER READINGS

Blake, W. (1970). *Songs of innocence and of experience.* Oxford University Press. (Original work published 1789 and 1794)

Dickens, C. (1995). *Hard times.* Wordsworth Editions. (Original work published 1854)

Engels, F. (2009). *The condition of the working class in England* (D. MacLellan, Ed.). Oxford University Press. (Original work published 1845)

Gaskell, E. (2010). *Mary Barton.* Wordsworth Editions. (Original work published 1848)

London, J. (2001). *The people of the abyss.* Pluto Press. (Original work published 1903)

Orwell, G. (1958). *The road to Wigan Pier.* Houghton Mifflin Harcourt. (Original work published 1937)

Sinclair, U. (1951). *The jungle.* Harper and Row. (Original work published 1906)

Tressell, R. (2008). *The ragged-trousered philanthropists* (P. Miles, Ed.). Oxford University Press. (Original work published 1914)

Twain, M., & Warner, C.D. (2006). *The gilded age.* The Modern Library. (Original work published 1873)

CHAPTER TWO

What Is Poverty? Conceptualizing, Defining, and Measuring Poverty

There is scarcely among the evils of human life, any so generally dreaded as poverty; the mind and body suffer together; its miseries bring no alleviations; it is a state in which every virtue is obscured, and in which no conduct can avoid reproach.

– *Samuel Johnson (1750/2013)*

WHAT IS POVERTY?

Although we may intuitively know what it is, and readily recognize it when we see it, poverty can be difficult to define. There is little consensus, even among social policy experts and researchers, about how poverty should be understood and measured. But the way that poverty is viewed is not simply an academic matter; it determines who, and how many, will be accepted as "truly" poor; how poverty will be approached; who will be appraised as deserving of support; and the form and character that this support will assume. Consequently, it is not surprising that the meaning of poverty, like the explanations for its causes and the proposals for its eradication, has always been a contentious and highly politicized issue. Awareness of poverty and social policy efforts to address it – from the allotments of low-cost wheat to the poor through the public granaries of Ancient Rome to repressive laws outlawing begging in late medieval Europe to social assistance and other public supports provided by modern welfare states today – have a very long history. The close study of poverty is much more recent. Detailed accounts of poverty were underway in Europe by the late 1700s and 1800s, spurred on by both evangelical preaching and mounting labor unrest, but rigorous, comprehensive surveys of the living conditions of the poor and the causes and consequences of poverty were not conducted until the late nineteenth and early twentieth centuries, when new research methods and techniques were developed. Since then, there has been considerable discussion and debate about the best way to conceptualize, define, and measure poverty.

CONCEPTUALIZING POVERTY: INCLUSIVE OR RESTRICTIVE?

Poverty can be understood broadly or narrowly. Broadly conceived, poverty is an inclusive and multifaceted phenomenon, comprising a dense network of material and nonmaterial losses, denials, privations, hardships, and disadvantages. Most plainly, people living in poverty have inadequate resources (such as income, food, clothing, housing, a clean and safe environment, education, and healthcare), difficult and degrading living conditions, and increased rates of illness, morbidity, and mortality, with few opportunities to improve their situation. But they may also experience other highly consequential nonmaterial deprivations and affronts that are overlooked in most accounts and studies of poverty. These include a lack of respect and an assault on their dignity; diminished rights, freedoms, opportunities, and "life chances"; social exclusion; and much less power, determination, and control over their lives. From this more comprehensive perspective, poverty encompasses many different *aspects* – cultural, social, political, legal, and psychological – and *levels* of deprivation and dispossession, as well as the numerous and often tightly interlocked and compounding conditions that help to perpetuate it, including low wages, lower levels of education, unemployment, and a lack of social supports. Philosophers Amartya Sen and Martha Nussbaum were among the first and most influential theorists to conceptualize poverty inclusively, highlighting the

greatly reduced "capabilities" and "functioning," heightened vulnerabilities, restricted rights and entitlements, and eroded dignity of people living in poverty (Nussbaum, 1997, 2000; Nussbaum & Sen, 1993;
Sen, 1992, 2006).

The Nordic nations and several other European countries have
systematically conducted annual or periodic "level of living" surveys
over the past few decades, examining a wide range of social indicators
to assess the overall "well-being" of their residents and to track developments and trends over time. Most nations, however, largely restrict
their purview to narrow economic concerns, such as the consumption
of goods and services, which, in turn, are typically examined indirectly. Expenditure or income data, which allow for a simple monetary
summary, are often used as proxies for records of consumption. Un-
derstandably, income is the most widely employed indicator in cross-
national poverty studies because it is the most easily standardized and
is routinely collected by governments for fiscal purposes, and it has a
significant impact upon our well-being. Income is a central precon-
dition for a decent standard of living in virtually all market societies,
but it is not a *direct* measure or indicator of poverty and deprivation. An exclusive focus on income may obscure or distort reality to
some extent. For example, if their household debt level is very high,
families with somewhat higher incomes may be more impoverished
than families that have lower incomes. Furthermore, the receipt of
"in kind" or "near cash" benefits and the availability of social services may be overlooked when income is the sole measure, but they
can be critical to the living standards of low-income families. Moreover, household income levels, which are typically examined for a
single year, might be underestimated or overestimated if the income
level recorded is atypical that year due to unemployment, underemployment, temporary illness, the birth of a child, an abundance of
overtime work, or the receipt of generous bonuses. Despite these
limitations, in the absence of other measures or as a supplement to
them, low income is a useful indicator that can help us to gauge the
breadth and depth of poverty, especially in rich and very highly commodified nations where there is much greater reliance upon markets
for essential goods and services (Halleröd, 1995; Kenworthy, 2007;
Ringen, 1988).

DEFINING POVERTY: ABSOLUTE, RELATIVE, AND SUBJECTIVE DEFINITIONS

Definitions of poverty allow researchers to determine its rate in a nation (or among various subgroups within nations). But poverty researchers, institutes, and governments often adopt strikingly different definitions of poverty to ascertain the poverty levels that their studies report. Three broad, central approaches to defining poverty are commonly distinguished in the literature on poverty: absolute, relative, and subjective (Ruggles, 1990). *Absolute* definitions of poverty, the earliest category employed, define people as poor if they have less than some fixed minimum standard; people are poor if they lack the most basic resources needed to sustain life. *Relative* definitions define people as poor if they have significantly less than others in their society. From this view, deprivation and need are understood within specific sociocultural and temporal contexts. Although both absolute and relative definitions of poverty are sometimes considered to be "objective," they invariably involve some intuitive interpretations by professionals, experts, and politicians of what is required for a "minimum" or a "decent" standard of living. *Subjective* definitions of poverty, in contrast, are based upon peoples' own perceptions and assessments of whether they, or others in their community, are poor. Researchers who use subjective definitions and approaches include the voices and insights of the poor themselves, going outside the conventional focus upon income levels, consumption patterns, and other strictly material or economic concerns. These three approaches to defining poverty and the forms of poverty measurement that they have spawned are examined more closely below.

Absolute and Relative Definitions of Poverty

One of the most prominent issues of contention among poverty researchers concerns whether poverty should be defined in "absolute" *or* "relative" terms. This debate typically revolves around which definition best captures the character of poverty, and erroneously implies that the two definitions are mutually exclusive. In fact, both approaches are indispensable. Each highlights a different but vitally important facet of poverty and has its own strengths and weaknesses. Both of these orientations can be traced back to the pioneering poverty studies conducted in

England in the late nineteenth century by Charles Booth (1840–1916) and (Benjamin) Seebohm Rowntree (1871–1954). These two researchers and social reformers are often portrayed as strong advocates of an exclusively absolute, "minimum needs" approach, but each of them, at least indirectly and to some degree, also acknowledged the wider living standards associated with relative definitions of poverty. In his study of poverty in London, Booth (1897) distinguished between the "poor" and the "very poor." The "poor," he noted, may have access to some basic necessities or goods beyond the reach of the "very poor," but their "means are barely sufficient for decent independent life" and their "lives are an unending struggle" (p. 5). Rowntree's (1901, pp. 86–87) early research, which demonstrated that extensive and deep poverty was not restricted to London, also distinguished "primary" from "secondary" forms of poverty in his studies of York. Their seminal research prompted many more poverty surveys in the UK and well beyond its borders (Veit-Wilson, 1986).[1]

ABSOLUTE POVERTY

Absolute definitions appear to provide the simplest and most objective accounts of poverty. From this perspective, people should be considered poor if they and their dependents do not have access to those goods designated as essential for survival. In the narrowest, most restrictive interpretation of absolute poverty – aptly referred to as "subsistence poverty" – food, clothing, and shelter are typically viewed as the three central "basic necessities." Advocates of this approach suggest that a strict focus upon such "survival" criteria provides a useful, fixed, and universal yardstick that allows us to more readily and discretely identify who is poor: i.e., only those people who do not have these basic necessities or whose income is too low to access them. Regardless of which nation, region, or century they live in, it is *only* those people who should be considered truly poor from this vantage point.

When scrutinized more closely, a strictly absolute approach is not nearly as straightforward, objective, or easy to apply as it initially appears. Determining *which* needs are the ones that must be satisfied and *which* goods to include in any "basket of essentials" is a complex and controversial task. It is also highly dependent upon both time and place. Even the three most definitive necessities that are typically identified by advocates of a strict absolute approach cannot be provided in a truly objective manner because the quantity and quality that people require cannot be easily ascertained for all people, across all societies, in all time periods. Consider food, arguably *the* most essential of all basic necessities. The caloric intake that humans need to meet simple daily energy requirements is partly dependent upon their size, gender, and age, as well as the demands of their work and other pursuits. Moreover, the quantity and quality of the food that people require for mere "survival" may leave them severely undernourished, undermine their long-term health, render them much more susceptible to illness and disease, and significantly shorten their life expectancy. The foods considered acceptable to meet the identified daily requirements are also culturally specific; eating domestic animals (such as dogs or cats), livestock (such as cows, pigs, or horses), or insects may be illegal, sacrilegious, taboo, or considered abominable in many societies, whatever their nutritional value.

It is equally difficult to "objectively" determine universal clothing and shelter needs. They most obviously depend upon the type of climate and weather conditions that people confront daily, but convention, custom, and the level of technological development are also very important considerations in our evaluations of what is "acceptable" here too. Judgments about the adequacy of clothing, for example, are as subject to prevailing standards of decency and sociocultural and religious practices as they are to prevalent climate conditions. "Adequate" shelters in developed nations are expected to provide their inhabitants with more than just basic protection from hostile elements. A proper residence should also address needs and concerns related to food storage, water supply, and garbage disposal, and should not present a fire hazard or other danger to its inhabitants or to their neighbors. Although not common in the British working-class households examined by Booth and Rowntree in the 1800s, the flush toilets, hot and cold running water, washing machines, dryers, refrigerators, and other appliances and utilities once regarded as luxuries in the past are considered basic essentials for homes across wealthy nations today. The homes of families may be deemed inappropriate and overcrowded if male and female siblings beyond a certain age must share a bedroom. Apart from the relative aspects of even the most basic physiological needs, it has long been acknowledged that humans also have critical social needs.

The well-known psychologist Abraham H. Maslow (1943, 1970), for example, identified a range of "deficiency needs" and "growth needs" that he arranged in a hierarchy of immediacy. Even his lowest and most urgent "deficiency needs" category included safety, belongingness, and self-esteem as critical to human well-being. Social inclusion, social security, a sense of empowerment, and control over one's life, as well as freedom from fear, humiliation, oppression, and coercion, are also commonly considered *essential* for humans. The United Nations' Universal Declaration of Human Rights (1948) and later UN international covenants (e.g., the International Covenant on Civil and Political Rights [1966] and the International Covenant on Social and Cultural Rights [1966]) also identify a more inclusive list of core needs that must be met for all people, including healthcare, education, security, and participation in the cultural life of their communities (Olsen 2011). Many of these considerations, such as getting an education, were less salient for many families just a century ago but are of great concern today. Crucial long-standing and emergent human needs and concerns are neglected or sidelined when the emphasis is on the considerations and provisions required for survival.

Despite these evident limitations, absolute definitions of poverty can be invaluable. They allow us to estimate the size of the population that is in very deep, severe poverty – the group that Charles Booth referred to as the "very poor." Wealthy nations, like Canada, the UK, and the US, have sizable groups of extremely impoverished people – living on the streets, in slums and ghettos, on reserves and reservations, in big cities, and in remote rural areas – in desperate conditions that can closely approximate those found in many poor, low-income nations. It is crucial for governments and organizations that furnish assistance to poor families to know how many people living in their countries experience privations and suffering so acute that their lives are in immediate danger. They also must be able to evaluate the effectiveness of their social programs in addressing extreme poverty. But narrow, absolute definitions are often wielded by governments, intergovernmental organizations, and international institutions to lower poverty rates administratively (rather than actually) and make their further reduction a more attainable goal for which they and their policies can be acclaimed, even though relatively little genuine progress may be in evidence. Absolute poverty definitions also allow conservative and neoliberal research institutes and think tanks to marginalize the more far-reaching policy recommendations of progressive anti-poverty organizations and activists that acknowledge a considerably larger poverty-stricken population extending beyond the most desperately poor – and to discredit their demands for more aggressive responses and greater resources to address this pressing issue.

RELATIVE POVERTY

The limits of absolute poverty definitions have led many researchers to advocate a relative definition of poverty. Some variant of this approach is widely applied around the globe today, especially in cross-national studies examining poverty rates and conditions across the nations of the advanced capitalist world. The relative approach to examining poverty – acknowledging particular sociocultural norms – has a long history too. In his classic study, *Inquiry into the Nature and Causes of the Wealth of Nations,* Adam Smith, one of the most influential and prominent early political economists, was among the first to highlight the relative aspects of poverty. Writing in the late 1700s, he insisted that the category of essential goods or "necessaries" included more than those items required for mere subsistence:

> By necessaries I understand, not only the commodities which are indispensably necessary for the support of life, but whatever the custom of the country renders it indecent for creditable people, even of the lowest order, to be without. A linen shirt, for example, is, strictly speaking, not a necessary of life. The Greeks and Romans lived, I suppose, very comfortably, though they had no linen. But in present times, through the greater part of Europe, a creditable day-labourer would be ashamed to appear in public without a linen shirt, the want of which would be supposed to denote that disgraceful degree of poverty, which, it is presumed, no body can well fall into without extreme bad conduct. Custom, in the same manner, has rendered leather shoes a necessary of life in England. The poorest creditable person of either sex would be ashamed to appear in public without them. (Smith, 1776/2003, pp. 1102–1103)

Smith recognized that a society's customs and established rules of decency determine which goods are considered indispensable for people to avoid degradation, humiliation, and stigma. Two centuries later, John K. Galbraith (1908–2006), the influential Canadian economist who served in the administrations of US presidents Franklin D. Roosevelt,

Harry S. Truman, John F. Kennedy, and Lyndon B. Johnson, emphatically endorsed a relative approach, stressing poverty's abasing facets:

> People are poverty-stricken when their income, even if adequate for survival, falls radically behind that of the community. Then they cannot have what the larger community regards as the minimum necessary for decency; and they cannot wholly escape, therefore, the judgement of the larger community that they are indecent. They are degraded for, in the literal sense, they live outside the grades or categories which the community regards as acceptable. (Galbraith, 1958/1976, p. 245)

The prominent contemporary British poverty researcher Peter Townsend also amplified and elaborated upon the importance of societal conventions and social inclusion in his groundbreaking work on poverty:

> Individuals, families and groups in the population can be said to be in poverty when they lack the resources to obtain the types of diet, participate in the activities and have the living conditions and amenities which are customary, or are at least widely encouraged or approved, in the societies to which they belong. Their resources are so seriously below those commanded by the average individual or family that they are, in effect, excluded from ordinary living patterns, customs and activities. (Townsend, 1979, p. 31)

Unlike absolute definitions of poverty, relative definitions acknowledge that what it means to be poor will change as societies develop and expectations and social conventions change over time.

SUBJECTIVE DEFINITIONS OF POVERTY

Rather than relying on absolute or relative levels of income or consumption patterns to determine if people are poor, subjective definitions employ interviews and surveys to find out what people believe is required to get by in order to establish who is poor. "Consensual" definitions of poverty – a variant within the subjective category – are based upon the idea that there is broad agreement in society about the items deemed "essential," things that everyone must be able to readily access. Households that cannot afford these socially perceived necessities are considered poor. Of course, there is clearly a "relative" dimension to subjective poverty definitions because survey and interview respondents must rely upon "socially established norms" and a commonly held set of expectations and values when they define poverty. As leading UK poverty researchers Joanna Mack and Stewart Lansley (1985) suggest, there may be "no such thing as an 'objective' as opposed to a 'socially perceived' measure: items become 'necessities' only when they are *socially* perceived to be so" (p. 38). Moreover, these social perceptions are determined by prevailing social conditions and context, including the distribution of resources and living standards, as well as the messages and images promoted by the media and other institutions.

A subjective approach has a certain appeal. After all, those facing daily deprivation and hardship should be well qualified to assess the minimum goods or income needed to support themselves and their families in their own communities. However, there are a number of drawbacks to defining poverty subjectively. First, given the infinite variety of short and long-term economic demands and conditions faced by individuals and families (including mortgages, debts, interest rates, and other aspects of family budgets), survey and interview respondents often have widely differing interpretations of what would constitute a level of income sufficient to "make ends meet." People who are "getting by" without an adequate diet or other basic amenities may not consider them necessary; they may not view themselves as poor if their expectations are low. Those who are deprived and exploited may learn to bear their burdens so well that they overlook them, and "discontent is replaced by acceptance" (Sen, 1984, p. 309). At the same time, formerly wealthy people downgraded by circumstance to a middle-class position may consider themselves poverty stricken. As the sociologist and poverty researcher Robert Erikson (1993) notes, "the problem with an approach based on people's own assessment of their degree of satisfaction is that it is partly determined by their level of aspiration, that is, by what they consider to be their rightful due" (p. 77). Studies also suggest that low-income families may be disinclined to identify themselves as "poor" in surveys. Perhaps this should not come as a surprise; popular media depictions of the poor often associate poverty with ignorance, laziness, immorality, and criminality. Some studies also indicate that repeated polling in a country produces substantially different accounts of poverty, making it difficult to track poverty trends accurately over time. Moreover, there are different levels of tolerance for poverty across nations. In the end, because survey data must be interpreted and aggregated by researchers, a subjective approach still relies upon experts to construct poverty lines (Gustafsson & Lindblom, 1993; Hagenaars, 1986; van Praag et al., 1982).

Despite these limitations, subjective approaches can give people living in poverty a voice and provide a means to examine the relationship between public opinion and the outcome of political processes. They also can provide useful information about the conditions, struggles, and strategies of poor families. Although rarely utilized as the central or "official" approach in most nations, subjective definitions have occasionally been employed as auxiliary poverty measures in many nations, including Canada, the UK, and the US, and they are more routinely used in several other countries to learn more about the character of poverty. There is a general consensus among most poverty researchers today that a relative approach is most useful in the developed world, and particularly for comparative studies of poverty. But absolute and subjective methods provide valuable complementary insights.

MEASURING POVERTY: COUNTING THE POOR

"Definitions" of poverty are more focused than "conceptualizations" of poverty; they reflect specific aspects of poverty that researchers consider important, but they are still somewhat abstract. They tell us *what* it is that we should attend to, but they do not precisely indicate *how* poverty will be gauged or the poor counted. Poverty *measures* provide precise "operational definitions" of poverty – working definitions that allow estimates of poverty levels. They do this by establishing *poverty lines*; people living below these thresholds are considered poor. Subjective measures – often used by polling companies such as Gallup, Ipsos MORI, or EKOS, which conduct surveys on behalf of governments, media outlets, and other organizations – ask respondents how much income (or which goods) families need to "get along" in a particular community. But the official or "quasi-official" poverty measures most routinely employed are derived from absolute and/or relative assumptions in most nations, including the United States (absolute), the United Kingdom (relative), and Canada (quasi-relative). Understanding these varying measures is critical.

Absolute Poverty Measures

Absolute poverty measures are based upon some notion of subsistence, but the ways that basic needs are satisfied can differ dramatically across, and even within, nations. Many of the resources that might be essential to families living in more remote villages and rural areas may be less central to most households living in large, rich, urbanized, industrialized metropolises. Researchers seeking to measure poverty in absolute terms typically estimate the cost of a "basket of goods" that meets basic subsistence needs identified in a particular country or across a region or group of broadly similar nations.

The World Bank was among the first organizations to establish an *international* absolute poverty line to allow for cross-national comparisons of poverty and serve as a benchmark to assess global progress in its eradication. International poverty lines attempt to hold the real value of poverty lines constant across nations, as is done in cross-temporal comparisons of poverty within single nations. In order to estimate the share of the world's population living in acute poverty, the World Bank first examined the national poverty lines in those low-income nations that were using them to track domestic poverty levels. It then used purchasing power parity (PPP) exchange rates to convert them all to a common currency and established an international poverty line based on the average of those national thresholds. This culminated in the World Bank's highly publicized "$1-a-day" international poverty line, introduced in 1990 in its flagship publication, the *World Development Report*. Using this measure, people are deemed poor if their required daily income or consumption level is $1 or less. Periodically recalibrated, this absolute approach is still employed by the World Bank today to determine the prevalence and severity of poverty in developing nations. Its revised "$1.25-a-day" measure is now used as its indicator of "extreme" poverty.[2] Apart from being a very narrow "subsistence" metric – largely ignoring actual living and working conditions, access to health, education, and other quality of life indicators – it is often castigated as an arbitrary and immorally low poverty line, "in the order of *one-hundredth* of the average income in the UK ... equivalent to around 37 people living on a single wage, with no recourse to welfare benefits" (Woodward, 2010).[3]

Absolutely Poor: Measuring Poverty in the United States

For practical and political reasons, governments are typically much less concerned with global poverty standards established by international research institutes such as the World Bank than with domestic measures. However, the official poverty measure used in the United States is at least broadly similar in its design to that used by the World Bank. Employed by the US Census Bureau, it is perhaps the best-known *national* absolute poverty measure.

The US absolute poverty line was developed in the early 1960s by Mollie Orshansky, an economist with the Social Security Administration (SSA) when President Lyndon Johnson's "War on Poverty" was underway. She first examined several different food budgets assembled by the US Department of Agriculture (USDA) and chose the most basic and least expensive "Economy Food Plan" – a "food basket" based upon 1955 spending patterns – to represent an adequate subsistence diet. Since previous surveys indicated that families typically devoted approximately one-third of their income toward food, she simply multiplied the cost of the economy food budget by three to approximate the costs of clothing and shelter, the two other widely acknowledged central necessities, in order to determine the *minimum* income level that a household required. From this, she constructed a set of poverty lines for families of various size and type, taking both the age and sex of family members into account. These thresholds were then compared to the Current Population Survey (CPS) estimates of families' pre-tax, cash income in order to determine how many families in the United States were living in poverty.

Orshansky had developed her poverty standard as an interim research instrument, but the thresholds she established were soon adopted by the Office of Economic Opportunity, the agency responsible for administering most of the "War on Poverty" programs in the United States, and became the official national poverty measure. Although these thresholds are updated annually for price inflation, based upon changes in the Consumer Price Index (CPI), they do not change in "real dollar" terms. Consequently, the "purchasing power" of the income levels that they recommend today is the same as when the poverty lines were originally established well over half a century ago (Fisher, 1992; Iceland, 2013; Ruggles, 1990).[4]

This narrowly defined official measure used by the Census Bureau underestimates the level and severity of poverty in the United States in several ways. First, while poverty thresholds are adjusted up or down with inflation, these adjustments do not reflect the fact that the cost of many necessities, such as shelter, utilities, childcare and medical care, has risen much faster than the *average* price increase of the broader bundle of commodities included in the CPI. Moreover, because prices of food relative to those of other necessities have declined markedly since Orshansky conducted her studies over six decades ago, the living standards derived from multiplying the greatly reduced cost of food by three have deteriorated in tandem. Finding and maintaining a job, for example, requires greater expenses for transportation and communication, including the costs of cell phones and computers. Second, the amount of money allocated to food is based upon estimates of what is required for "subsistence," not for maintaining long-term health. Third, these poverty lines do not take into account the variation in both patterns of consumption and the cost of living across the different regions and communities of the US mainland.[5] Fourth, this poverty measure considers only pre-tax income, overestimating the amount of money that many families are left with to survive on. But it also excludes income received from government programs, creating an even more confusing picture of the numbers of the poor in the United States and the impact of social programs on poverty rates.[6] Finally, the measure misses both the large "near poor" population living on incomes that are only a few dollars above its poverty thresholds and the acutely poor populations who live very far below them but are not easily located or surveyed – the homeless population (Haveman, 1987; Iceland, 2013; Ruggles, 1990). In order to address some of these issues the United States has employed an additional Supplemental Poverty Measure (SPM) since 2011.[7]

Advocates of absolute measures often maintain that strong economic growth invariably leads to marked declines in poverty rates. Of course, it is easier to bring poor families above a very low absolute poverty line than to address their broader needs and concerns. But even the modest goal of raising families above these thresholds cannot be reached without organizations and social policies that promote a fairer distribution of the wealth created through growth.

Relative Poverty Measures

Accounts of poverty in Europe tend to favor relative measures. Although they can assume several forms, relative measures are all based upon some type of comparison or contrast among people or households within the same society. Some examine prevailing patterns of expenditure and consumption for a lengthy list of commodities to determine how far individuals, families, or households fall below social norms. Most relative measures, however, utilize poverty lines that are statistically constructed. Some arbitrarily label the bottom 10 percent or 20 percent of an income distribution in society as poor. More commonly, relative measures are based upon an income cutoff that can be expressed as a proportion of the average income for a given society as a whole. Studies from the Organisation for Economic Co-operation and Development (OECD); the United Nations Human Development Reports (UNHD); research from Eurostat, the European Union's (EU) statistical agency; and many other cross-national poverty studies operationally define poverty to include those households with an income that is less than a particular fraction (typically 50 percent or 60 percent) of the average (median or mean) income in each of the countries being examined in order to take broader societal living standards into account. Although poverty researchers using these relative approaches still have to make some arbitrary decisions to establish poverty lines, they typically make fewer subjective judgments than required by those constructing absolute thresholds (Fellegi, 1997; Iceland, 2013; Ruggles, 1990).

Purely relative measures of poverty have some disadvantages. Some critics argue that relative measures identify and address "income inequality" in society, not poverty, which, they maintain, must be measured on the basis of scientific anthropometric and physiological criteria (e.g., Rector & Sheffield, 2011; Sarlo, 1992, 2019).[8] They also point out that relative measures cannot easily register the incidence of poverty in nations in which most people are destitute. Critics of relative poverty measures argue that they tend to inflate levels of poverty. But they might also underestimate the level of poverty in some situations; in a society in which most people have very low incomes and few are well off, the percentage of those with less than the average (the "relatively" poor) will be low.

Some statistically defined relative measures of poverty make it difficult to assess just how poor some people are relative to others or to monitor and track changes in poverty rates and conditions. For example, if the bottom 10 percent of income earners is defined as poor, we do not know – without employing additional measures – how large the difference is between the income level of this group and that of the next 10 percent (or any other decile) in that society. Moreover, no change in the position of the lowest decile would be registered even if the income level of every household in society increased tenfold. In *relative terms*, the bottom 10 percent would still be the bottom 10 percent; it would appear to be no better off than it was before, even though its purchasing power and quality of life (assuming price stability) could have improved markedly. The same would be true if the living standards of every household were to decline drastically in tandem. Purely relative poverty measures, their opponents suggest, present a "moving target," so poverty can never be eliminated or even diminished. They argue that, while it is possible for everyone in a society to rise above an absolute, subsistence income or consumption level, relative measures do not allow us to track poverty reduction because a certain, statistically defined part of the population will always be defined as relatively poor (Huston et al., 1994; Sarlo, 1992). Of course, from the perspective of most researchers who endorse relative measures, even if everyone's income goes up tenfold, those at the bottom will still be *relatively* deprived. In many ways, little will have changed for them (especially if the cost of living has also risen). We could more fully determine if this bottom group is actually any better off by examining other central dimensions of poverty, such as their life chances, degree of social exclusion, and other forms of social degradation relative to others in their society.

Although some of these objections are valid, relative poverty measures are very useful when employed properly. The criticisms of the relative approach noted above best apply to definitions based on a certain set percentage of all households as poor – such as "the bottom 10 percent." Unless the distribution of income is greatly equalized, there always will be a bottom 10 percent that is defined as poor. But this type of relative poverty measure is rarely employed. More commonly, people or households are defined as poor when they have less than 50 percent (or 60 percent) of the median or average income of families in a society. Of course, it does not make sense to use relative measures in comparative studies of poverty across all of the nations of the developed and developing worlds. But relative measures are invaluable for comparing rates and trends within and across rich developed nations. Further, it is simply inaccurate to suggest that changes in poverty levels cannot be detected using relative measures. Such an argument is premised upon the entirely erroneous neoliberal idea that the only way to reduce poverty is through economic growth. Poverty researchers David P. Ross et al. (2000) clearly illuminate the flaws with this popular but false assumption:

> [I]magine a society of 100 people ranged on an income ladder according to their levels of income. The person with the highest income is on the first rung at the top and the person with the lowest income is on the 100th at the bottom. If everyone's income increases equally because of general economic growth, then the ladder shifts up, but people will stay on the same rungs. Thus, those on the bottom rungs will always be poor; they will never rise above the 75th rung (assuming this rung represents a poverty line defined as one-half of average income). However, if redistribution of income (through direct income transfers or jobs) is the major means for resolving poverty, then it is quite possible to move all people above the level of income formerly marked by the 75th rung. In this case, shifting income from the top to lower rungs of the ladder does not increase the target average income, it just rearranges the same total amount. (pp. 7–8)

In fact, relative poverty has been markedly reduced in many nations through progressive fiscal and social policies that promote a fairer distribution of income and wealth in society, and via labor market programs designed to promote full employment. Strong unions and labor movements also have played a crucial role in reducing levels of inequality and poverty, however measured, in many developed nations. A review of trends in the Nordic lands, among others, clearly indicates the impact that such measures can have upon relative poverty rates (e.g., Brady, 2003a, 2009; Moller et al., 2003; Olsen, 2002, 2011). And poverty rates among the elderly and other subpopulations have been dramatically lowered in many countries through the development of pensions and other social programs.

Of course, studies that rely solely on economic indicators to set relative poverty lines will miss "life chances," "quality of life," and other important aspects of poverty. In the Nordic lands and many other nations, there is a much wider range of supports, services, and protections for poor and low-income households, an important detail often overlooked when these nations' notably lower poverty rates alone are contrasted with those in the Anglo nations; poor people are considerably better off in nations that provide greater social services and other social supports and legal protections for their residents. If used in conjunction with other poverty indicators and considerations, relative measures are indispensable to studies of poverty within and across the wealthy, developed nations of the world. They also have been invaluable for tracking poverty trends over time, assessing which groups are overrepresented among the poor, and assessing the impact of social policies in cross-national comparisons.

Measuring Poverty in the United Kingdom and Canada: Relative and Absolute Considerations

The United Kingdom has been a pioneer and a long-standing leader in the study and measurement of poverty. Poverty research in the UK established traditions that have had a profound and enduring impact in Canada, the US, Australia and New Zealand, and outside these former British colonies. The principal source of data on income poverty in the UK today is an annual report called *Households Below Average Income* (HBAI), produced by the Department for Work and Pensions (DWP) using low-income data derived from the Family Resources Survey (FRS). The HBAI reports, which provide information on the size and characteristics of the low-income population in the UK, employ both relative and absolute income thresholds, based upon both median and mean household incomes, for income measured both before and after housing costs (Townsend, 2004). Although not an "official" poverty series, the annual HBAI reports provide low-income poverty data using thresholds that are widely accepted as poverty lines in many international studies, such as those produced by the OECD and Eurostat. The most commonly employed poverty metric in the UK is a relative measure that defines households (adjusted for size) as "poor" if their income is 60 percent or less of the national median income.

One contentious aspect of the UK's measure is that the poverty threshold changes each year as the median income changes, affecting both the number of people defined as poor and the poverty rate. If the median income falls, for example, the number of people below this new median income (60 percent of the lower median) will be reduced, lowering the poverty rate. Many households that were previously listed as poor, consequently, will no longer be recorded as poor, even though their incomes and their living standards remain the same as they were before. In order to address this issue, the HBAI report also uses an "anchored" threshold based upon 60 percent of the median income from a previous year. Although referred to as an "absolute" measure in the HBAI reports, this "anchored" threshold is not a true absolute measure; that is, it is not based upon the cost of a few basic necessities, such as the absolute measure used by the US Census Bureau. But it serves as a kind of proxy for one, addressing a concern raised by critics of relative poverty measures (that relative poverty is a "moving target") and allowing poverty researchers to track trends over time. Useful studies of the prevalence, distribution, and root causes of poverty in the United Kingdom are also provided through the Joseph Rowntree Foundation, a prominent charitable institution with roots that go back to 1904 (MacInnes et al., 2014; Parekh et al., 2010).[9]

Until recently, Canada, like the UK, has not employed an "official" poverty measure. Rather, three very different metrics have been in play to address this issue. In an attempt to sidestep political controversy, all of them were said to provide estimates of the prevalence of families with "low income" or living in "straitened circumstances." But these approaches have been widely accepted as indicators of the scope and severity of poverty (Canadian Council on Social Development, 2001; National Council of Welfare, 2009; Statistics Canada, 2010).[10]

The Market Basket Measure (MBM), Canada's most recent poverty metric, was developed by the Federal/Provincial/Territorial Working Group on Social Development Research and Information under the auspices of Human Resources Development Canada (HRDC). As the name suggests, the MBM is an *absolute* poverty approach based upon the cost of purchasing a specified basket of essential goods. Introduced in a 2002 report, its basket of goods included estimates of the costs of basic telephone service, transportation, school supplies, books and other reading materials, recreation and entertainment, and other personal care and social service expenses, in addition to food, clothing, and shelter – a considerably more expansive "basket of necessities" than that used in the US Census Bureau's absolute poverty estimates.[11] Because they are based upon the cost of purchasing these goods and services in the *local* marketplace, MBM thresholds are sensitive to variation in the cost of living across Canada, and they have been periodically readjusted.

They reflect a "modest," basic standard of living, falling somewhere between the strict, "subsistence" standard used in the United States, and a more generous basket designed with greater social inclusion in mind. In 2018, the federal Liberal government revamped its MBM to establish Canada's first official poverty line.

Canada also employs a strictly relative approach – the Low Income Measure (LIM) – that is very similar to the official metric used in the UK, and subject to the same concerns and issues. But LIMs are based upon 50 percent of the median family income threshold (adjusted for family size) rather than the 60 percent used in the UK. And, unlike Canada's MBM, they are uniform across the nation. However, the primary sources of poverty data in Canada have been Low Income Cut-Offs (LICOs), uniquely Canadian measures based upon *both* absolute and relative considerations.

The LICO, Canada's oldest, most widely recognized, and most cited poverty metric, was introduced in a 1968 report by the Economic Council of Canada, but LICOs originate in poverty research carried out by Statistics Canada in the late 1950s and early 1960s. A 1959 Statistics Canada survey suggested that the average Canadian family spent about 50 percent of its income on food, clothing, and shelter, the three "basic necessities" emphasized in absolute measurements of poverty. Jenny Podoluk, an economist at Statistics Canada, then proposed that families devoting 70 percent or more of their income to these essentials (i.e., 20 percent or more than what the average family was spending on them) should be viewed as poor. Podoluk's suggestion that poverty be defined in relation to what the *average* Canadian family spent on "basic necessities" added a "relative" dimension to the poverty measure.

Unlike the absolute poverty metric in the United States, which is based upon estimates of an appropriate *minimum* level of income necessary for survival, LICOs are based upon estimates of an appropriate *maximum* proportion of family income directed toward subsistence goods, a proportion that is defined relatively, namely, in relation to what the average family spends on them. Families spending disproportionate amounts of their income on basic necessities, it was reasoned, have very little money left for other essential purchases, such as transportation, health, dental and personal care, prescription drugs, childcare, and recreation. Consequently, they are substantially worse off than average Canadian families and are deprived and excluded from full participation in their society – concerns highlighted by researchers advocating relative poverty measures. Podoluk then calculated a series of LICOs set at the points where families of different sizes would likely spend 20 percent or more of their income on basic necessities than would the average family.[12] These thresholds were then compared with Statistics Canada's annual household survey income estimates to determine how many families were living in "straitened circumstances," the official euphemism for poverty in Canada. As in the United States, the proportion of income spent on the three "basic essentials" in Canada has declined over time. But, unlike in the United States, this prompted several revisions to update ("rebase") Podoluk's original calculations. The last revision occurred in 1992 when Statistics Canada's Family Expenditure Survey (FAMEX) indicated that average family expenditure on the three basic necessities had dropped to 34.7 percent of their income. Following Podoluk's "20%-or-more" formula, Statistics Canada established a new series of low-income thresholds set at income levels where families spend 54.7 percent or more of their income on the three basic necessities.

Although it originally focused upon gross, *before-tax* income to establish LICOs, Statistics Canada began to include *after-tax* LICOs as well in 2000 (and retroactively calculated them back to 1976). After all, it seems logical to define individuals and families as poor ("low income") in relation to the actual amount of money they have left to spend. Given the progressive nature of income tax, the rate of poverty is reduced when post-tax income is examined. However, these new post-tax LICOs do not provide an entirely complete or accurate picture of consumable income because Statistics Canada's after-income-tax definition of income does not consider (1) regressive taxes, such as sales and consumption taxes, which bear most heavily upon the less affluent; (2) payroll taxes (such as unemployment insurance and pension premiums), which are deducted from employment income up to a threshold level and are thus somewhat regressive in nature; and (3) the considerably higher proportion of income spent by the less affluent on employment expenses, such as childcare and transportation. In short, they take only the progressive aspects of the taxation system into account while ignoring the regressive or flat aspects of it, thereby underestimating the incidence of poverty (Canadian Council on Social Development, 2001).

Despite its initially more "relative" orientation, the LICO approach has become more like its absolute American counterpart over the past two decades and now more blatantly shares many of its problems. First, because the thresholds have not been recalibrated since 1992, LICOs have become increasingly distant from average expenditure levels and, thereby, less relative. Second, as in the United States, LICOs are not adjusted to reflect the greater needs and broader patterns of consumption today – a crucial "relative poverty" concern. Third, the adjustments made for community size in the calculation of LICOs do not acknowledge differences in the cost of living across the range of cities grouped together in the "large city" category (500,000 or more inhabitants); living costs can vary markedly across major metropolitan centers such as Calgary, Edmonton, Montreal, Ottawa, Toronto, Vancouver, and Winnipeg. Finally, like other poverty measures, LICOs neglect, or greatly underrepresent, poverty on reserves and amongst the large homeless population in Canada.

HOMELESSNESS: ACUTE, ENCOMPASSING POVERTY

> Do not ask the name of the person who seeks a bed for the night.
> He who is reluctant to give his name is the one who most needs
> shelter.
> – Victor Hugo (1862/2001)

Homelessness is one of the deepest and most severe forms of poverty. It most immediately refers to the absence of regular, adequate, and appropriate housing but typically includes myriad forms of other related privations and social exclusions. As with poverty, there is no universal definition of homelessness across all nations; indeed, there can be considerable variation in the ways that it is conceptualized, defined, and measured over time and place by various official organizations and other research institutes across and even within nations. The United Nations distinguishes two broad categories of homelessness, *absolute* homelessness and *relative* homelessness, paralleling the two dominant definitions of poverty. The absolute definition of homelessness is the most restrictive, including only people who are without any physical shelter in the most literal sense. From this perspective, the homeless are those who "live on the street," sleeping on sidewalks and under tunnels; in subways, bus stations, and train depots; in vacant buildings, family cars, and old abandoned vehicles; in tents and cardboard boxes; and in parks and campgrounds within or outside city limits. This narrow understanding fits the popular image of severe or "acute" homelessness commonly depicted in the media – images of people on busy streets and other public spaces in large urban centers who may have mental health or substance abuse problems. But the majority of the people living on the streets, or "sleeping rough," do their best to avoid the public and stay out of sight and, thereby, are commonly missed in studies of the prevalence and conditions of homelessness. They constitute one group of the "hidden homeless" that is not included, or is significantly underrepresented, in virtually all estimates of homelessness.

Relative definitions of homelessness are much broader, including people who sleep in shelters, hostels, welfare hotels, refuges, missions, lodging houses ("flophouses"), and other temporary and insecure forms of accommodation, as well as those who involuntarily live in the basements or sleep on the floors and couches of friends and family members. Although these people are not literally without shelter, their tenure is unstable, inadequate, and/or insecure, and they typically have no private space of their own. Relative homelessness also may include people who have substandard housing that provides little protection against hostile weather, lacks basic amenities, or is overcrowded, unsafe and unsanitary, infested with rodents or insects, or otherwise unfit for human habitation. A relative definition, therefore, includes several other forms of "hidden homelessness," embracing large numbers of people who are typically left out of official estimates of the size of homeless populations.

The European Federation of National Organisations Working with Homeless People (FEANTSA) has developed one of the most useful ways to conceptualize and understand different forms of homelessness. FEANTSA's European Typology on Homelessness and Housing Exclusion (ETHOS) is based upon a definition of a "home" in relation to three key domains: the *physical*, the *social*, and the *legal*. If the criteria of all three domains are met, a dwelling can be considered a "home."

Having a home can be understood as: having an adequate dwelling (or space) over which a person and his/her family can exercise exclusive possession (*physical domain*); being able to maintain privacy and enjoy relations (*social domain*) and having legal title to occupation (*legal domain*). (Edgar et al., 2004, p. 5)

The ETHOS typology identifies four conceptual categories of homelessness on the basis of how closely they satisfy or approximate the criteria in each of them. The *roofless* category includes people living on the streets, who are excluded from all three domains – physical, social, and legal ("absolute homelessness"). The *houseless* category comprises people who are living in temporary accommodations, such as interim or short-term shelters, and people living in prisons, hospitals, and treatment centers that will have nowhere to live when they are discharged. People in the houseless category have a dwelling (physical domain) but are excluded from the legal domain because they do not have legal title to their space and from the social domain because they do not have a private or safe space for social relations. The *insecure housing* category includes people who are without legal tenancy or are living under the threat of eviction as well as those whose circumstances render them vulnerable to physical or sexual violence and abuse. The members in this category are excluded from the legal domain and are always at great risk of becoming homeless. Finally, the *inadequate housing* category is composed of people who live in dwellings that are hazardous to their well-being. Although the ETHOS typology identifies the last two categories (insecure housing and inadequate housing) as forms of "housing exclusion," rather than homelessness per se, other researchers note that the living conditions of people in these situations can be just as extreme and difficult as those endured by roofless and houseless people (Amore et al., 2011; Sahlin, 2012). Based upon their relationship to these three domains, ETHOS groups people into seven different conceptual categories of homelessness and housing exclusion that address variations in the character, extent, and depth of homelessness (see Figure 2.1). People may be excluded from one domain, some combination of two domains, or all three domains (see Table 2.1).

Conditions and Context of Homelessness

The starvation and lack of shelter I encountered constituted a chronic condition of misery that is never wiped out even in periods of greatest prosperity.

– Jack London (1903/2001)

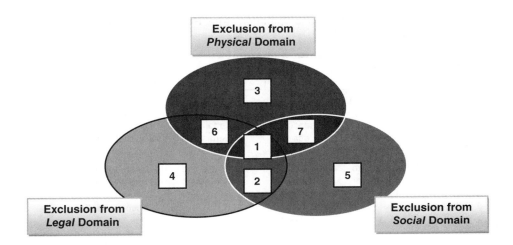

1 Rooflessness

2 Houselessness

3 Inadequate Housing (with secure tenure)

4 Insecure Housing (with adequate housing)

5 Social Isolation within a Secure and Adequate Context

6 Insecure and Inadequate Housing

7 Inadequate Housing and Social Isolation within a Legally Occupied Dwelling

Figure 2.1. The Three Domains of Homelessness/Housing Exclusion (ETHOS)
Source: Adapted from Edgar and Meert (2006).

Of course, like poverty, homelessness is associated with a broad range of conditions and deprivations beyond inadequate housing. These include a low income (a central consideration in market societies because almost everything has to be purchased, including the most basic essentials), inadequate social supports, few entitlements and rights that can actually be enjoyed or exercised, and near-total social exclusion from society. The homeless have no substantial private property or space and none of the basic rights and privileges these assets confer, such as a personal place to eat, rest, sleep, store belongings, or be with family and friends. They can only carry out these activities in public spaces, but anti-vagrancy laws, harassment, and the threat of incarceration prevent them from sleeping, "loitering," eating, and

Table 2.1. Conceptualizing and Operationalizing Homelessness and Housing Exclusion (ETHOS)*

Conceptual Category	Physical Domain	Legal Domain	Social Domain	Operational Definitions
1. Rooflessness	no dwelling (roof)	no legal entitlement to space for exclusive possession	no private and safe personal space for social relations	– living on the streets ("living rough") – staying in overnight shelters or emergency accommodations
2. Houselessness	a place to live, fit for habitation	no legal entitlement to space for exclusive possession	no private and safe personal space for social relations	– living in homeless shelters, hostels, refuges, and other temporary accommodations – due for release from institutions or residential care centers (penal, medical, children's home)
3. Inadequate Housing (with secure tenure)	dwelling unfit for habitation	has legal title and/or security of tenure	has space for social relations	– living in tents, makeshift shelters, shacks or shanties, overcrowded housing, or other dwellings not intended for human residence or deemed unfit by legislation or building regulations
4. Insecure Housing (with adequate housing)	a place to live	no security of tenure	has space for social relations	– temporarily living with family or friends – living with no legal (sub) tenancy – illegally occupying land – eviction or repossession orders underway
5. Social Isolation (with secure and adequate housing)	a place to live	has legal title and/or security of tenure	no private and safe personal space for social relations	– living in overcrowded conditions
6. Insecure and Inadequate Housing	dwelling unfit for habitation	no security of tenure	has space for social relations	– unlawfully occupying shelters unfit for human habitation (e.g., barns, sheds)
7. Inadequate Housing and Social Isolation (legally secure)	dwelling unfit for habitation	has legal title and/or security of tenure	no private and safe personal space for social relations	– families doubling up in inadequate dwellings

* The shaded cells show the deficits experienced by people in each category of homelessness or housing insecurity.
Source: Adapted from Edgar and Meert (2006) and Olsen and Benjaminsen (2019).

performing other activities necessary to live. These laws and practices strip the homeless of their rights, freedom, and autonomy. As political philosopher Jeremy Waldron (1997) notes, "No one is free to perform an action unless there is somewhere he [or she] is free to perform it" (p. 446). Other severely deprived and degraded groups at the bottom of historical social hierarchies, such as slaves, feudal serfs, and "untouchables" or outcasts of caste systems, have experienced a similarly sweeping denial of rights and almost complete social exclusion, but even they had a widely acknowledged function and purpose in their societies. The homeless, in contrast, are depicted as a surplus population whose only value is to serve as a warning to others (Olsen & Benjaminsen, 2019).

Nations vary greatly in the ways that they conceptualize and define homelessness, ranging from narrow absolute approaches to more inclusive approaches similar to the ETHOS typology. The decision to conceptualize homelessness very strictly often reflects attempts by governments and other organizations and agencies to minify a serious problem or define it away. However, as with measuring poverty, the use of discrete or restricted definitions may also reflect a genuine concern with addressing desperate immediate needs, such as the number of beds or meals that are required each day. Broader definitions of homelessness are more concerned with urgent "at risk" populations and the precariously and provisionally housed, not only the "houseless" group of people living on the streets. This approach targets both the current and future needs of homeless populations, placing greater emphasis upon preventing, not just managing, homelessness. It entails identifying and addressing the many risk factors (including mental health issues and substance abuse disorders), pathways (such as domestic and sexual abuse and childhood trauma), and structural conditions (discrimination, shortages of adequate and affordable housing stock, high rates of unemployment, stagnating wages, declining levels and forms of social supports, and so on) that can lead to homelessness. But more inclusive studies are considerably more difficult and costly to carry out, which discourages researchers from conducting them.

Because the homeless lack permanent addresses and are highly mobile, censuses, surveys, and other traditional means of measurement and data collection are not well suited for identifying and studying homeless populations. Large numbers of homeless people, including most of those living on the streets, staying with friends, or poorly housed – three prevalent forms of "hidden homelessness" across virtually all wealthy nations – are difficult to find and unlikely to be identified and counted by researchers. Those who are more readily located may not always want to cooperate with those who are studying them. Consequently, researchers often estimate homelessness rates by using records of the numbers of people they can more easily monitor, such as those who use shelters, soup kitchens, and hostels, but the quality and accuracy of these data can vary greatly. Ironically, the size of homeless populations will tend to be most seriously underestimated in those nations, and in those regions within nations, that have the least developed networks of benefits, services, and organizations to support the homeless. Nations with limited spaces in shelters and minimal services available for homeless people can only acknowledge a number equal to the restricted capacity of their spaces – a phenomenon referred to as the "service statistics paradox." Those who do not use these amenities at all, or who use them only infrequently, will be entirely overlooked.

Some studies provide "snapshots" of homelessness, recording the number of people that are "unhoused" on a particular night ("point prevalence" measures). Other studies focus on people who are homeless for longer periods of time, such as a week, a month, or a year ("period prevalence" measures). Both approaches miss people who are no longer homeless but have experienced homelessness at some point in their lives. Telephone surveys asking about homelessness over respondents' lifetimes produce higher estimates. But this approach typically excludes many people who are *currently* homeless, and inaccessible by phone. The challenges of studying homelessness in a single nation and time frame are greatly amplified in cross-national research on homelessness, given the notable variation in how homelessness is defined and data are collected. Consequently, comparative studies are less frequently undertaken, but they have provided valuable insights (e.g., Benjaminsen & Dyb, 2008; G. Daly, 1996; M. Daly, 1999; Shinn, 2010; Toro et al., 2007).

Canada, the UK, and the US have used different approaches to estimate the scope of homelessness and to track ongoing patterns and trends over time. Indeed, uniform definitions and measures have been elusive even *within* these three countries among various branches and levels of government, nongovernmental research centers, and advocacy organizations. In the United States, there is not even a single federal definition of homelessness. The definition set out by the McKinney-Vento Homeless Act of 1987 (and subsequently amended) to determine eligibility for the array of programs and services it authorized was adopted by the Department of Housing and Urban Development (HUD), the Department of Labor, and the Department of Veterans Affairs. It considers people homeless if they are living in a temporary shelter or sleeping in a place not appropriate for shelter. But other departments, such as Education, Health and Human Services (HHS), and Justice, have employed definitions that are more inclusive or highlight other dimensions of homelessness for access to their programs. In Canada, various levels of government and agencies (such as Statistics Canada), as well as independent, nonprofit organizations (such as the Canadian Council on Social Development), have also utilized disparate approaches and metrics. In the United Kingdom, homelessness data can reflect the divergent definitions and measures employed within and across England, Ireland, Scotland, and Wales (Congressional Research Service, 2018; Frankish et al., 2005; Government Statistical Service, 2019).

Homelessness has been increasingly acknowledged as a serious and growing problem in Canada, the UK, and the US since the 1980s. But, until recently, they all greatly underestimated the scope of homelessness because they primarily addressed only two forms of it ("rooflessness" and "houselessness"). Moreover, their estimates of those two forms of homelessness were decidedly inadequate because they were based on the numbers of people who used a homeless shelter or service on a given night or were openly living on the streets and easily located. Their measures did not reflect the full extent and gravity of the problem, discounting several pathways and manifestations of homelessness. The studies undertaken in the three Anglo nations, documenting the number of homeless people in shelters or living on the streets in urban centers and encampments, primarily spotlighted white adult males who often have mental health and substance abuse issues. But they overlooked the increasing numbers of women, children, and youth fleeing various forms of domestic violence, abuse, neglect, and rejection who were living in transitional homes and women's shelters or provisionally doubling up with friends and relatives in order to escape harm. LGBTQ2S people, greatly overrepresented among homeless youth, were also missed because they typically avoid using homeless shelters where policy, staff, and patrons may be homophobic and transphobic. Homelessness estimates in the three Anglo nations have also excluded women who are precariously housed and at considerable risk of homelessness – those whose income is so low they would be destitute if their partner was no longer living with them due to separation, divorce, or death – and more likely to be the head of single-parent families when partners split up (Abramovich & Shelton, 2017; Bretherton, 2017; Johnson et al., 2017; Scott, 1984).

Although all three Anglo nations have adopted more inclusive definitions, measures, and data collection practices, ones that better address some of the concerns set out in the ETHOS typology, the US approach remains more restrictive than those employed in Canada and the UK. Yet despite its less inclusive approach, poverty and homelessness rates are notably higher in the United States, reflecting its policy orientation and other underlying conditions. In Chapter 3, poverty levels, patterns, and trends in Canada, the United Kingdom, and the United States are explored using each nation's poverty data. This exploration is followed by a discussion illuminating comparative contrasts among the three national approaches to poverty and homelessness, which are then compared with those of other wealthy nations that have been more successful addressing poverty and homelessness.

NOTES

1   Booth's chief assistant, Hubert Smith, produced a nine-volume study of London in the 1930s, and Rowntree published sequels to his 1899 study of York in 1935 and 1951. Other economists, such as Arthur Lyon Bowley and Frederick Scott, studied the conditions of the working class and the poor in other cities and towns in the UK, including Reading, Northampton, Warrington, Stanley, Manchester, and Salford, in the first half of the twentieth century (Gillie, 1996; Hennock, 1987).

2   The World Bank recalibrated its lower level poverty line to $1.08 a day or less (in 1993 prices) in 1999 and again to $1.25 a day or less (in 2005

prices) in 2008, as more national poverty lines and more accurate data became available (World Bank, 2008).

3 A "$2-a-day" standard serves as an "upper level" poverty line in developing nations. For the nations of the wealthy, developed world, the World Bank set its poverty line at $11 a day.

4 The US Department of Health and Human Services (HHS) has also employed "poverty guidelines" to determine financial eligibility for more than 20 federal programs, including Head Start, the Food Stamp Program (now known as the Supplemental Nutrition Assistance Program/SNAP), the National School Lunch Program, the Low Income Home Energy Assistance Program, and some parts of Medicaid (Fisher, 1992; Ruggles, 1990).

5 Between 1966 and 1970, separate poverty guidelines were established for Alaska and Hawaii.

6 During the Reagan-Bush era, it was commonly argued that poverty would be nonexistent in the United States if "in-kind" benefits, such as food stamps and healthcare (Medicaid), were included as part of a family's income. However, access to most programs for the poor is dependent upon an income level considerably lower than the official poverty line. Including the cost of some social programs for people in poverty, such as the publicly provided medical care that some of the poor receive as part of their income, also can create confusion; according to this logic, a person might no longer be considered poor if that individual receives a significant amount of financial support to address a serious illness.

7 Although developed earlier, the current Supplemental Poverty Measure (SPM) was created in 2010 based on the recommendations of a panel of experts from the National Academy of Sciences. Employed since 2011, it includes a broader basket of essentials and takes into account many government programs designed to assist low-income families and individuals that are not included in the official poverty measure. It has a relative cast because its thresholds are adjusted for variations in costs by state and metropolitan area and updated annually to reflect real growth in expenditures on this basket of goods (Iceland, 2013; Johnson & Smeeding, 2012; Meyer & Sullivan, 2012).

8 These criticisms of relative poverty measures are most commonly made by neoliberal think tanks in Canada (e.g., the Fraser Institute), the UK (e.g., the Adam Smith Institute), and the United States (e.g. the Heritage Foundation). They conceptualize and measure poverty narrowly to reduce the gravity of the problem and redirect state resources.

9 Entrepreneur and member of the renowned Rowntree confectionary family, Joseph Rowntree (1836–1925) was also a noted philanthropist and social reformer. He was the father of B. Seebohm Rowntree and a friend to Charles Booth, the influential researchers who laid the groundwork for poverty research in the United Kingdom that would be adopted and adapted in many other nations.

10 The new MBM defines poverty as the conditions faced by people who are "deprived of the resources, means, choices and power necessary to acquire and maintain a basic level of living standards and to facilitate integration and participation in society" (Employment and Social Development Canada, 2018, p. 8). It "reflects the combined costs of a basket of goods and services that individuals and families require to meet their basic needs and achieve a modest standard of living. The basket includes items such as healthy food, appropriate shelter and home maintenance, and clothing and transportation. It also includes other goods and services that permit engagement in the community, particularly for children, youth, parents and seniors" (p. 11). Using this definition, a household or family lives in poverty if it does not have enough income to purchase this basket of goods and services in its community. The MBM uses a more inclusive basket than the US absolute measure but still excludes important items such as childcare and prescription medicines.

11 The MBM is an "absolute" poverty metric because it is not constructed on the basis of where people stand in relation to others in their society. But it has a "relative" cast because it is based upon an updated and broader conceptualization of what is considered "essential" today.

12 LICOs (Low Income Cut-Offs) are adjusted to accommodate seven family sizes, four different community sizes, and a rural/urban distinction, yielding thirty-five poverty or low-income thresholds.

SONGS ABOUT POVERTY AND HOMELESSNESS

However useful, accounts of poverty and homelessness that focus only on income levels below an established official threshold or the numbers of people finding refuge in a crowded shelter miss the character of destitution – the unrelenting quotidian hardships, miseries, and grief that can undermine mental and physical health and truncate life expectancies; the solitude and alienation; the loss of rights and freedoms; the struggle to reclaim public space; the assaults on human dignity; the heartache and the contempt endured; the resignation; and the resistance. Poets, songwriters, musicians, and other artists can profoundly distill this complex picture, or more effectually illuminate particular dimensions of it, in ways that transcend statistics. It should not be surprising that so many poignant and powerful songs come from the United States, where poverty has been more widespread, entrenched, and unchecked than in most other nations in the wealthy capitalist world – and where it has been long and intimately connected to racism. The songs listed below capture various aspects and dimensions of poverty and homelessness.

Listen to the playlist here: https://spoti.fi/3cCF8fb

B.B. King, "Why I Sing the Blues" (1969)
Ben Harper, "Homeless Child" (1997)
Bessie Smith, "Homeless Blues" (1992 [1927])
Bessie Smith, "Poor Man's Blues" (1993 [1928])
Bruce Springsteen, "Brothers Under the Bridge" (1998)
Bruce Springsteen, "The Ghost of Tom Joad" (1995)
Candlebox, "He Calls Home" (1993)
Craig Morgan, "Almost Home" (2003)
Ed Sheeran, "The A Team" (2011)
Emerson Drive, "Moments" (2006)
Gil Scott-Heron, "Whitey on the Moon" (1970)
Grandmaster Flash and Furious Five, "The Message" (1982)
Harry Nilsson, "Mournin' Glory Story" (1969)
Immortal Technique, "The Poverty of Philosophy" (2001)
John Mellencamp, "Jackie Brown" (1989)
Ralph McTell, "Streets of London" (1969)

FURTHER READINGS

Abramovich, A., & Shelton, J. (Eds.). (2017). *Where am I going to go?: Intersectional approaches to ending LGBTQ2S youth homelessness in Canada and the US*. Canadian Observatory on Homelessness.

Daly, G. (1996). *Homeless: Policies, strategies and lives on the street*. Routledge.

Kusmer, K.L. (2002). *Down and out and on the road: The homeless in American history*. Oxford University Press.

Peters, E.J., & Christensen, J. (Eds.). (2016). *Indigenous homelessness: Perspectives from Canada, Australia, and New Zealand*. University of Manitoba Press.

Teixeira, L., & Cartwright, J. (Eds.). (2020). *Using evidence to end homelessness*. Policy Press.

PERSONAL ACCOUNTS OF HOMELESSNESS

Bishop-Stall, S. (2005). *Down to this: Squalor and splendor in a big-city shantytown*. Vintage Books.

Dickens, C. (2010). *Night walks*. Penguin Books. (Original work published 1860)

Eighner, L. (1993). *Travels with Lizbeth: Three years on the road and on the streets*. St. Martin's Press.

Karp, B. (2011). *The girl's guide to homelessness: A memoir*. Harlequin Enterprises.

London, J. (2001). *The people of the abyss.* Pluto Press. (Original work published 1903)

Orwell, G. (1961). *Down and out in Paris and London.* Harcourt Brace Jovanovich. (Original work published 1933)

Scott, S. (2007). *All our sisters: Stories of homeless women in Canada.* University of Toronto Press.

Stringer, L. (1999). *Grand Central winter: Stories from the street.* Pocket Books.

Thistle, J. (2019). *From the ashes: My story of being Métis, homeless, and finding my way.* Simon and Schuster.

PART TWO

Identifying and Addressing Poverty: The Dimensions, Character, and Impact of Poverty

Poverty in Three Anglo Nations: The Dimensions, Character, and Impact of Poverty

> You discover boredom and mean complications and the beginnings of hunger, but you also discover the great redeeming feature of poverty: the fact that it annihilates the future.
>
> *– George Orwell (1933/1961)*

Examining poverty across a range of rich nations illuminates the extent to which poverty is inevitable, as well as what can be done to mitigate it. If the prevalence and character of poverty differ markedly across countries with similar levels of wealth, we can learn from these nations' policy approaches. But, as noted in the previous chapter, poverty is defined and measured very differently in Canada, the United Kingdom, and the United States, making it difficult to compare their rates and other dimensions of poverty directly. While it is impossible to standardize poverty measures completely, several international institutions and agencies, such as the Organisation for Economic Co-operation and Development (OECD), the LIS Cross-National Data Center (LIS), and Eurostat (the statistical office of the EU), provide "harmonized" data that allow invaluable cross-national comparisons of poverty rates, inequality, and well-being over time.[1] However, these research centers do not typically collect data about several key dimensions of poverty, such as the vulnerable groups that are most likely to be poor or how long people live in poverty. This chapter closely examines the degree, depth, duration, and distribution of poverty (the 4 Ds) in Canada, the UK, and the US over time using each nation's domestic poverty measures. These detailed national narratives are then supplemented with harmonized international data to compare poverty rates and trends across these three countries and among a wider range of nations, allowing for fuller understanding of the character and sources of poverty and the viability of existing or proposed solutions.

FOUR KEY DIMENSIONS OF POVERTY

The *degree* of poverty refers to both the number of people in a nation who are poor and the proportion of its population (poverty rate) that is poor. National poverty rates usefully indicate the percentage of a population that is living below a country's poverty line. But they do not tell us how poor those people are; they do not address how far below the poverty line their income falls. They treat all poor people as equally poor, missing both the severity of poverty and the distinction between the "poor" and the "very poor" first highlighted by Booth and Rowntree in their pioneering UK poverty studies. Examined over time, poverty rates reveal trends indicating whether the percentage of the population defined as poor has been stable, declining, or rising. But they do not indicate whether the poor are becoming poorer or better off over time. For example, in a country with a poverty rate of 10 percent, if every poor person's income were cut in half, the poor's living conditions would dramatically decline, but the national poverty *rate* (the percentage living below the poverty line) would remain 10 percent.

Consequently, poverty researchers often use *depth* of poverty measures to ascertain the severity of poverty endured by poor people. The income of poor families may be a few dollars below the poverty line or thousands of dollars below it. Some depth-of-poverty measures provide simple "incidence estimates" of the number and percentage of people who are living at a certain fraction of national poverty income thresholds. The US Census Bureau, for example, indicates what percentage of the total population, as well as what percentage of the poor population, has an income level below 50 percent of its established poverty lines. In Canada, the "poverty gap index" is used to measure the depth of poverty by calculating the *average* shortfall in the income of poor families from the poverty threshold. Thus, it summarizes the range of incomes of the people living below poverty lines.[2] The UK has used a more stringent application of its main relative measure to estimate the depth of poverty; it identifies those with an income that is 40 percent or less of the average income (instead of 60 percent) as living in deep poverty.

The *duration* of poverty episodes that people experience – and the related flow patterns of people transitioning in and out of poverty – is another vital concern. Although much less frequently reported than poverty rates, the length of time that people are in poverty clearly matters. The impact of long-term or chronic poverty is far greater than that of transitory and less frequent poverty spells. Chronic poverty is closely associated with significantly poorer physical and mental health and markedly greater risks for a wide range of social and health problems (Chernomas & Hudson, 2013; Gupta et al., 2007; Murali & Oyebode, 2004; Pagani, 2007; Raphael, 2013; Wilkinson & Pickett, 2006). People who are poor for protracted periods are much more likely to have exhausted or depleted stocks of consumer durables, credit lines, public transfers, financial and social support from friends and family, and other forms of protection that can help to buffer the experience and keep them out of deeper poverty. Consequently, chronic poverty is more difficult to escape and more likely to be passed on from one generation to the next (Blanden & Gibbons, 2006; Pressman, 2011; Pressman & Scott, 2009). In addition, cross-sectional ("point in time") poverty snapshots often conceal the numbers of poor families who have just transitioned out of or are about to enter poverty. Estimates of annual poverty rates often grossly underestimate the actual number of people who experience poverty every year. An annual poverty rate of 10 percent, for example, typically encompasses far more than 10 percent of the population because there is a significant amount of turnover in the families that are poor over the course of a year.

Poverty is not randomly or evenly dispersed in any nation. Researchers often focus on the *distribution* of poverty among key groups or subpopulations. Some of them, including children, women, single-parent families, the elderly, racialized groups, ethnic minorities, immigrants, and people with disabilities, are often significantly overrepresented among the poor because of their greater labor market vulnerability, a dearth of social supports available to them, and various forms of discrimination. They are more likely to be unemployed or underemployed and tend to have more precarious, lower-wage jobs that provide fewer benefits and services – problems greatly compounded by social policy retrenchment over the past few decades. These conditions place them at heightened risk of poverty. Well-established poverty triggers, such as relationship breakup, family dissolution, serious injuries or health problems, and discrimination in job and housing markets, may submerge them in deep poverty.

THE CHARACTER OF POVERTY

Although most definitions of poverty focus on low income or inadequate resources, the experience clearly encompasses much more than this. Poverty comprises a dense web of risks, vulnerabilities, stresses, deprivations, and disadvantages that are cumulative, interactive, and compounding, rendering it corrosive and intractable. Indeed, many of these conditions are both *causes* and *consequences* of poverty. The cheaper, highly processed, less nutritional foods; substandard housing; unsafe neighborhoods; and reduced access to healthcare, which are often associated with poverty, for example, can impair children's physical and mental health, begetting higher levels of absenteeism from school, lower grades, diminished self-esteem and subverted aspirations, and elevated school dropout rates. All of this, in turn, can lead to more precarious lower-income employment or unemployment when poor children become adults and can greatly increase their risk of remaining poor or falling back into poverty. Persistent and deep poverty is considerably more pernicious than more transient and less extreme forms of poverty. People who are critically and chronically poor are much less likely to escape poverty. The impact and consequences of poverty can be observed across several interacting groups and spheres, including children, families, residential neighborhoods, and communities.

The Impact of Poverty on Children and Families

> Poverty ... is extremely unfavourable to the rearing of children. The tender plant is produced; but in so cold a soil, and so severe a climate, soon withers and dies.
>
> – *Adam Smith (1776/2003)*

Many adverse factors and hardships closely associated with poverty can affect cognitive development and the physical, emotional, and mental health of children and other family members. The "timing" of poverty is a crucial consideration. Human development in the early years of life occurs at an extraordinary scale and pace, establishing the base for further growth and progress. Children are disproportionately sensitive to their environments. Poverty in the prenatal stages and first five years of life can be especially harmful, providing an unstable and fragile foundation that can greatly amplify risks for developmental delays, learning disabilities, and other developmental health challenges. Its repercussions, if unacknowledged and unaddressed, can reverberate over a lifetime and across generations (Gupta et al., 2007; Hertzman, 2010; Pagani, 2007).

Virtually all aspects of family life and their outcomes are negatively affected by the myriad adversities, deprivations, and disadvantages associated with poverty. For many poor families facing unemployment, underemployment, inadequate income and resources, the threat of eviction or homelessness, and other chronic deprivations, life can be unpredictable, unstable, and chaotic. The daily strain of living in poverty can foster a wide range of mental and physical health problems. Poverty's impact on health and overall well-being is reflected in lower birth weights and higher rates of infant mortality and morbidity, including a wide range of chronic conditions and infectious diseases (such as anemia, meningitis, rheumatic fever, haemophilus influenza, parasitic diseases, and gastroenteritis) and greater risks of asthma and obesity. It may also be reflected in visual and hearing difficulties, learning disabilities and delays in motor and cognitive development (including attention deficit disorder, hyperactive disorder, memory deficiency, lower language development and problem-solving skills, emotional and behavioral problems, and weaker verbal and math skills). It is crucial to remember that risks to cognitive and social development can be dramatically reduced if dense scaffoldings of proactive and preventive social supports and services are mounted to address the interlocking conditions endured in low-income environments that coalesce to help keep families entrenched in poverty (Lipina & Posner, 2012; Luby et al., 2013; National Center for Infants, Toddlers and Families, 2014).

Parents in poor families also tend to have poorer health, lower levels of education, less time and energy to engage in cognitively enhancing activities (reading with their children, helping them with their home-work, and participating in school activities), and fewer resources, such as books and quiet study spaces. Under the burden and strains of poverty, they may be less likely to adopt interactive "serve and return" parenting styles that can promote emotional development and social competence (Engle & Black, 2008; Evans, 2004; Gupta et al., 2007; Pagani, 2007). People in poor families also have higher rates of academic failure and higher school dropout rates, increasing the likelihood that, as adults, they will earn less money, work fewer hours, be employed in more precarious jobs, and have higher rates of unemployment. Nations that have developed a more comprehensive range of proactive income supports, social services, and other anticipatory and preventive programs have had significantly more success in mitigating many of these conditions, consequences, and causes of poverty (Duncan & Brooks-Gunn, 2009; Duncan et al., 2012; Hertzman, 2010; Huston, 1994) – a central concept that is more fully explored in the next chapter.[3]

LOW-INCOME NEIGHBORHOODS AND COMMUNITIES

> Anyone who has ever struggled with poverty knows how extremely expensive it is to be poor.
>
> – James Baldwin (1961/1992)

Low-income neighborhoods and communities are often characterized by the synergistic effects of multiple adverse risk factors, such as substandard housing with inadequate safety features; under-resourced schools; fewer recreation centers, parks, and libraries; greater distance from markets and urban centers; greater exposure to toxins and other hazardous conditions (such as air and water pollutants and waste); excessive noise levels; and higher rates of crime. Without cars or easy access to efficient public transportation, poor families often pay much more for groceries and other necessities because they are reliant upon smaller local stores, where economies of scale and the higher cost of doing business in poor neighborhoods can greatly inflate the price of food and other necessities. Poor families may not have the storage facilities to save money by buying in bulk when products are on sale, or they may lack the income to purchase the most nutritious foods and higher quality, more durable shoes, clothing, and other items. They may pay rent that is equivalent to or higher than a mortgage because they do not have the credit or down payment required to purchase a house or the security deposit and advance rent payment required to move to more adequate rental housing. Obtaining housing insurance is more difficult and costly in low-income neighborhoods. Poor families often need to purchase essentials such as appliances and furniture through costly rent-to-own lease agreements. They cannot always afford to pay all of their bills, so they are often charged late fees, and they often pay much higher interest on their credit cards because they are only able to meet the minimum payments each month. In many cases, the income of working-poor families is considered "too high" for them to qualify for income supports and services, which have been rapidly declining in many nations over the past few decades – and most notably in the three Anglo nations under scrutiny here. In place of these once-offered supports, check-cashing outlets, pawnshops, rent-to-own stores, and other "poverty industries" have proliferated, often owned or bankrolled by large corporations and financial institutions that routinely prey upon the poor. These developments are well underway in most rich capitalist countries today but are especially prominent in the United States and other Anglo nations where they originated and have rapidly multiplied (Caplovitz, 1963; Hirsch, 2013; Hudson, 1996a, 1996b; Williams, 1977; Wimer et al., 2019).

Although poverty is widespread in the Anglo nations and in many others across the wealthy, developed world, its prevalence and severity is not on the same scale as in the poorest countries, where a large majority of residents may be acutely poor throughout their lives. But its *character* is broadly similar in many respects. The World Health Organization (WHO, 1995) describes poverty as "the greatest cause of suffering on earth," exerting "its destructive influence at every stage of human life from the moment of conception to the grave" (p. 1). The United Nations (UNDP, 1997) highlights poverty's close links to poor health, low education, an inability to exercise basic rights, and a denial of the choices and opportunities necessary for living a "tolerable life" (p. 2). These descriptions capture the general conditions, injustices, and violence of poverty across both poor and wealthy nations. But the face of poverty in these two worlds, and the nature of the daily struggles of the poor families who dwell in them, is very different.

In the wealthy and heavily monetized developed world, there is much greater reliance upon purchasing essential goods and services in the market, and those without resources have few alternative means of obtaining them and participating in society. Without an adequate income, poor people in rich nations often live in exile, with minimal survival skills and few opportunities to provide even the most basic essentials for themselves; they typically cannot grow their own food, access clean water, build their own shelters, or make their own clothing. They are among the most defenseless against natural disasters, from major snow and ice storms in the north to tropical cyclones in the south such as Hurricane Katrina, which devastated the city of New Orleans, Louisiana, in 2005. They are also much more vulnerable to major manufactured disasters caused by corporate decisions and government policies and mismanagement, as witnessed in Detroit, Michigan (see Box 3.1).

The next section provides an overview of the key dimensions and character of poverty and homelessness in Canada, the UK, and the US over the past few decades and then explores some similarities and differences across these measurements and aspects. This examination is augmented by cross-national contrasts that indicate more striking variation between these three nations and some others in Europe. These comparisons suggest that, while it may not be possible to abolish poverty in capitalist societies, the long-standing, pronounced levels and extreme forms of poverty in the Anglo nations can be mitigated and poverty's pernicious impact greatly attenuated. The accounts of poverty in the three Anglo nations presented below are based upon their official or most widely employed "quasi-official" measures of poverty, but also considered are these nations' main alternative or supplementary metrics. Although Canada, the UK, and the US use very different poverty measures, they all define poverty as an inadequate income. Despite the limitations of this somewhat narrow approach, a focus on inadequate income can provide insight into the nature of poverty in these three heavily commodified, wealthy capitalist countries because most of their residents are highly dependent upon income to access most essential goods and services and to participate in society. The data also clearly demonstrate that poverty is not evenly or proportionately distributed across demographic groups in each of these countries. However, as the next chapter will show, this dependence upon market income is less salient in nations with considerably more developed social supports and

BOX 3.1 STRANDED IN DETROIT: THE IMPACT OF INVESTMENT DECISIONS IN THE UNITED STATES

The American automobile industries based in Detroit – once one of the largest, wealthiest, and most vibrant cities in the United States – undermined the local economy by gradually shifting production to low-wage, low-tax, high-repression nations and to other anti-union ("right-to-work") states within the United States. The low-wage auto parts suppliers to whom they had been outsourcing much of their production, as well as other auto-related industries, soon followed them. While the more affluent, mostly white families were able to escape to the suburbs, the poor, disproportionately Black families were left stranded in Detroit's urban center. The relocation of jobs that ravaged the "Motor City" and culminated in its filing for bankruptcy in 2013 – the largest city to do so in the nation's history – was enabled by US governments at all levels. When auto giants GM and Chrysler ultimately went bankrupt, due to the miscalculations and blunders of their boards of directors and the major shareholders that chose them, the state bailed them out with little effort to promote employment or to protect workers, the city, or its residents.

The flight of industry, small businesses, and the middle class significantly eroded the tax base in Detroit, leading to a severe slashing of investment in essential infrastructure, including the police, the fire department, utilities, and public schools – and to higher taxes and costs for services for the families left behind. Then, in the spring and summer of 2014, the Detroit Water and Sewerage Department shut off service to thousands of poor families unable to pay their water bills. Deprived of running water and functioning toilets, parents could not cook or clean or properly care for their children, making them vulnerable to having their children taken away by Child Protective Services. Families evicted from their homes faced new laws that banned and criminalized their attempts to survive through panhandling on the streets, sleeping outdoors in public spaces, or squatting in the multitude of abandoned buildings and ruins that have constituted a large part of the city's core for decades.

welfare states. The provision of interlocked networks of generous income programs, high-quality social services, and protective legislation designed to support and protect all citizens or residents in a nation goes some considerable distance toward diminishing people's dependence upon the market – decommodifying them – and creating greater equality.

POVERTY IN THE UNITED STATES

The United States is one of the few nations in the wealthy capitalist world that employs an *absolute* official poverty metric. This measure is more closely linked to significant material deprivation and the struggle to meet basic needs than to continually evolving social living standards and comparative disadvantage. Data from the US Census Bureau (2019a) in Table 3.1 indicate that the US poverty rate has been high and stable for over four decades, with relatively minor fluctuations. In 1975, 12.3 percent of the population in the United States was living in poverty – almost 25.9 million people. In 2018, the poverty rate was about the same (11.8 percent), but there were over 38 million people living in absolute poverty.

The official poverty rate in the United States is high compared to that in most other rich developed nations. Yet it is significantly underestimated. The use of a strict absolute poverty measure based upon an entirely inadequate assessment of the costs of subsistence living has resulted in poverty thresholds that are far too low. If the United States used a less stringent poverty metric, like those adopted in most other wealthy countries, its already high poverty rate would be considerably greater. If the sharp climb in consumer debt over the past few decades was taken into account – along with the impact of interest payments on that debt – the poverty rate would be higher still because families have even less income available for essentials (Pressman & Scott, 2009; Scott & Pressman, 2013; Wimer et al., 2019).[4]

Even more disturbing than the persistently high level of poverty in the United States is the increase in its depth or severity (Shaefer & Edin, 2013; US Census Bureau, 2013).[5] In 1975, 3.7 percent of the population in the United States had incomes lower than 50 percent of its poverty threshold – i.e., this group had less than half the income level

Table 3.1. Poverty Rates (%) and Depth in the United States: Official Measure and SPM[a]

	1975	1983	1993	2003	2013	2018	SPM 2018
All People	12.3	15.2	15.1	12.5	14.5	11.8	12.8
Female	13.8	16.8	16.9	13.7	15.8	12.9	13.4
Male	10.7	13.6	13.3	11.2	13.1	10.6	12.1
Depth of Poverty							
% of all people below 50% of poverty level	3.7	5.9	6.2	5.3	6.3	5.3	4.2
% of all *poor* people below 50% of poverty level[b]	29.9	38.5	40.7	42.6	43.8	45.2	32.8[c]
Families	10.9	13.9	13.6	10.8	12.4	9.0	n/a[d]
Single Parent Families (female householder)	37.5	40.2	38.7	30.0	33.2	24.9	25.0
Children (under 18 years)	17.1	22.3	22.7	17.6	19.9	16.2	13.7
Elderly (65 years +)	15.3	13.8	12.2	10.2	9.5	9.7	13.6
Race							
White	8.6	10.8	9.9	8.2	9.6	8.1	8.7
Hispanic	26.9	28.0	30.6	22.5	23.5	17.6	20.3
Black	31.3	35.7	33.1	24.4	27.2	20.8	20.4

Sources: US Census Bureau (2014) *Income and Poverty in the United States: 2013*; US Census Bureau (2019a) *Income and Poverty in the United States: 2018*; US Census Bureau (2019b) *The Supplemental Poverty Measure: 2018*
[a] SPM = Supplemental Poverty Measure, adopted in 2011 as an additional poverty metric
[b] Calculated from US Census Bureau (2014, 2019a)
[c] Calculated from US Census Bureau (2019a, 2019b)
[d] SPM measures poverty among married couples (7.7 percent) and cohabiting couples (13.9 percent) not primary families

that the government deemed necessary for subsistence. By 2018, 5.3 percent of the (now much larger) US population was living on incomes that were less than 50 percent of that threshold. The percentage of the *poor* population with incomes that were 50 percent or less of the poverty threshold increased even more markedly, from 30 percent in 1975 to 45 percent in 2018. How do families survive on such low incomes? They do so by cutting back on the very essentials that the US poverty definition underscores as required for survival: skipping meals; buying cheaper, less nutritional food; not turning up the heat in the winter; wearing worn out, inadequate clothing; walking for miles to and from work; taking on greater debt; not always paying their bills. Of course, many acutely poor people do not survive. According to statistics from the Los Angeles County Coroner's office, at least 2,815 homeless people died in Los Angeles County alone between 2000 and 2007. Another study found that approximately 700 people who are homeless, or at risk of being homeless, die every year across the United States from exposure-related conditions such as hypothermia and frostbite (Hawke et al., 2007; National Coalition for the Homeless, 2010). The popular sentiment suggesting that "poor" people in rich nations would be "well off" if they were living in a poor country furnishes little comfort for them.

Poverty is not distributed evenly or indiscriminately across all groups in any nation; some groups are much more likely to live in serious poverty for extended periods. Women have long experienced greater poverty than men. This is one manifestation of a dense and entrenched network of gender inequalities that exist, to varying degrees, across virtually all wealthy capitalist nations. In the 1970s, with women's rapidly increasing presence in the paid labor force, researchers highlighted the "feminization of poverty" (e.g., Brady & Kall, 2008; Goldberg, 2010a, 2010b; Goldberg & Kremen, 1990; Pearce, 1978). They documented the markedly higher levels, greater severity, and more enduring forms of poverty among women, and their greater barriers to escaping it – particularly as heads of single-parent families. They also identified an array of closely interrelated reasons for the increasing feminization of poverty, including women's higher rates of unemployment and part-time employment, occupational segregation in job ghettos, discrimination in the labor market, lower earnings even when doing the same work as men, and outsized responsibility for unpaid domestic or care work in families. In 2016, almost 20 percent of workers earned poverty-level wages in the United States, but the percentage was higher among women (28 percent) than men (24 percent) (Economic Policy Institute, 2019).

Although these conditions are endured by women in virtually every nation, they are especially acute in the United States, where unionization rates have long been relatively low and declining. Women in the United States also have had access to far fewer social services and supports, such as childcare, labor-market training programs, public transportation and healthcare, parental leave programs and family allowances. They have been largely reliant upon meager, means-tested, and highly stigmatized social assistance programs (Abramovitz, 1988; Fraser, 1989; Gordon, 1988, 1994). Some of these labor market conditions and barriers have improved over the past few decades, but poverty still has a female face in the United States today.

The US poverty rate was 12.9 percent for females and 10.6 percent for males in 2018. As shown in Table 3.1, the poverty rate for females has consistently been higher than that for males for over four decades, and this gender difference is evident across all ages. In 2018, the poverty rate among those 65 years of age and older was 11.8 percent for females and 8.1 percent for males. The family poverty rate has been slightly lower than the poverty rate for all people, but it too held steady between 1975 (10.9 percent) and 2018 (9.0 percent). The poverty rate is starkly higher among single-parent female-headed families than among two-parent families. In 1975, the rate of poverty among single-parent "female householders" (37.5 percent) was more than triple the rate among two-parent families (10.9 percent). By 2018, it had declined markedly (24.9 percent), but it remained close to three times the two-parent family poverty rate. Unlike in many other nations, child poverty rates in the United States have always markedly exceeded the total population poverty rates. In 1975, the child poverty rate was 17.1 percent, encompassing 10.2 million children; by 2018, the rate was about the same (16.2 percent) but included almost 12 million children. Cross-national research suggests that these extreme gender and age disparities can be significantly reduced, but they are often accepted as unavoidable.

Many of the same labor market disparities and conditions faced by women have also played a central role in sustaining high rates of deep poverty among immigrant, ethnic, and racialized groups and other minorities in the United States – buttressed by a protracted and ongoing history of intense discrimination and racism. The destructive and enduring impact of these conditions was greatly amplified and singularly evident for "involuntary minorities" – groups assimilated into a society against their will and brutally subordinated (Ogbu, 1992, p. 8).[6] In the United States, two of the most prominent involuntary minorities are Native Americans and African Americans. Although the histories of these two groups are painfully familiar to many people, the oppressively heavy and enduring weight of their stories – sometimes lost, dismissed, or minified in poverty discourses today – is briefly rehearsed here.[7]

The genocidal invasion of North America by Europeans involved the violent appropriation of Native Americans' lands and brutal crushing of their resistance. The many atrocities they endured in the United States included their forced march westward, culminating in the death of thousands, and their segregation via relegation to federal reservations. Their cultures, so thoroughly incompatible with that of the acquisitive, imperious colonizers, were viewed as primitive and barriers to progress to be methodically decimated in boarding schools and churches (Davidson, 2012; Russell, 2009). Despite the horrendous conditions they have endured, Native Americans have received relatively little attention in US poverty research and are often neglected in major studies, partly due to the numerically small size of the population (about 2 percent of the US population) and partly due to the concentrated focus on other severely deprived groups, such as African Americans and Hispanic Americans. But their poverty rate and corresponding living conditions and opportunities for advancement have long been among the worst in the nation. In 2016, the poverty rate among Native Americans was 23 percent; it was 36 percent among those living on federal reserves. Native Americans also have the highest morbidity and suicide rates and the lowest levels of education, home ownership, and life expectancy of all population groups in the United States (Huyser et al., 2014; National Congress of American Indians, 2020; Sarche & Spicer, 2008; Stromwell et al., 1998).

It is similarly difficult to convey the full-scale, destructive impact of the horrific conditions imposed on African Americans. The popularity of poverty narratives that blame the poor for their plight today – targeting Black people in particular – also warrants a concise but incisive recapitulation of the successive, sordid chapters of African American history. Ripped from their homelands, Africans were sold into slavery and pressed into long, grueling, labor-intensive work; their families torn apart; their cultures and languages suppressed; the most basic human rights denied to them. The adoption of the Thirteenth Amendment to the US Constitution formally ended slavery in 1865, but that was not the end of involuntary servitude. A clause in the amendment left open the possibility for it to continue as a form of punishment for people who were convicted of a crime. Slavery was soon superseded by "convict leasing"– another intensely brutal form of forced labor that compelled thousands of falsely imprisoned Black men and women in many Southern states to work on plantations and in quarries, mines, mills, lumber camps, and other industries. Aptly referred to as "neo-slavery," it would endure for several decades, to be gradually displaced by the widespread use of "prison farms" and chain gangs, perpetuating the brutal treatment of Black prisoners. Concomitantly, a dense network of "Jim Crow" rules, codes, practices, and ideas enforcing and rationalizing racial segregation and affecting almost every aspect of social life was formalized and legalized and would persist throughout most of the twentieth century (Blackmon, 2009; Foner, 2005; Oshinsky, 1997; Parish, 1989; Wilkerson, 2020). Parts of this network remain informally entrenched today, and the traumatic legacy of these practices endures in many forms, including high rates of poverty, homelessness, and incarceration, despite ongoing resistance and challenges to them over the centuries.

Racialized groups, minorities, and immigrants in the United States, like women, have often been excluded from the relatively few and miserly social programs that constitute the nation's comparatively restricted welfare state, or they have been included in ways that have secured their position at the bottom of the stratification ladder. This is most conspicuously true for African Americans. The federal structure of the US state allowed powerful planters in the South, and the governments and politicians that have represented them, to ensure that any national social programs that might weaken their hold over Black labor would not be accessible to agricultural and domestic workers – the occupational areas where most African Americans were employed – and that the state-level benefits they were eligible for were inconsequential (Alston & Ferrie, 1999; Goldfield, 1997; Lieberman, 1998; Quadagno, 1994).

Black people and Hispanics have long been disproportionately represented among the destitute in the United States. The occurrence of poverty-level wages among Black people (33 percent) and Hispanics (34 percent) is notably higher than among white people (19 percent) (Economic Policy Institute, 2019). As seen in Table 3.1, the 2018 poverty rates for these two groups have declined since 1975, but the Hispanic poverty rate (17.6 percent) was still over twice as high as that among white people (8.1 percent), and the Black poverty rate (20.8 percent) was higher yet. One recent study indicated that "of black Americans who reach age 75, 91 percent have been touched by the experience of poverty" (Rank, 2005, p. 96). The shockingly high child poverty rate (16.2 percent) in the United States is also highly correlated with "race." In 2018, the poverty rate among white children was 8.1 percent, but it was 23.7 percent among Hispanic children and 29.5 percent among Black children.

One of the most striking trends in the cross-sectional poverty rates in the United States reported in Table 3.1 is their stability across almost all groups. Periods of strong economic growth and higher rates of GDP per capita, a dramatic rise in the number of women in the labor force, an increase in the number of two-income families, and higher average levels of education – some of the most highly touted remedies for poverty put forward by proponents of neoliberalism – have had relatively little impact on the poverty rate in the United States. Why? Research points to the proliferation of low-wage, part-time, and precarious employment; the rising costs of increasingly crucial needs such as education, childcare, healthcare, transportation, and housing; and the decline of unions and of the public income supports, services, and protections that fostered a fairer distribution of the wealth created during earlier periods of economic expansion. The elderly and single-parent families (female custodial) were two groups that experienced an appreciable decline in poverty due to the end of the recession and improved social benefits (McGarry, 2013).

Aware of some of the problems with its long-standing poverty measure, the US Census Bureau introduced a supplemental metric in 2011. The Supplemental Poverty Measure (SPM) extends the official measure, using updated and adjusted poverty thresholds and taking into account some government programs designed to assist low-income families (US Census Bureau, 2019b).[8] However, the poverty data obtained through the two metrics are very similar; only the percentage of all poor people below 50 percent of the poverty line is strikingly different (Table 3.1, columns 6 and 7). The 2018 poverty rate for "all people" using the SPM (12.8 percent) was only slightly higher than the rate based on the official poverty measure (11.8 percent). Among the elderly, the SPM poverty rate was notably higher (13.6 percent) than the official poverty rate (9.7 percent), partly due to lower official thresholds used for this group (Iceland, 2013, pp. 32–34; US Census Bureau, 2019b). The SPM child poverty rate (13.7 percent), however, was lower than the official child poverty rate (16.2 percent) because it includes some benefits not considered in the official rate. Although US social programs are not as generous as those in many other nations, they have still had a significant impact. Social Security, the "most important anti-poverty program" moved 27.2 million people out of poverty; refundable tax credits moved 8.8 million people out of poverty (US Census Bureau, 2019b, p. 2).

The snapshots in Table 3.1 depicting stable rates of poverty over the past four decades in the United States do not capture poverty dynamics. They do not indicate whether the same individuals and families are poor over time; they do not reveal patterns of movement in and out of poverty, or tell us if poor individuals and families live in poverty for short or long periods. Research using the Panel Study of Income Dynamics (PSID) does track some of these changes. The PSID is a household data panel survey that has collected social, economic, and demographic data from the same families since 1968 – making it the longest running longitudinal household survey in the world. It indicates that there has been a continual, significant flow in and out of the ranks of the poor in the United States. Unlike in many low-income countries (LICs) in the developing world, where majorities or near majorities of the population may remain destitute for very long periods, most poor people in the United States fall below the poverty thresholds for relatively short periods and manage to rise above them after just a year or two. However, many of them drift just above the poverty threshold, and significant numbers of them will fall back into poverty – and many poor families do experience chronic poverty (Bane & Ellwood, 1986; Stevens, 1999).

These are pivotal observations. First, they suggest that there is a core group of chronically poor people in the United States who endure the physical, psychological, and emotional hardships associated with extended periods of poverty. Second, they indicate that the actual number of people who experience a period of poverty is much higher than that suggested by the relatively steady percentage of the population that is poor (the official poverty rate). This means that the risk of falling into poverty is far greater than most people in the United States believe it to be. The percentage of the population that will fall into poverty within a six-year period is at least twice as high as the annual poverty rate (Jäntti, 2009). Some studies suggest that a *majority* (58 percent) of all Americans between the ages 20 and 75 will experience at least one year living below the official poverty line (Hacker, 2008; Rank, 2005; Sandoval et al., 2009).

The knowledge that many families continually slip in and out of poverty helps to offset the commonly expressed cynical observation that some poor households are not "truly" poor because they may own vehicles, telephones, air conditioners, or microwave ovens. Most poor families acquired their consumer goods *before* they fell into poverty. Moreover, these popularly reported and often begrudged "luxuries" are often purchased secondhand and in disrepair. Families are frequently admonished in the media, and by those who are better-off, for not selling their few possessions when they become poor, but it would be imprudent to do so because they will have to be replaced by costlier consumer goods two or three years later when they have escaped absolute poverty. And these goods are often essential to promoting employment, social inclusion, and a more tolerable existence (Pressman, 2011).

Official accounts of poverty also underestimate the large homeless population in the United States. The Census Bureau only addresses homelessness every ten years, and it only acknowledges one segment of the homeless population. The last US Census indicated that there were 209,000 people in the United States using emergency and transitional shelters in 2010 (US Census Bureau, 2012). But a more inclusive study by the US Department of Housing and Urban Development (HUD) suggested that there were 610,042 homeless people in the United States in January of 2013, which equates to approximately 19 out of every 10,000 people in the population (US Department of Housing and Urban Development, 2013; National Alliance to End Homelessness, 2014). The HUD study used a "point-in-time" count of the number of homeless people who were found in sheltered locations (394,698 people, or 65 percent of the homeless population) and unsheltered locations (215,344 people, or 35 percent of the homeless population) on a single night in January of 2013. Children constituted 23 percent of the total homeless population (138,149 people), and 36 percent of the homeless population (222,197 people) lived in families.[9] By 2017, HUD reported 554,000 homeless people – 193,000 of whom were living on the streets, without access to emergency shelters, transitional housing, or safe havens (US Department of Housing and Urban Development, 2017). But even HUD's more inclusive estimates fall short because a significant portion of the homeless population is hidden or inaccessible.

Homelessness is an extreme and highly consequential form of poverty. It is associated with a wide array of vulnerabilities and mental and physical health outcomes and risks, including cancer, diabetes, hepatitis C, HIV, hypothermia, seizures, pulmonary disease, oral health problems, skin problems, "street feet," respiratory ailments such as asthma and bronchitis, hypertension, drug and alcohol dependencies, and lower life expectancy (Hwang, 2001; Rimawi et al., 2014). Black people, who often face many of these same problems and are grossly underserved by social programs, are also overrepresented among the homeless population, suggesting that they face a "double dose" of vulnerability. Centuries of systemic racism and the dense tangle of closely interrelated forms of oppression it unleashed – including mass incarceration and multiple barriers after release from prison, such as restrictive housing policies and a raft of other discriminatory social programs and practices – have ensured that homelessness has remained a prevalent and durable problem across Black communities in the United States (Alexander, 2012; Egleton et al., 2016; Johnson, 2010; Jones, 2016).

For many reasons, homeless people are far more difficult to count than those with very low incomes. The number of homeless people found in shelters will depend upon the number of beds available. But homeless shelters are often filled to capacity in the United States, so many people are turned away. A study of hunger and homelessness in twenty-three US cities found that most shelters had to deny spaces to homeless people because they could not accommodate them (US Conference of Mayors, 2007). Communities that do not operate shelters, missions, or soup kitchens or provide other social services to the homeless – a situation that is especially common in many rural areas and small towns across the United States – have even fewer opportunities to track their local homeless populations. Moreover, homeless people often choose to avoid shelters, which can pose health risks and many other threats.[10] Because of their high turnover rate, with hundreds of people cycling through their beds, homeless shelters are often infested with parasites such as bedbugs, lice, and scabies. Hepatitis, tuberculosis, influenza, and other chronic illnesses and communicable diseases are also recurring problems in shelters because homeless people are often malnourished and inadequately clothed and cannot easily access healthcare. Homeless people fear that they will be raped, assaulted, or robbed of their few personal effects while sleeping in shelters. They also worry that they or their children will encounter drug addicts and drug dealers. There is little privacy in often overcrowded shelters, which typically have strictly regimented times for check-in, meals, and sleeping. Shelters may also segregate family members and require them to give up their pets (Fuller, 2011; Hartman, 2013; Homelessadvice.com, 2018; Mackie et al., 2017).

Given these conditions, many homeless people prefer to live on the streets. But counting unsheltered homeless people is considerably more difficult because of the myriad remote or secluded places that they might seek refuge. Moreover, the adoption of new laws and policies that penalize the homeless for sleeping, sitting, eating, panhandling, or engaging in other unavoidable survival activities in public spaces – and the increasingly aggressive police crackdowns and sweeps these laws foster – have pushed the homeless even further underground and out of sight (Charles, 2009; Gaetz, 2013; O'Sullivan, 2012). The HUD homeless estimates are limited to just two groups of homeless people in the United States: (1) those using emergency and transitional shelters and (2) those that can be located "on the streets" on a particular night. These estimates do not include many other large groups of homeless people (identified in the ETHOS typology described in the previous chapter), such as individuals and families who live doubled up with other families or those who continually cycle through the homes of friends and relatives. However, the US Department of Education's National Center for Homeless Education monitors how many homeless children are enrolled in public preschools and primary and secondary schools (grades K to 12). It identified 1,258,182 homeless children in the public school system in 2013; this number had increased to 1,353,363 by 2017 (National Center for Homeless Education, 2014, 2017).[11]

The labor movement and welfare state in the US have played significant roles in the redistribution of income and slowing the spread of poverty. But they have not been as influential as their counterparts in most other rich nations, including Canada and the UK. Their ongoing erosion and the proliferation of low-wage, precarious jobs encouraged by neoliberalism and globalization have helped to sustain the magnitude and depth of poverty in the United States.

POVERTY IN CANADA

While poverty patterns in Canada are broadly similar to those observed in the United States, there are some noteworthy differences in the poverty levels, trends, conditions, and distributions across the two North American nations as well. The Canadian poverty figures presented in Table 3.2 are not derived from a strictly absolute poverty definition like that used in the United States; they are based on after-tax LICOs, Statistics Canada's long-standing, most frequently used, and widely cited poverty measure.[12] It is a hybrid or "quasi-relative" metric, combining aspects of both relative and absolute poverty measures. Individuals and families in Canada are considered "low income" – the long-standing official euphemism for "poor" in Canada – if they spend 20 percent or more than what the *average family* spends (a *relative* poverty consideration) on a basket of *basic necessities* (an *absolute* poverty consideration). However, because LICOs have not been rebased over the past two decades, like the official metric in the United States, they have become increasingly removed from mainstream consumption patterns.[13]

As in the United States, poverty is strikingly higher and deeper among certain groups in Canada. The feminization of poverty is related to a constellation of labor market conditions, disadvantages, and burdens largely similar to those found in the United States, compounded by an ongoing decline in some social supports over the past few decades (e.g., Evans, 2010; Townson, 2000). Indigenous and Black populations closely fit the description of "involuntary minorities" in Canada too. But public awareness of the plight of these two groups, as well as their prominence in official poverty studies, is inverted in Canada; the historical treatment and circumstances of Indigenous peoples in Canada have received greater national and international attention than the history of Black people in Canada – including their enslavement – which still has a relatively low profile.

Poverty rates among Indigenous peoples in Canada have always been significantly higher than those for "all people" and those for all other subpopulations in the nation.[14] The high poverty rates and greatly diminished life chances found among Indigenous peoples are intimately linked to largely similar patterns of domination and oppression as those endured by Native Americans south of the border – institutionalized racism and a litany of indignities and abuses, cultural genocide, and physical genocide. In the United States, American and European settlers could easily access the West with the support of the federal government. The Homestead Act of 1862 allowed them to claim 65 hectares of land if they built a home on it and farmed it for five years, and settlement was replete with ongoing violent wars against Native Americans. In Canada, the state instituted a policy of starvation to control Indigenous peoples and push them onto reserves, so it could build a national railroad and open the West. Expansion into the Prairie Provinces hinged on the Royal Proclamation of 1763. It established the principle that settlers could access land only after the government negotiated treaties with the Indigenous peoples living on them, purchased their land from them, and guaranteed them rights to reserve lands. While legal, and ostensibly principled, the negotiation of treaties in Canada was marked by relentless fraud and coercion. Furthermore, the Indigenous peoples who signed the treaties have often been forced to relocate from reserves found to be rich in natural resources (Daschuk, 2019; Frideres, 2016; Russell, 2009; Truth and Reconciliation Commission of Canada, 2015).

Indigenous languages and cultural and spiritual practices were outlawed, and sacred objects were destroyed; full participation in Canada's political, social, and economic life was contingent upon the abandonment of Indigenous identity. By forcing children into residential schools and day schools, the Canadian government aimed to assimilate them into the mainstream and erase its legal and financial obligations set out in the treaties. Many of the children forced into these schools by law were subject to extreme abuse. In the 1960s, as the schools were phased out, Indigenous children became victims of the "Sixties Scoop," a child-welfare policy that removed them from their homes, separating siblings, and placed them with non-Indigenous families across Canada and the United States. Official commissions, reports, and studies over the past few decades – from both within and outside Canada – have consistently documented the extensive and severe poverty levels, horrendous living conditions, and lack of services on many reserves. They have also highlighted widespread discrimination, mirroring the situation of Native Americans and African Americans in the United States (e.g., Canadian Human Rights Commission, 2013; Erasmus & Dussault, 1996; Truth and Reconciliation Commission of Canada, 2015; UN HRC, 2014; Wilson & Macdonald, 2010).

While Canada's history as the terminal station of the "Underground Railroad" and a safe haven for runaway slaves from the US South is widely known and often publicly proclaimed, its sustained and firm embrace of slavery is not as familiar. The history of slavery in what is now Canada began in the 1600s and endured until the British Parliament abolished it in 1833–34. African Americans were enslaved in New France, known as Lower Canada and then Québec, and in British North America, comprised of Upper Canada (Ontario) and all of the Maritime provinces (Newfoundland, New Brunswick, Nova Scotia, and Prince Edward Island). Canada's harsh climate and geography were not suitable for the kind of large-scale agricultural pursuits that promoted the enslavement of thousands of African Americans and Indigenous people on plantations in colonies in the United States, the Caribbean, Brazil, and Spanish America. But slaves in Canada worked and lived under largely similar conditions. Stripped of their rights, they were forced to endure long hours clearing land, chopping wood, and working in the fields, in the trades, in domestic service, and in many other forms of labor. After slavery ended, they endured discriminatory and racist treatment in places such as Africville, a destitute Black community north of Halifax whose inhabitants were denied basic services and amenities and eventually forced out when it was razed as part of a program of urban renewal (Clairmont & McGill, 1974; Nelson, 2009).[15] Canada's sustained history of slavery, spanning over two hundred years; its treatment of Black communities; and their ongoing resistance are still under-researched, largely hidden and unknown even to most Canadians. But, as with other "involuntary minorities," those in Canada faced widespread discrimination and racism; higher rates of poverty and unemployment, lower levels of education, and poorer health have been the legacy (Cooper, 2007; Russell, 2009; Trudel, 2013; UN HRC, 2017; Winks, 1997).

As indicated in Table 3.2, poverty levels and trends in Canada are disturbing but not as bleak as those in the United States. The Canadian poverty rate for "all people" decreased from 13 percent in 1976 to 7.3 percent in 2018.[16] The poverty rates for female-headed single-parent families, children, Indigenous/Aboriginal Canadians, and, especially, the elderly, also dropped markedly. Yet despite these notable reductions, poverty remains a very serious problem in Canada. A poverty rate of 7.3 percent for all people is still high (encompassing close to 2.7

Table 3.2. Poverty Rates (%) and Depth in Canada: LICOs[a] and MBM[b]

	1976	1981	1991	2001	2013	2018	MBM 2018
All People	13.0	11.6	13.2	11.2	9.8	7.3	11.0
Female	14.8	13.3	14.2	12.1	9.9	7.2	10.9
Male	11.1	9.9	12.1	10.3	9.7	7.5	11.1
Depth of Poverty Average gap ratio[c]	33.5	32.8	32.1	33.6	36.2	37.9	33.4
Families	10.4	8.8	10.0	8.1	6.8	4.1	7.7
Single Parent Families (female lone parent)	58.7	48.7	52.7	37.4	29.4	19.5	31.7
Children (under 18 years)	13.4	12.6	15.2	12.2	11.1	5.9	10.8
Elderly (65 years +)	29.0	21.0	11.1	6.7	3.7	4.0	5.6
Aboriginal Canadians[d] (off reserve)	n/a	n/a	28.8[e]	15.5[f]	14.2	13.6	19.5

Source: Statistics Canada Table 11-10-0135-01 (formerly CANSIM Table 206-0041) accessed January 4, 2021
[a] LICOs (Low Income Cut-Offs, 1992 base, after taxes and transfers)
[b] MBM = Market Basket Measure adopted as Canada's official poverty line in 2018 (2018 base)
[c] The average gap ratio measures how far, on average, people or households fall from the poverty line
[d] Statistics Canada, Canadian Income Survey, Custom Tabulations (2013, 2018, MBM 2018)
[e] Data from 1996 Survey of Labour and Income Dynamics
[f] Data from 2001 Survey of Labour and Income Dynamics

million people), reflecting a decline of less than 6 percentage points in the poverty rate across a span of over four decades. Moreover, because Canada's LICOs have not been adjusted since 1992, the data in Table 3.2 underestimate the number and percentage of individuals, families, and subgroups living in poverty. General living standards in Canada have risen, and the percentage of income that families spend on basic necessities has declined since that time, but the LICOs were not raised in accordance with these improved economic standards and conditions. Updating the LICOs would raise the poverty thresholds and increase the number of people that fall below them (Mitchell & Shillington, 2008). Furthermore, while the poverty rate in Canada for all people declined between 1976 and 2018, the depth of poverty increased. In 1976, the average income of the population of poor people was 33.5 percent below the poverty threshold. By 2018, with only minor fluctuations over this period, the depth of poverty increased to 38 percent.

Through its Survey of Labour and Income Dynamics (SLID) – a household survey that provides national data on fluctuations in income over time – Statistics Canada is able to track the duration of poverty spells. As in the United States, poverty is a transitory experience for the majority of poor people in Canada. About one-third of the people who are living in poverty at a given time will *not* be poor one year later, and only 2 percent of them will be poor for six or more years. But more than 20 percent of Canadians will experience poverty sometime over a six-year period (Murphy et al., 2012, p. 9). As in the United States, poverty in Canada is more persistent among particular subpopulations, such as single-parent families (especially when the single parent is female) and Indigenous people.

Despite substantial declines since 1976, by 2018, the percentage and number of poor children (5.9 percent; 407,000 children) and poor female-headed single-parent families (19.5 percent; over 140,000 families) remained strikingly high in Canada, and notably higher than in many other wealthy nations. The decline in poverty among these families has been attributed to a marked increase in the employment levels of single parents (e.g., Richards, 2010). But single parents often have to take on two or more low-paying jobs, working long, hard hours to lift their families above the poverty threshold. Moreover, these declines are often accompanied by a pronounced, but more rarely acknowledged, increase in "time poverty" and stress levels in low-income families – which is greatly exacerbated in nations such as Canada that furnish relatively few social services and supports for them.

The 1996 poverty rate of Indigenous people living off reserves (28.8 percent) was almost double the rate of poverty for "all people" that year. In 2011, the Indigenous poverty rate was 15.8 percent; it declined to 13.6 percent in 2018, but it remained much higher than the overall poverty rate in Canada. Moreover, the poverty rates shown in Table 3.2 do not include Indigenous people living on reserves and in remote communities – where conditions are often the most desperate – because Statistics Canada has not established LICOs for these areas. However, the 2006 Census included an incomplete enumeration of reserves in Canada in its calculation of poverty among Indigenous communities. Using Canada's purely relative poverty metric, the Low Income Measure (LIM), the poverty rate was 40 percent for Aboriginal children and 50 percent for status First Nations children (Collin & Jensen, 2009; Macdonald & Wilson, 2013).[17] At 12.3 percent, the relative poverty rate (LIM) for non-Indigenous children in Canada greatly exceeds the child poverty rates in many wealthy capitalist nations. But it appears almost modest when contrasted with these startling Indigenous child poverty rates.

Of course, as stressed in Chapter 2, poverty rates based solely upon low income cannot adequately capture the character of poverty. The Royal Commission on Aboriginal Peoples conducted in the 1990s noted that "Aboriginal people in Canada endure ill health, insufficient and unsafe housing, polluted water supplies, inadequate education, poverty and family breakdown at levels usually associated with impoverished developing countries" (Erasmus & Dussault, 1996, p. 1). Two decades later, a United Nations Human Rights Council report, based on the work of UN Special Rapporteur James Anaya, suggested that there had been little improvement, noting "the distressing socioeconomic conditions of [I]ndigenous peoples in a highly developed country" and the stark contrast between the well-being of Indigenous and non-Indigenous people in Canada (UN HRC, 2014, p. 7). Severe housing shortages; dilapidated, overcrowded, mold-ridden housing without indoor plumbing, proper heating, or reliable power; and inadequate water and sewage systems that pose high health risks are commonplace on many reserves, as are myriad health and social ills, including high rates of infant mortality, respiratory illness, communicable and chronic diseases, depression, and suicide. These communities consistently have among the lowest rates of life expectancy in the country. The use of "portables" rather than permanent buildings for schools, high rates of dropout from high school, a lack of culturally appropriate child and family services, and roads that are in severe disrepair are among countless severe deprivations and conditions endured across many reserves in Canada. These appalling conditions, and the systemic racism and discrimination that generates them, were revealed yet again in the report of the Truth and Reconciliation Commission of Canada (2015). The poverty data for Canada in Table 3.2 excludes Indigenous peoples on reserves, who are among the poorest people in Canada, often living in "Third World" conditions in this wealthy nation.

Poverty rates remain high and living conditions desperate for many poor people in Canada, and there has been remarkably little change over the past few decades. Because the LICOs have not been rebased for some time, the Canadian poverty rates presented in Table 3.2 are more akin to a measure of deep or absolute poverty now. However, an examination of poverty levels using the new official absolute poverty measure in Canada – the market basket measure (MBM) – presents an even bleaker picture in some respects. The poverty rates for all people and for all subgroups are notably higher using the MBM (column 7) than for LICOs (column 6) in 2018, but MBM poverty is not as deep.[18]

Other measures reinforce these disturbing rates. The proportion of households relying upon food banks increased by 19 percent between 2001 and 2014. By March of 2014, 841,191 people were dependent upon food banks, which fell far short of meeting needs in Canada. In 2012, 4 million people in Canada, including 1.15 million children (16 percent of all children), experienced "food insecurity" – defined as an inability to afford a balanced diet, being forced to miss meals, going hungry, or experiencing anxiety about running out of food – a problem that has grown or persisted in every province or territory since 2005 when the collection of data on food security began. Moreover, most food insecure households (62.2 percent) were reliant upon wages or salaries from employment – in other words, they were members of the "working poor."

As in the United States, the underestimation of poverty generated by the character of Canada's poverty metrics is further exacerbated by the exclusion of the sizeable homeless population from its poverty data. Mass homelessness has become an increasingly pressing issue since the early 1980s, with Canada's embrace and acceleration of neoliberal policy, including tax cuts for corporations and wealthy individuals, the discrediting and restructuring of the welfare state (leaving fewer and less generous social supports in place), deregulation, and a marked shift in housing policy from social housing to the private sector. The severe shortage of affordable housing this new orientation fostered was further exacerbated through gentrification – the conversion of buildings into expensive condominiums and hotels.

Recent studies suggest that over 235,000 people experience homelessness each year in Canada (Food Banks Canada, 2014; Gaetz et al., 2014, 2016; Tarasuk et al., 2012). Increasing numbers of homeless people are readily observed today in the busy downtown districts and commercial centers of virtually all large cities in the nation, often in close proximity to some of the wealthiest neighborhoods. As in the United States, the homeless crisis is openly reflected in the rapid proliferation of "tent cities" across the nation. In the absence of affordable housing and neighborhoods, homeless people have created makeshift homes and villages in an attempt to seek refuge from harsh weather and to escape the judgment and harassment they endure on the streets and the hassles and limits to their freedom they often encounter in shelters. They also seek to regain a sense of community through mutual support and cooperation. Comprising a crush of tents, shacks, lean-tos, and other forms of semipermanent, substandard housing made from pieces of cheap wood, strips of corrugated metal, and other repurposed detritus and debris, the largest encampments may hold more than 125 people in Canada – and over twice that many in the United States (Herring, 2014, 2015; Hunter et al., 2014; UN HRC, 2009).

Reminiscent of earlier squatter camps that spread across North America in the late nineteenth and early twentieth centuries (popularly referred to as "hobo jungles" or "tramp colonies"), most tent cities are illegal.[19] Although some of them have existed for five or more years and may be informally permitted by local authorities, most of them are routinely shut down, their residents evicted and their shelters dismantled. But they frequently reappear soon afterward, often in the same location or in close proximity to it. In Toronto, Canada's most populous metropolis, large-scale tent cities have taken root in parks, green spaces, and fields and in abandoned areas on the city's outskirts, while smaller encampments continually appear, vanish, and reemerge on city streets and below underpasses and bridges. Toronto's largest community, "Tent City," situated on several acres of waterfront land near the harbor, was home to hundreds of people from the time it emerged in 1998 to when it was shut down in 2002. The Downtown Eastside (DTES) of Vancouver, one of the poorest parts of Canada's largest western city, is another center of substandard housing where enclaves of homeless people and families abound (Bishop-Stall, 2005; Shelter, Support and Housing Administration, 2018; Urban Matters & BC Non-Profit Housing Association, 2018).

Determining the magnitude of homelessness – which can assume several, often easily overlooked "hidden" forms – is inherently challenging, as underscored in the previous chapter. Until recently, the Canadian government had not set out an explicit definition of homelessness and had focused largely on chronic homelessness. However, through Reaching Home, a community-based program introduced as part of a new National Housing Strategy, Canada has adopted a more inclusive definition of homelessness that is a modified version of that proposed by the Canadian Observatory on Homelessness (2012). It sets out four distinct forms of homelessness: (1) the unsheltered, (2) the emergency sheltered, (3) the provisionally housed, and (4) the precariously housed.[20] Although the federal government has focused to date on broadening its understanding and measures of the first two forms, it has recently expressed some interest in addressing the latter two forms. It also has expended considerable effort to coordinate the way homelessness is measured and tracked in 61 communities across its provinces and territories in recent years; in 2018, most of the nation's largest cities used a standard survey and a point-in-time count of various types of indoor and outdoor homelessness (Gaetz, 2020).

Not surprisingly, the groups that are overrepresented among the poor are typically overrepresented among the homeless, including women, youth (especially LGBTQ2S youth), and, particularly, Indigenous peoples. Although they comprise only 4.3 percent of the population of Canada, Indigenous peoples constitute between 28 percent and 34 percent of the nation's homeless population (Gaetz et al., 2016). Their numbers are especially high, and living conditions strikingly dire, in larger urban areas, such as Vancouver, Regina, Saskatoon, Winnipeg, Toronto, Ottawa, and Montreal, as well as on reserves, and in the Western provinces (Belanger et al., 2013; Gaetz et al., 2016; UN HRC, 2009). The elderly population is one of the few groups in Canada that experienced a dramatic reduction in poverty over the past thirty-five years, reflecting the impact of Canada's multitiered system of old age pensions and other income supports for the elderly. However, this trend has begun to reverse in recent years as social supports for the elderly have declined and the numbers of homeless among the older population is expected to rise (Grenier et al., 2016; Myles, 2013).

POVERTY IN THE UNITED KINGDOM

The way that poverty is understood, defined, and measured in the United Kingdom is strikingly different from the narrow, fixed absolute poverty metric of the US Census Bureau and the quasi-relative LICOs and absolute MBM used in Canada. Both the United States and Canada calculate and highlight the costs of a basket of identified "necessities"– a hallmark of an absolute poverty approach. The Department for Work and Pensions (DWP) in the UK employs a purely relative measure as its principal poverty metric; people are defined as poor if they have an income that is below 60 percent of the median (midpoint) income in the nation. They are poor because their income is deemed to be significantly lower than the average income in the UK, not because they do not have enough income to meet a circumscribed range of "basic needs" that have been identified by poverty and policy experts. This relative approach places greater emphasis on predominant living standards, the norms of everyday life, and social inclusion than the metrics that are used in the other two Anglo nations. The principal source of data on "low income poverty" in the United Kingdom is the Households Below Average Income (HBAI) series produced by the Department for Work and Pensions (2014; Townsend, 2004).

The UK poverty rates for individuals and groups presented in Table 3.3 are based upon their income level *after* housing costs have been deducted. These costs include rent, mortgage interest payments (net of tax relief), housing insurance premiums, water rates, and other housing expenses and service charges. Focusing on "after housing costs" (AHC) income levels as the main standard of living measure avoids the perverse but familiar situation in which people who receive increases in housing benefits to keep up with their rent increases are no longer considered poor because their income has gone up, even though their financial circumstances have not changed. It also avoids treating households with similar income levels but very different housing expenses as equivalent: for example, two elderly households might receive the same pension but have very different living standards because one of them has paid off a mortgage while the other must continue to pay rent.[21]

In addition to its distinctly relative poverty metric, several of the subgroups identified in Table 3.3 are also defined differently in the UK than in Canada and the US. Children are individuals who are under 16 years of age, rather than under 18 years of age.[22] The HBAI reports also refer to "pensioners," rather than the "elderly," highlighting the age at which people become eligible to retire and receive a state pension in the UK. Moreover, while the pensionable age for men has been

consistent at 65 years of age, the pensionable age for women was originally 60 years of age but has gradually increased over time. Finally, the
ethnic and minority groups highlighted in the UK poverty reports are
not the same as those identified in the two North American nations.[23]
Despite these divergent ways of defining population subgroups and determining poverty rates, Table 3.3 shows that poverty *trends* in the UK
are remarkably similar to those observed in the US and Canada. For
the most part, UK poverty levels have been relatively stable or remained
high even after marked declines.

As indicated in Table 3.3, there has been little change in the UK
poverty rate among all individuals between 2003/2004 (21 percent;
14 million people) and 2017/2018 (22 percent; 14 million people) –
reflecting a small but disheartening increase.[24] The poverty rate for children in the United Kingdom has remained high between 2003/2004
(28 percent) and 2017/2018 (30 percent). Moreover, as in the United
States, the poverty rates for children have been consistently higher than
those for all individuals over this period. A study of poor children in the
UK across a ten-year period (1998–2008) underscored the all-encom-
passing impact of poverty: "The experience of poverty is clearly damaging and it permeates every facet of children's lives from economic and
material disadvantages, through social and relational constraints and
exclusions to the personal and more hidden aspects of poverty associated with shame, sadness and the fear of difference and stigma" (Ridge,
2009, p. 91). Only the elderly (pensioners) experienced an appreciable
decline in poverty between 2003/2004 (20 percent) and 2017/2018
(16 percent), but the rate remained very high.

All poverty measures have some drawbacks. The UK approach sets
the poverty threshold as a proportion of the population's average income each year; by definition, it can therefore fluctuate each year in
line with annual changes in the average median income. Consequently,
a decline in the number of people in poverty (low income) can occur
not only if people's income rises, lifting them above the threshold, but
also if the median income declines. In the latter instance, the poverty
rate can go down when people with low incomes experience a decline
in income that is less than the fall in the average income – creating a
somewhat misleading impression of progress. Between 2007 and 2013,
for example, the median income declined by 9 percent, rendering the
poverty threshold 60 percent of a 9 percent lower base than it was in

2007. If the 2007 median income threshold were used for 2013, an additional 3 million people would have been in the "low-income poor" category (MacInnes et al., 2014). This ongoing problem prompted the DWP to introduce another, more stable, supplemental poverty metric based upon 60 percent of the median income from one consistent previous year – 2010/2011 (adjusted for inflation). This supplemental metric measures the number and proportion of people who have incomes below this stable or "anchored" 2010/2011 threshold, rather than against a new median income every year (Department for Work and Pensions, 2014, 2019a, 2019b).[25] However, as Table 3.3 shows, the differences in poverty rates using the central and supplemental measures have been relatively minimal (columns 4 and 5).

Although the United Kingdom employs a very different poverty metric than those used in Canada and the United States, the uneven distribution of poverty across various subpopulations is strikingly similar in all three countries. The UK, too, has experienced a feminization of poverty with higher poverty rates among women than men due to women's greater responsibility for children, discriminatory practices, and gendered labor market conditions, including horizontal segregation (different areas of employment from men) and vertical segregation (lower status and pay when working in the same jobs as men). Women have also been more reliant upon meager means-tested benefits while men have had greater access to relatively generous social insurance supports (Millar, 2010; Reiss, 2018). However, the poverty rates for men and women have become more similar over the past few decades. The poverty rate among lone parent families declined notably over this fifteen-year period (from 52 percent to 45 percent), but it remains disturbingly high. Like the elderly poverty rates in Canada – and, to a lesser extent, in the United States – the level of poverty among pensioners in the United Kingdom dropped from 20 percent in 2003/2004 to 16 percent in 2017/2018, due to the introduction of better income supports.

Like Canada and the US, the UK is a highly racialized capitalist society, which is reflected in its much higher rates of poverty among some minority groups. Discrimination, racism, and many other manifestations of inequality are legacies of Britain's colonial era, when it controlled vast territories across Africa, Asia, and the Caribbean and dominated the Atlantic slave trade. Its racialized concept of nation, implanted in North America and elsewhere in its empire, fixated on its destiny to rule the Indigenous peoples of its colonies, whom it deemed both biologically and culturally inferior. As in the United States and Canada, the success of this idea hinged on its firm embrace, across all classes, by the dominant white "race."

The majority of Black and Asian people in the United Kingdom migrated there from its colonies to meet the demand for labor. Many were originally recruited to fight in WWI, and those who stayed on after the war's end experienced high levels of unemployment, poverty, and racism – and the brutal shutdown of the civil unrest that these conditions engendered. However, the great majority migrated from the Indian subcontinent and the Caribbean after WWII, as the UK sought to rebuild and expand its shattered economy. Over the ensuing decades, with rapid economic growth, white workers began moving into service sector and manufacturing jobs with higher pay and better working conditions. As British subjects, migrants from Britain's colonies had privileged access to the UK labor market, and their numbers escalated, but they almost invariably assumed positions in the lowest-paid jobs (Cole, 2016; Fryer, 2018; Ramdin, 2017).

Like their racialized counterparts in North America, minorities in the UK face discrimination and many other disadvantages, reflected in higher rates of unemployment, underemployment, and part-time work; overrepresentation in low-wage sectors and occupations (such as sales, catering, personal services, hairdressing, textiles, and clothing); lower pay (even with similar qualifications as white workers); and poorer health, shorter life expectancies, and much higher rates of poverty. Ethnic minorities in the United Kingdom are far more likely than white workers to receive less than the living wage. They are also less likely to be covered by social insurance benefits and occupational pensions. All of these conditions have been especially prevalent among people of Bangladeshi and Pakistani origin (Barnard, 2014; Berthoud, 2002; Brynin & Longhi, 2015; Francis-Devine, 2020; Vlachantoni et al., 2015, 2017; Weeks-Bernard, 2017). Higher rates of over-policing and incarceration complete a picture that is very similar to that of racialized involuntary minorities in North America. In 1965, the year after the United States established its Civil Rights Act (1964), the UK finally introduced its Race Relations Act, the first legislation addressing discrimination. This was followed by the Race Relations Act of 1968 to address discriminatory practices in employment and housing. But neither the

UK's history of racism and discrimination nor the emergence of anti-racist groups such as the British Black Panthers (inspired by the US Black Panther Party) has garnered as much attention as have similar developments in the United States.

The poverty level among ethnic minorities in the UK – mirroring those for Black people and Hispanics in the US and for Indigenous people in Canada – has declined over the past fifteen years, but has remained almost twice as high as that among white people. In 2003/2004, the poverty rate among ethnic minorities in the UK was 41 percent. This rate declined to 38 percent in 2017/2018 but was still much higher than for white people (20 percent). For some minorities, however, the poverty rate is over three times as high as that for white people. In the early 2000s, the poverty rate among white people was 20 percent but almost 70 percent for Pakistani/Bangladeshi people. By 2007, the poverty rate was still 20 percent among white people but 45 percent among Black people (African, Caribbean, other), 55 percent for Pakistanis, and 65 percent for Bangladeshis (Kenway & Palmer, 2007; Platt, 2007). A decade later, the poverty rates for these groups remained very high, at 42 percent for Black people, 46 percent for Pakistanis, and 53 percent for Bangladeshis (Francis-Devine, 2020). As in North America, higher rates of unemployment, precarious employment, lower wages, far fewer social supports, discrimination, and social exclusion are still central factors that lead to higher levels of poverty among ethnic groups, minorities, and immigrants in the UK.

Longitudinal studies suggest also that poverty dynamics in the UK are broadly similar to those in Canada and the US.[26] Using data from the British Household Panel Survey (BHPS) – a multipurpose survey that was initiated in 1991 and inspired by the long-standing Panel Study of Income Dynamics in the United States – UK poverty researcher Stephen Jenkins (2011) notes that the poor population in the UK is continually changing:

> [I]t is not the same people who are poor always. There is substantial turnover and churning in the low-income population between one year and the next ... [and] over the period of several years, many more people experience poverty than are poor in any single year. (Jenkins, 2011, p. 360–361)

The fact that people continuously cycle in and out of poverty in the three Anglo nations should help to dispel the myth that people are

Table 3.3. Poverty Rates (%) and Depth in the United Kingdom (under 60 percent of median income/AHC)[a]

	2003/ 2004	2008/ 2009	2012/ 2013	2017/ 2018	Anchored[b] 2017/ 2018
All Individuals	21	22	21	22	20
Female	20	21	19	20	18
Male	18	19	19	18	16
Depth of Poverty (under 40% of median income)	8	10	9	10	9
Two Parent Families	22	24	23	23	21
Lone Parent Families	52	50	42	45	41
Children (under 16 years)[c]	28	30	27	30	26
Pensioners (65 years + for men; 60 years + for women)[d]	20	16	13	16	14
Ethnicity[e]					
White	20	20	19	20	17
Ethnic Minorities	41	43	38	38	34

Sources: Department for Work and Pensions (2014); Table 3.5db & Table 4.1ts, Supporting data tables; Department for Work and Pensions (2020)
[a] AHC = after housing costs
[b] Incomes under 60 percent of median in 2010/2011
[c] Unmarried or non-cohabiting 16- to 19-year-olds who are in full-time, non-advanced education are also considered children
[d] The data for female pensioners are not consistent because the pensionable age for women has increased from 60 years + to become increasingly more in line with that for men.
[e] Data are based on three-year averages

poor because they are lazy, make bad decisions, or have adopted a dysfunctional subculture, eschewing mainstream values. Of course, as noted earlier, children raised in chronically poor families typically endure a range of disadvantages and hardships, including poorer health, higher levels of stress and anxiety, social exclusion, higher levels of unemployment, and more precarious employment. They are more likely to be poor as adults, and they are more likely to pass on their disadvantaged positions across generations. But this is much less likely in the Nordic and other rich European nations with well-developed networks of social programs than it is in the UK and the US, where intergenerational mobility and levels of social supports are *both* relatively low.[27]

Finally, as in Canada and the United States, the depth or severity of poverty (measured relatively as 40 percent or less of median income) has increased over time. Disturbing income-based conclusions about rising and deepening poverty trends are buttressed by data obtained through survey research from projects such as Breadline Britain and Poverty and Social Exclusion (e.g., Lansley & Mack, 2015). These data indicate that the percentage of households deprived of various items, routines, and opportunities – identified through large-scale public surveys as "necessities" – had increased between 1999 and 2012. For example, the percentage of households had increased in many categories of concern: households that were unable to adequately heat their homes, were living in damp homes, could not afford three meals a day for children or two meals a day for adults, could not replace or repair broken electrical goods, could not afford household contents insurance, did not have appropriate clothes for a job interview, did not have enough bedrooms for their children, did not have suitable age-appropriate books or study spaces for their children, could not afford hobbies or leisure activities for their children, and/or could not afford to send their children on school trips. A majority of the UK population lacked at least one of these necessities; 30 percent of the population lacked three or more (Lansley & Mack, 2015; UN HRC, 2019).

The UK data and trends presented in Table 3.3 resemble those for Canada and the United States in yet another crucial way: they underestimate poverty levels. They do not reflect the impact of recent cuts to benefits for the poor and – as in Canada and the US – they do not include the sizable homeless population. The UK has no comprehensive estimates of homelessness because it is defined and measured differently in each constituent country or region. But recent studies indicate that the number of identified "rough sleepers," statutory homeless, and people at risk of homelessness has risen steeply over the past few years in England, trended upward in Wales, and climbed significantly in Northern Ireland. Only Scotland experienced a decline in its rate of homelessness by strengthening its safety net, but the prolonged recession, recent reductions in social supports, and a declining supply of affordable housing may halt this trend (Department for Communities and Local Government, 2014; Fitzpatrick et al., 2012, 2013, 2014, 2015).

Not surprisingly, there are some striking similarities in the levels, character, and distribution of poverty across the three Anglo nations, but, in most instances, the UK and Canada are more similar to each other than to the US. Their more muted antipathy toward the state and correspondingly less strident defense of individualism and "independence" are reflected in their more developed welfare states and lower poverty rates. But neoliberalism has arguably made greater inroads in the United Kingdom where, as in the United States, it was established earlier and more firmly, and many subsequent leaders and policy makers have emulated the leads of Thatcher and Reagan.

CROSS-NATIONAL CONTRASTS: WITHIN AND BEYOND THE ANGLO WORLD

The central poverty measures used in the United States (absolute), Canada (quasi-relative), and the United Kingdom (relative) are very different, so their national poverty data are not truly comparable. But we can still readily observe strikingly similar *trends* across the three nations over time: (1) they all have high poverty rates that have endured for several decades, (2) there has been relatively little or no decline in their *total* poverty rates (all people), and (3) the most vulnerable groups (children, single-parent families, and particular racialized or ethnic groups and minorities) remain overrepresented among the poor. In all three nations, poverty levels were, to some degree, contained by the array of social programs and supports that were in place – however minimal by comparative, international standards, as shown in the next chapter. Moreover, the national poverty measures used underestimate the poverty levels in all three states, and the depth of poverty has held steady or increased in all of them. The United States has fared the worst over time; its higher poverty rates across virtually all categories and subgroups and its notably deeper poverty were sustained. Canada has been perhaps the most successful of the three nations in reducing poverty among some of its most vulnerable groups. But, in most instances, its poverty rates have remained high over time, even where there was a notable decline (e.g., among children, single-parent families, and Indigenous people). Moreover, the depth of poverty was higher in 2018 than it was more than four decades earlier. Canada did extremely well in reducing poverty among its elderly population between 1976 (29 percent) and 2018 (4.0 percent), and the UK had some notable success reducing its child poverty rates during this period (see Waldfogel, 2010). Overall, however, their national poverty data indicate that the three wealthy Anglo nations have made relatively little progress and have little to celebrate.

Common trends notwithstanding, some notable distinctions among the three Anglo nations can be observed by contrasting the harmonized poverty and inequality data furnished by the LIS Cross-National Data Center in Luxembourg. Table 3.4 presents one popular measure of income inequality in the Anglo nations, the GINI coefficient. It summarizes the relative size of income inequality, indicating where a nation's distribution of income falls between two hypothetical extremes, 0 and 1. A coefficient of 0 indicates "perfect equality"; all individuals or households in a nation have exactly the same income. A coefficient of 1 indicates "perfect inequality"; all of the income generated in a nation accrues to just one individual or household. While neither of these two conditions ever obtains in reality, the GINI can tell us where a nation stands in relation to these two theoretical polar positions. Table 3.4 provides an overview of income inequality in the three Anglo nations using GINIs over time (columns 1 and 2). The GINIs in Canada, the UK, and the US are relatively high, and, as expected given their prominent standing in the plethora of inequality studies that have emerged over the past decades (e.g., Bradley et al., 2003; Brady et al., 2016; Collins, 2018; Dorling, 2018; Esping-Andersen & Myles, 2009; Gangl, 2005; Heisz, 2016), there has been a marked increase in income inequality in all three of these Anglo nations since the mid-1980s. However, there is also notable variation across them, with the highest level of income inequality in the United States, followed by the United Kingdom, then Canada.

Table 3.4 also indicates that, when a standard, relative measure of poverty is applied across Canada, the United Kingdom, and the United States (people with 50 percent or less of the median income in their nation), there has been very little change in the total poverty rate (for all people) in any of them over the past three decades. However, as in the 1980s, the poverty rate was highest in the United States (17 percent) in 2018. The US child poverty rate (20 percent) remained even higher than its total poverty rate, and greatly exceeded the high child poverty rates in the UK (13 percent) and Canada (12 percent). The elderly poverty rates in Canada and the UK were not nearly as high as that in the US (22 percent) but increased in both nations.

Table 3.4. Inequality and Poverty Rates in Canada, the United Kingdom, and the United States, 1987 and 2018

Nation	GINI Coefficient		Poverty Total (%)		Poverty Children (%)		Poverty Elderly (%)	
	1986	2018	1986	2018	1986	2018	1986	2018
Canada[a]	0.283	0.313	11.0	12.0	13.9	11.9	10.9	12.6
United Kingdom	0.303	0.328	9.0	11.0	11.6	13.4	7.0	10.5
United States	0.339	0.384	17.5	17.3	24.7	19.8	21.2	22.1

Source: LIS Cross-National Data Center (2021), *Inequality & Poverty Key Figures* (accessed January 5, 2021)
[a] Data for Canada are from 1987 and 2017

The use of common, harmonized measures allows us to compare the three poverty rates and trends across the three broadly similar Anglo nations, identify variation, and begin to investigate what is behind the variation. Examining the three nations together provides context and insight. Although they are all liberal nations with similar histories and cultures, the variation in their levels of poverty and inequality are not negligible. These variations reflect other differences in fiscal policy, social policy, and labor movement strength that, even when relatively minor, can have a disproportionate impact (Blundell et al., 2018; Card & Freeman, 1993/2009; Olsen, 2011; Zuberi, 2006). This is explored further in subsequent chapters.

However, the performance of these three Anglo nations is especially dismal when it is juxtaposed with that of other wealthy capitalist nations. As Table 3.5 indicates, employing a standard relative poverty measure (an income that is less than 50 percent of the median income) shows that rates of poverty varied markedly across nine rich capitalist nations in 2018.[28] The total population poverty rates in Canada and the UK were almost twice those in Denmark and Finland; the US poverty rate was nearly three times as high.[29] Differences in child poverty rates are equally striking. Child poverty rates in Canada and the UK (about 12 percent) were much higher than those in Norway and over twice those in Denmark (5 percent) and Finland (3.5 percent). The US child poverty rate (21 percent) was almost twice that in the other two Anglo nations, over four times the rate in Denmark, and six times the rate in Finland. Moreover, unlike in Denmark and Finland, the child poverty rate was higher than the poverty rate for the total population in the United States.

Table 3.5. Relative Poverty (%) in Nine Nations in 2018 (under 50 percent of median income)

Nation	Total Population Poverty Rate	Depth of Poverty (poverty gap)	Child Poverty Rate	Elderly Poverty Rate
Canada	11.8	29.8	11.8	11.9
United Kingdom	11.7	36.8	12.4	14.9
United States[a]	17.8	38.8	21.2	23.1
Denmark[a]	6.1	29.4	4.7	3.0
Finland	6.5	21.2	3.5	7.2
France	8.5	24.2	11.7	4.1
Germany[a]	10.4	25.1	11.3	10.2
Norway	8.4	33.7	8.1	4.3
Sweden	8.9	23.0	9.0	10.9

Sources: OECD (2021b), *Poverty rate*, doi: 10.1787/0fe1315d-en (accessed January 5, 2021); OECD (2021a), *Poverty gap*, doi: 10.1787/349eb41b-en (accessed January 5, 2021)
[a] Data are for 2017

Poverty rates among the elderly are also strikingly higher in the Anglo nations than in Denmark (3.0 percent), Finland (7.2 percent), France (4.1 percent), and Norway (4.3 percent). However, the elderly poverty rate in Canada (11.9 percent) was lower than that in the UK (14.9 percent), and it was strikingly lower than the rate in the US (23.1 percent). But recent policy changes and developments have rendered elderly poverty a growing concern again in Canada and other nations, including the United States and the United Kingdom (Myles, 2000, 2013; OECD, 2013). The "poverty gap" – an OECD "depth of poverty" measure that indicates the percentage by which the median income of the poor in each nation falls below the poverty line – is also much lower in the non-Anglo nations. Finland and Sweden (and France) stand out here. The median income of poor people is between 21 and 23 percent below the poverty lines in Finland and Sweden, but almost 30 percent below the poverty line in Canada, almost 37 percent of the poverty line in the UK, and almost 40 of the poverty line in the US.

There are several noteworthy trends and observations within and across the three Anglo countries and the comparator nations. First, poverty rates are high in Canada, the UK, and the US. However, there is variation in the degree and depth of poverty across these states; income inequality, rates of poverty, and the severity of poverty have consistently been markedly worse in the United States than in the other two Anglo nations. But the three Anglo countries have not done as well as many of their European counterparts, especially the Nordic nations. Finland, in particular, has sustained its relatively low rates of poverty since 1988 for all people (5.6 percent) and children (2.9 percent), and it has been one of the few nations in the wealthy capitalist world to steadily reduce the size of its homeless population, which declined by over 74 percent over this period (ARA, 2020). However, it is also noteworthy that poverty levels have been fairly stable across all nations for several decades, and that no nation has come close to eradicating poverty. The cross-national variation and trends observed here are, in part, related to the character and development of national social policy approaches and the character of each nation's welfare state, which are addressed in the next chapter.

NOTES

1 The LIS Cross-National Data Center was formerly known as the Luxembourg Income Study (LIS).

2 However, since this measure indicates the "average" shortfall among the poor, two countries with the same "poverty gap" may have very different configurations of low-income groups among their poor populations. For example, the poverty gap in a nation in which all of the poor people have incomes that are 50 percent of the poverty line income may look the same as that in a nation in which half of poor people have incomes that are 75 percent of the poverty line income and the other half have incomes that are 25 percent of the poverty line income. The *average* "depth" of poverty can be the same for both countries, but the lived experience of poverty is not the same for everyone in the two nations. Higher order indices provide estimates of the way that poverty is dispersed across the poor population in a nation. Statistics Canada addresses this dispersion by calculating the square of the poverty gap ratio. This "squared poverty gap index" places greater weight on households that are further below the poverty line, addressing the *intensity* of poverty. Other popular poverty gap indices calculate the average gap from poverty thresholds for the whole population.

3 Some research suggests that the severe stresses and strains associated with managing poverty can be all consuming and reduce people's capacity to address other issues and problems in their lives fully and adequately (Mani et al., 2013).

4 A study from the Center on Poverty and Social Policy at Columbia University (Wimer et al., 2019) suggests that official aggregate measures of inflation mask the fact that prices and price increases are higher for poor people. The overall poverty rate in the United States and that among vulnerable subpopulations, such as children, women, racialized groups, and immigrants, would be markedly higher if "inflation inequality" were taken into account. Moreover, many more people and families would qualify for benefits such as the food and housing assistance provided through anti-poverty programs.

5 Using the World Bank *extreme* poverty measure for developed nations (an income lower than $2.00 a day), Shaefer and Edin (2013) showed that "the prevalence of extreme poverty rose sharply between 1996 and 2011" (p. 265).

6 The term "minority" has been used in a number of different ways, variously referring to groups that are numerically or statistically smaller than the majority, groups with different cultural traits from the majority, and groups that are subordinated and/or face discrimination and endure unequal conditions in society. Women, for example, while not typically a numerical minority in most societies, are considered a minority in the latter sense. "Voluntary" minorities are groups who have voluntarily migrated to a new society, often in search of greater opportunities and well-being. Of course, they too often face discrimination and other barriers (Fleras, 2017; Ogbu, 1992).

7 In the United States, the term "Native Americans" is used to refer to the Indigenous peoples within the present borders of the continental United States, Alaska, and Hawaii.

8 Although the new Supplemental Poverty Measure (SPM) was developed in the early 1990s, the US Census Bureau did not release a report using this metric until 2011, under the Obama administration. It has a somewhat more "relative" dimension than the official measure because its thresholds have been updated to include additional costs (such as household supplies, personal care, and nonwork-related transportation), and it is adjusted for variations in housing costs across states and metropolitan areas. Consequently, some US researchers argue that it provides a more accurate depiction of poverty in the United States.

9 Many studies indicate that the number of homeless people is considerably higher than single night "point-in-time" estimates convey. Rather than counting the number of people found on the street and in other non-shelter locations on one night, researchers with the Urban Institute went to soup kitchens and shelters over the course of a month in 1987 to talk with homeless people about where they slept and ate for each of the seven days prior to the interview (Burt & Cohen, 1989). Establishing estimates for both *one-day* and *one-week* periods, they found that the homeless count for the latter period was 75 percent higher. The number of people

who experience homelessness over an extended period, such as a year, is strikingly higher. One Urban Institute (2000) study suggested that "even in a booming economy, at least 2.3 million adults and children, or nearly 1 percent of the U.S. population, are likely to experience a spell of homelessness at least once during a year" (p. 1). See also Burt et al. (2001) and National Law Center on Homelessness and Poverty (2017).

10 In the city of New York, there were 1,687 "critical incidents" in 2015. Almost half of them were violent, including assault, child abuse, and domestic violence, but nonviolent physical disputes and theft were also common. The number of these incidents and the occurrence of violence increase with the size of the shelter population (Sandoval et al., 2016).

11 When the younger, nonschool-aged homeless are taken into account, the total number of homeless children in the United States in 2013 was almost 2.5 million – a staggering 1 in every 30 children – and a dramatic increase from the level in 2010, when 1 in 45 children was homeless (National Center on Family Homelessness, 2011, 2014).

12 Although Canada has not had an official poverty measure, the government has acknowledged that LICOs are typically employed as proxies (Shillington & Stapleton, 2010). In 2018, the federal Liberal government introduced an official poverty line measure based on a revamped version of the market basket measure (MBM), a more inclusive type of absolute measure of poverty. But the MBM's "basket" of goods and services still excludes indispensable needs such as childcare and prescription medicines.

13 Canadian poverty thresholds for its LICOs have been periodically recalculated to account for the declining percentage of income spent on basic necessities and for improvements in the general standard of living in Canada over time. The thresholds were "rebased" in 1969, 1978, 1986, and 1992, but they have not been adjusted since.

14 In Canada, the terms "Indidgenous people(s)," "Aboriginal people(s)," and "Aboriginal Canadians" or "Native Canadians" are commonly employed. The Canadian Constitution identifies three groups of Indigenous people with Aboriginal rights: (1) the First Nations people, the original inhabitants of the land that is now Canada (including status Indians, who are subject to the Indian Act and have the right to live on reserves, and non-status Indians); (2) the Métis, people of Indigenous and European ancestry; and (3) the Inuit, who inhabit the Arctic and northern regions of Canada.

15 The population of Africville included slaves from the area and their descendants, former slaves from the United States who were refugees after the War of 1812 between the Americans and the British, and freedom-fighting Maroons (escaped slaves) deported from Jamaica by the British in the late eighteenth century.

16 The progress suggested by the decline in LICO "poverty rates" between 1976 and 2018 is not endorsed when Canada's Low Income Measure (LIM) – a relative metric similar to those used by the OECD and LIS,

defining poverty as less than 50 percent of the median income – is employed. Using the LIM, Canada's poverty rate was 13 percent in 1976 (over 3 million people) and remained almost the same in 2018, over forty years later, at 12.3 percent (over 4.4 million people).

17 Indian status is the legal status of a person who is registered as an Indian under the Indian Act.

18 Employing the MBM, one study indicated the depth of poverty was just as severe for the working poor as it was for the nonworking poor because the former's wages and benefits were so low, even though they worked, on average, as many hours as nonpoor workers did (Fleury & Fortin, 2006).

19 Dignity Village in Portland, Oregon, was among the first homeless camps to be legally recognized.

20 The Canadian Observatory on Homelessness (COH) is a nonpartisan research and policy partnership among academics, policy and decision makers, service providers, and people with lived experience of homelessness. It evolved from the Canadian Homelessness Research Network (CHRN) and is housed at York University in Toronto. Its typology, inspired by the European ETHOS typology discussed in Chapter 2, sets out four groups: (1) *the unsheltered,* people living on the streets or living in places unfit for human habitation; (2) *the emergency sheltered,* people staying in homeless shelters and shelters for people experiencing domestic violence or fleeing from disasters; (3) *the provisionally accommodated,* people who are provisionally housed in accommodations that are temporary or insecure, such as those who are "couch surfing" or in institutional care with nowhere to go upon release; and (4) *those at risk of homelessness,* people whose current housing situations are dangerously lacking security, such as people in danger of losing their job or being evicted.

21 There can be some advantages to using "before housing costs" (BHC) measures too. As the Department for Work and Pensions (2014) notes, they are "useful when there has been an increase in housing costs because of better quality housing, and so living standards have improved" (p. 14). Its HBAI reports include low-income poverty estimates based on both "after housing costs" and "before housing costs."

22 Unmarried or non-cohabiting 16- to 19-year-olds who are in full-time, non-advanced education are also registered as children in the HBAI reports; 19-year-olds have only been included in this group since 2006.

23 In addition, the ethnic group categories have not been entirely consistent over time in the HBAI reports.

24 The UK poverty data in Table 3.3 begins in the early 2000s; HBAI data from 1994/1995 to 2001/2002 were for Great Britain rather than the United Kingdom.

25 The Department for Work and Pensions (DWP; 2011) routinely refers to this alternative metric as an "absolute" poverty measure. However, it acknowledges that it is really an "anchored" poverty measure (tied to a

constant, previous median or threshold) rather than a true absolute poverty measure based on the costs of a small basket of basic necessities.

26 The only longitudinal low-income poverty data available through the British Household Panel Survey (BHPS) are "before housing costs" (BHC) because the survey does not collect sufficient data on housing costs to include "after housing costs" estimates (Townsend 2004).

27 The growing literature on social mobility includes studies by Blanden and Gibbons (2006), Blanden et al. (2005), d'Addio (2007), Esping-Andersen (2015), Gangl (2005), and Serafino and Tonkin (2014).

28 Table 3.5 uses data from the OECD, which employs a similar relative measure (under 50 percent of the median income) to that used by the LIS Cross-National Data Center. However, LIS data do not include some nations or are less current than the OECD data. Sweden, for example, has not been included in the LIS statistics since 2005 when it was a low-poverty exemplar – a position it no longer holds (Olsen, 2013).

29 The 2011 poverty rates using thresholds anchored to 2005 did not differ notably from those presented in Table 3.4 (OECD, 2015).

FURTHER READINGS

Brittain, M., & Blackstock, C. (2015). *First Nations child poverty: A literature review and analysis.* First Nations Children's Action Research and Education Service.

Desmond, M. (2016). *Evicted: Poverty and profit in the American city.* Broadway Books.

Iceland, J. (2013). *Poverty in America: A handbook* (3rd ed.). University of California Press.

Kenworthy, L. (2011). *Progress for the poor.* Oxford University Press.

Lansley, S., & Mack, J. (2015). *Breadline Britain: The rise of mass poverty.* Oneworld Publications.

Lister, R. (2004). *Key concepts: Poverty.* Polity Press.

Mishel, L., Bivens, J., Gould, E., & Shierholz, H. (2012). *The state of working America* (12th ed.). Economic Policy Institute/ILR Press.

Rank, M.R. (2005). *One nation, underprivileged: Why American poverty affects us all.* Oxford University Press.

Raphael, D. (2011). *Poverty in Canada* (2nd ed.). Canadian Scholar's Press.

Silver, J. (2014). *About Canada: Poverty.* Fernwood Publishing.

USEFUL RESEARCH REPORT AND DATA SITES

Canadian Observatory on Homelessness (COH)/Homeless Hub, York University, Toronto: http://www.homelesshub.ca

Center for Poverty & Inequality Research, University of California–Davis: https://poverty.ucdavis.edu

Economic Policy Institute, State of Working America Data Library,
  Washington, DC: https://www.epi.org/data

European Federation of National Organisations Working with the Homeless
  (FEANTSA), Brussels: https://www.feantsa.org/en

Institute for Research on Poverty, University of Wisconsin–Madison: https://
  www.irp.wisc.edu

LIS Cross-National Data Center, Maison des Sciences Humaines,
  Luxembourg: http://www.lisdatacenter.org

Organisation for Economic Co-operation and Development (OECD), Paris:
  http://www.oecd.org

Population Studies Center, Institute for Social Research, University of
  Michigan: https://www.psc.isr.umich.edu

Stanford Center on Poverty and Inequality, Stanford University: https://
  inequality.stanford.edu

Statistics Canada, Ottawa: https://www150.statcan.gc.ca/n1/en/subjects

UNICEF, New York: https://www.unicef.org/research-and-reports

United States Census Bureau, Washington, DC: https://www.census.gov
  /topics/income-poverty/poverty.html

CHAPTER FOUR

Poverty and the Welfare State: Comparative Contrasts

[U]ntil the great mass of the people shall be filled with the sense of responsibility for each other's welfare, social justice can never be attained.

– Helen Keller (1913, p. 35)

POVERTY AND THE WELFARE STATE

One of the most ubiquitous approaches to addressing poverty in afflu-ent capitalist nations has been the development of social policy and the creation of welfare states, but there can be pronounced variation in their character and efficacy over time and place.[1] While most welfare states have typically had broader aims than combatting poverty and the panoply of conditions and outcomes associated with it, poverty has typ-ically been a central catalyst for their advent and growth, particularly in the aftermath of the Great Depression and WWII. In the 1940s, British economist and social reformer William Beveridge identified "five giants of evil" that were closely associated with poverty: squalor, want, disease, idleness, and ignorance. His influential welfare state "blueprint," *Social Insurance and Allied Services* (Beveridge, 1942), advocated universal so-cial insurance, public healthcare and education, a greater commitment to full employment, and family allowances to address economic dis-tress. The pioneering social reforms it promoted propelled the United

Kingdom toward the international social policy forefront, even if they did not constitute a comprehensive "cradle-to-grave" welfare state. The "Beveridge Report," as it became popularly known, neglected some critical concerns and groups, such as single parents and those not in the workforce. It also sustained several preexisting policy instruments, such as targeted social assistance, user fees, and other more stigmatizing and punitive practices, which became entrenched to be extended and amplified later in the neoliberal era. But the report's ambitious agenda and implicit idea of liberal collectivism would profoundly influence social policy development in other nations, including Canada (Abel-Smith, 1992; Hills et al., 2001).

A distinct concern with poverty and social protection was also embedded in the "categories of social need" addressed by Leonard Marsh (1943/1975) in his *Report on Social Security for Canada* (the "Marsh Report") in 1943. Closely patterned on the report written by Beveridge – Marsh's mentor – this pivotal social policy cornerstone provided a foundation for Canada's welfare state. It was buttressed by two other crucial social policy documents addressing healthcare and housing respectively. The first, a report of the Advisory Committee on Health Insurance (the "Heagerty Report"), reviewed the provision of healthcare in nations across the globe and called for a joint federal-provincial program of health insurance. The second, a report on community planning and housing (the "Curtis Report"), documented the prevalence of overcrowded, substandard housing and slums in Canada and the shortage of affordable housing. It extolled the record of public housing in Britain and called for massive government intervention in the housing market. Together, these reports constituted Canada's first comprehensive anti-poverty and social security program for change, but several of their proposals and recommendations would be shelved or implemented later in a less far-reaching form (Finkel, 2006; Guest, 1997).[2]

In the United States in the mid-1960s, President Lyndon Johnson initiated a "war on poverty." As part of his "Great Society" vision, this arsenal of policy initiatives included Medicaid (for low-income families), Medicare (for the elderly), the Food Stamp Act, and the Elementary and Secondary School Act, which subsidized school districts with large numbers of poor students. Building upon and extending landmark "New Deal" social reforms initiated by President Roosevelt three decades earlier, these policies became core components of the US welfare state. While not as redistributive or supportive as the initiatives taken in many of the more comprehensive welfare states in Europe, the social programs emplaced across the three Anglo nations went some considerable distance toward reducing poverty rates and alleviating some of poverty's grim conditions. Even the United States – the country with the least developed and coordinated assemblage of social programs in the Anglo world today – made some impressive progress. In 1959, the year it began collecting poverty statistics, the US poverty rate was 22 percent (over 39 million people). By 1973, it had declined to 11 percent (23 million people). Since then, its social policy measures have helped keep millions of people from falling into poverty (Bailey & Danziger, 2013; Edelman, 2012; US Census Bureau, 2014). However, compared with their counterparts in other wealthy, capitalist nations, the welfare states are relatively undeveloped in the UK, Canada, and the US, where market and private sector provisions have been more firmly embraced and promoted. Poverty has remained a critical issue in these nations, and it has intensified over the past few decades with structural, institutional, and political changes. However, it has not generated the same sense of urgency, social policy focus, or public support that it did in the decades before neoliberalism took hold. As the welfare states in these three nations have been eroded and pared back over the past few decades, their deep roots in the Poor Law tradition have been increasingly exposed.

WELFARE STATE MODELS AND SOCIAL POLICY APPROACHES

As shown in Chapter 3, there is striking variation in the level and nature of poverty across the nations of the wealthy capitalist world, which is, in part, related to their diverse social policy approaches and the character of their welfare states. Welfare states are often defined as social support systems through which states assume some measure of responsibility for the promotion and protection of their residents', families', and communities' well-being.[3] But states' level of dedication to this goal and their range of responses – including the way they define and secure our welfare – can vary markedly over time and place. Welfare states exist in every developed, affluent capitalist nation, but they can assume a bewildering variety of sizes, shapes, and configurations. Social policy researchers have attempted to impose order on this complex and often chaotic tangle of social policy diversity. They have identified broad similarities and differences that allow for the organization of welfare states into clusters or "families."

One of the most useful and widely employed approaches is the "welfare regimes" (or "welfare worlds") typology, which sets out three distinct "ideal types" of welfare states: two comprehensive, "institutional" regimes (*conservative* and *social democratic*) and one basic or residual regime (*liberal*).[4] When the typology was first developed, its focus was primarily on the character and impact of the income support programs in each regime. Over time, other key measures and dimensions have been brought into the framework to distinguish welfare states more fully (Esping-Andersen, 1990; Olsen, 2002, 2019b). In practice, no nation's welfare state entirely matches the profile of any of these three models.[5] Rather, each is a hybrid that typically fits "best" into one of the three welfare regimes.

Broadly similar, the welfare states in Canada, the UK, and the US are categorized as belonging to the *liberal* regime, the least developed welfare state model. But there have been notable differences in their character and impact on poverty. The "intra-regime" variation across them helps to explain the differences in the rates and severity of poverty in these nations over time, a pattern observed in the previous chapter. Their increasingly similar policy approaches in the current period of neoliberal austerity helps to explain similarities in poverty trends today. Welfare states in the other two regimes, conservative and social democratic, are considerably more developed than those in the liberal regime and more effective in addressing poverty and other forms of inequality. Although they do so in distinctly different ways from each other, both of these more highly developed, institutional models provide policy lessons for the Anglo nations.[6]

Liberal Welfare States

Some of the central attributes of welfare states that have received attention in social policy research are their goals, orientation, scope, generosity, inclusivity, and impact. These attributes can be strikingly different across the three welfare state regimes or worlds, and these differences

greatly affect impacts on poverty and other forms of inequality. Perhaps the most definitive and important dimensions of a welfare state –
because these are distinctly imprinted on all of the others – are its central
goals. Liberal welfare states are largely geared to function as narrowly
circumscribed "last resort" safety nets. They primarily support people
in times of need, emergency, social dislocation, or crisis, and generally
provide relatively minimal support. Aptly described as "residual," or
"rudimentary," these basic welfare states are expressly designed to limit
dependence upon the state. Liberal welfare states furnish programs
designed to help markets work more efficiently, with an implicit or explicit expectation that this should benefit most people in society. Despite the existence of some policy areas or measures that fit somewhat
uneasily in the liberal welfare state family and some notable differences
across these policies in the three Anglo nations under study, Canada,
the UK, and the US are routinely, and befittingly, classified within this
family. In contrast to many other modern welfare states, they are more
reluctant to promote and defend strong social rights, including those
that would more effectively address poverty. Rather, they ensure the
dominance of the market by providing modest forms of public support
and encouraging and subsidizing private alternatives. Consequently,
the citizens of these nations are more "commodified"; that is, they are
considerably more dependent upon market forces and employers for
their well-being. This is especially true in the United States. Although
it departs from the liberal ideal in several respects, including in its social insurance programs and universal public provision of primary and
secondary education, the US welfare state most closely conforms to the
liberal ideal.[7]

Liberal welfare states are designed to modify or mitigate some of
the more negative consequences of capitalist markets, which, left to
their own devices, operate without a moral compass. Their *orientation*
is therefore more reactive, passive, and remedial, rather than anticipatory, proactive, and preventive. For example, they provide income
assistance to some poor families to attenuate some of the conditions
and consequences of destitution, rather than seriously committing to
redress, eliminate, and prevent poverty through a closely integrated
array of policy measures. They typically emphasize passive income support programs (such as social unemployment insurance and social assistance) over active measures designed to avert job loss and encourage

full employment. A curative, remedial healthcare orientation is also more prominent in the liberal regime than are health promotion and preventative approaches that address the impact of neighborhoods and the environment.

The *scope* or scale of liberal welfare states is also relatively limited or incomplete, addressing a much more restricted range of needs, contingencies, and risks. Since they are not as dedicated to securing a broad array of rights, entitlements, and freedoms, or to fostering greater social inclusion to ensure the full participation of all members of society, social services are generally less available, accessible, and comprehensive in liberal welfare states. None of the three Anglo nations examined here provide public, universal childcare, elder care, or tertiary education.[8] Active labor market programs, including measures designed to match unemployed workers with available jobs, create jobs, or provide training programs that address current and future needs for workers, have not been central parts of these nations' labor market policies. Universal healthcare does not exist in the United States; is notably incomplete in Canada (pharmacare, home care, and dental care are not included); and is moving toward greater privatization in the United Kingdom (via the Health and Social Care Act of 2012).[9] Families who cannot afford to purchase these and other essential social services in the market are left without coverage, or with inadequate supports, and are more likely to become and remain poor.

The welfare states of Canada, the UK, and the US are also considerably less *generous* than many others in several respects. Their income programs provide minimal benefits and have longer waiting periods before benefits can be claimed, as well as shorter periods of benefit receipt. The social services that do exist are often less extensive, of lower quality, and have fewer adjuvants or auxiliary supports in place. State authorities have more discretion over who receives social support because it is not typically provided as an entitlement or as firmly based upon social rights.

The programs available in the Anglo nations are also generally less *inclusive* than those in many other rich, developed nations. They place emphasis on targeting particular groups such as poor or low-income families (offering these groups selective programs) rather than on providing everyone with universal benefits. Programs that target the poor generally receive less public support in most nations. People who do not benefit directly from programs financed by their taxes are more likely to be persuaded to adopt accounts of poverty that portray poor families as lazy welfare "scroungers" and "skivers" who choose not to work. This rhetoric can generate vigorous pubic demands for reductions in social spending, more stringent eligibility rules, and lower taxes, culminating in lower levels of social expenditures and commitment and, ultimately, less support for poor families. Consequently, despite their explicit focus on poverty, the net *impact* of targeted programs can be notably lower than the impact of more comprehensive, universal, and considerably more popular programs that benefit everyone (Korpi & Palme, 1998).

It may be unfair to assess liberal welfare states as failures for not eliminating poverty since that task has not been central to their purpose or design. Most of them, however, *have* targeted poverty among some groups, such as children, with strikingly unsatisfactory results. Indeed, as noted in Chapter 3, the child poverty rates in Canada, the United Kingdom, and United States have long remained higher than population poverty rates – and the child poverty rates in the United States are perpetually notoriously high. Moreover, these nations can be censured for their steadfast faith in market forces as the best solution to this problem despite the existence of a vast accumulation of contradictory evidence over the past few decades. Conservative welfare states and, most notably, the social democratic welfare states of the Nordic nations have been considerably more effective in preventing and reducing high levels and extreme forms of poverty and mitigating their most pernicious forms of damage (e.g., Bradley et al., 2003; Brady, 2003b, 2009; Esping-Andersen & Myles, 2009; Huber & Stephens, 2014; Korpi & Palme, 1998; Olsen, 2002, 2011; Smeeding, 2006a, 2006b).

Conservative and Social Democratic Welfare States: Lessons for the Anglo Nations

Welfare states traditionally denoted as "institutional" are more developed and have considerably more ambitious objectives than liberal welfare states, and, consequently, their policies are more extensive and encompassing. In turn, they are far more effective at reducing the extent and intensity of poverty. One of the strengths of the tri-polar welfare regime typology is that it allows us to distinguish two different types of institutional welfare state models: (1) *conservative* welfare states and (2) *social democratic* welfare states (Esping-Andersen, 1990).

Conservative welfare states, found in continental European nations such as Belgium, France, the Netherlands, and Germany, its most quintessential exponent, are less redistributive than their social democratic counterparts.[10] Their emphasis upon earnings-related, occupational insurance programs and their relatively modest provision of social services can reinforce existing class, gender, occupational, nativity, and other hierarchies. However, compared with *liberal* welfare states, they have much higher levels of social spending and greater support for a more extensive array of social rights. They also reject the idea of market primacy as the key to well-being. Consequently, their poverty rates are generally lower than those of Canada, the UK, and the US (Jäntti & Danziger, 2000; Myles, 1998; Smeeding, 2006a, 2006b).

Despite some notable differences among the members of the *social democratic* cluster of institutional welfare states, they are typically characterized by a denser web of universal social programs and a greater emphasis upon addressing more forms of inequality than other welfare states. This model, found in the Nordic lands (Denmark, Finland, Norway, and Sweden), promotes the general well-being of the entire population by more fairly redistributing social resources, opportunities, and life chances and by securing and extending more social and political rights. Rights to (1) an adequate standard of living (including the right to food, clothing, housing, medical care, education, and other necessary social services) and to (2) employment and participation in the cultural life of communities – as set out in the United Nations Universal Declaration of Human Rights (1948) and reinforced in its International Covenant on Economic, Social and Cultural Rights (1966) – are often much more closely observed and implemented here (Olsen, 2011, 2019a). The greater emphasis upon rights-based social supports in social democratic welfare states has, in turn, allowed them to further "decommodify" their citizens and long-term residents, diminishing their reliance upon markets and employers for their well-being.

Social democratic welfare states, with Sweden as their most paradigmatic representative, have been the most committed to promoting greater equality, and among the most successful in reducing the prevalence and intensity of poverty.[11] They have also done more to eliminate or attenuate many of the conditions and consequences of poverty, such as poor health, inadequate housing, unemployment, and low levels of education. They provide systems of coordinated and mutually reinforcing proactive programs and services. Rather than relying primarily on passive unemployment insurance programs, which are actuated *after* workers lose their jobs, they pioneered and continue to place greater emphasis upon active labor market measures, such as job training, job creation, and occupational rehabilitation and youth programs, as well as universal postsecondary education to promote employment and citizenship. Besides comprehensive healthcare (including dental care, pharmacare, midwife services, vaccinations, prosthetics, wheelchairs, crutches, checkups, and consultations), they also provide generous sickness insurance that allows parents to stay home with sick children to promote their recovery and limit the exposure of teachers, childcare workers, and peers to contagious illnesses. Unlike in the Anglo nations, where poor and low-income parents and single mothers are often compelled to enter the labor market in nonstandard, low-wage jobs with few supports, social democratic welfare states provide accessible and affordable childcare, training, education, and other auxiliary programs (Graubard, 1986; Kangas & Palme, 2005; Kvist et al., 2012; Olsen, 2002, 2011).[12]

Furthermore, many of these programs have rendered social democratic welfare states more "women friendly" than welfare states in the other two regimes; universal family allowances and generous parental leave programs that require both parents to take part in order to receive full benefits help to account for women's higher participation rates in the labor force and their lower rates of poverty (Bergqvist et al., 1999; Borchost, 1994; Hernes, 1987; Kjelstad, 2001).[13] Service-intensive welfare states with universally high quality and high standards for all programs provide equal treatment for rich and poor families. But the quality of life improvement is typically greater for poor families. The comprehensive grids of generous, inclusive, coordinated, and synergistic programs that constitute social democratic welfare states necessitate higher levels of social spending, funded through higher levels of taxation, than in the liberal regime nations. Yet because of their more broadly encompassing and sheltering embrace, these programs have received strong public support, with relatively little "tax backlash" or resentment, and the Nordic nations have been able to sustain a strong commitment to ending poverty, reducing inequalities, and fostering greater well-being across their populations – although some of this has been undermined by globalization, the recalibration and restructuring of welfare states, and greater austerity (Brady & Bostic, 2015; Esping-Andersen & Myles, 2009; Jacques & Noël, 2018; Korpi & Palme, 1998; Larsen, 2006, 2008; Svallfors, 1997, 2003, 2012).

THE THREE PILLARS OF WELFARE STATES

Welfare states in the wealthy capitalist world today comprise three distinct but closely interlocked networks of institutional provisions, practices, and protections: (1) *income supports*, (2) *social services*, and (3) *protective legislation* (see Figure 4.1; Olsen, 2019b). But there is remarkable variation in the intent, magnitude, and essence of the welfare states in place across the nations of the rich capitalist world, as well as in the emphasis accorded to each of these three policy pillars. Across a range of interactive social policy domains with overlapping concerns and responsibilities – including family, labor market, healthcare, education, workplace injury, disability, housing, old age, and income policies – these pillars furnish a broad array of instruments that can have a profound impact on the breadth, depth, and distribution of poverty, and on the daily lives and well-being of poor families. Pensions and other old age *income supports* can reduce poverty by providing substantial economic support to the elderly and increasing the demand for workers in the paid labor market to replace those who have retired. The provision of public *social services*, such as healthcare, childcare, postsecondary education, social housing, public transportation, and other proactive measures, can also inhibit and diminish poverty by alleviating severe stresses and strains on poor children and families and promoting greater physical and mental well-being. *Protective legislation*, such as minimum wage laws, rent controls and other tenancy laws, statutory rights to housing, and other benefits can also establish and secure human rights and promote greater equality and social inclusion (Einhorn & Logue, 1989; Esping-Andersen, 1990; Ginsburg, 1992; Gould, 1993; Olsen, 2002, 2013). Some key measures from each of the three policy pillars of the liberal welfare states in Canada, the UK, and the US, and their impact on poverty, are examined below.

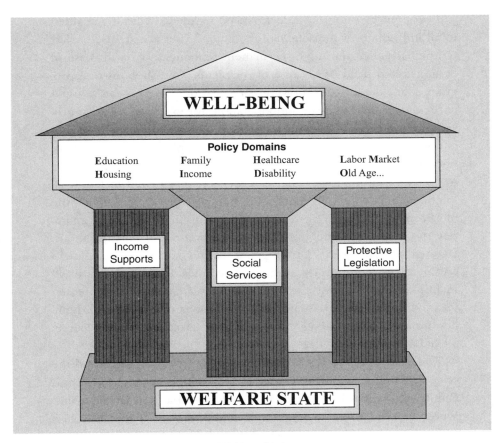

Figure 4.1. Three Pillars of the Welfare State

The Income Supports Pillar

Income programs encompass a broad spectrum of cash payments or "transfers," with varying conditions of eligibility, levels of generosity, and forms of financing, which can provide families with a greater measure of economic and social stability. They include three main categories of monetary or cash support: *demogrants, social insurance,* and *social assistance.* The way these three income transfers are accessed and designed, the people they are intended to reach, and their level of generosity vary markedly across nations. This policy pillar also includes the less direct forms of income support provided through the tax system, known as "fiscal welfare."

Demogrants are universal, tax-financed payments typically provided to all individuals or households in a nation. They are accessed solely on the basis of citizenship or permanent residency, not on the basis of demonstrated need or because of recipients' contributions to a program. Many demogrants, however, are provided to everyone within a particular demographic or subpopulation; for example, they are provided to everyone in a certain age group (children or the elderly), to people with a disability, or to families with multiple children. These are often referred to as "categorical universal" because they are accessible to everyone within a particular category. Universal child or family allowances, old-age supplements, and disability supports are among the most common forms of categorical demogrants that have played an important role in containing or reducing poverty rates in many nations. Demogrants have been relatively generous and helped to forestall high and deep levels of poverty in the Nordic lands. Because they are "all inclusive," public support for them is widespread; the resentment often fostered by programs that are targeted at poor individuals and families but financed through general taxation is avoided (Korpi & Palme, 1998; Larsen, 2006, 2008).

Nations with liberal welfare states provide few demogrants, and the ones that they have furnished, such as Old Age Security (OAS) and Family Allowances in Canada, have not been particularly generous. Moreover, some of the demogrants that did exist in Canada have been terminated, restructured as selective programs with more stringent conditions and reduced benefit levels, or displaced by fiscal measures over the past few decades. Canada's long-standing Family Allowance program for example – established in 1944 as the nation's first universal program – was replaced by the Canadian Child Tax Benefit (CCTB) in 1993. The UK's universal Child Benefit, introduced in 1975 (but rooted in the 1942 Beveridge Report), became means tested in 2013.[14] In the United States, universal income programs have not taken hold. Its Old Age Security program is a quasi-universal contributory insurance program, not a demogrant with eligibility based upon citizenship. Unlike Canada and the UK – and most other nations of the developed world – the US never had a universal family allowance or child benefit program. It has supported poor families through its targeted Aid to Families with Dependent Children (AFDC, 1962) program, an income benefit rooted in the 1930s New Deal. Although not a demogrant, and far from generous, it was provided as an entitlement, and it reached many poor families. But it was eliminated in 1996 via the Personal Responsibility and Work Opportunity Reconciliation Act (PWORA) and succeeded the next year by the more restrictive, punitive, and difficult to access Temporary Assistance to Needy Families (TANF) program, which offers discretionary, time-limited cash assistance and requires recipients to participate in work-related activities (a form of "workfare"). The Supplemental Nutrition Assistance Program (SNAP) – introduced in 1964 as the Food Stamp Program and renamed in 2008 – is now the only cash assistance program for poor families that is "guaranteed" (legally mandated) in the United States.

Social insurance programs are central components of virtually all modern welfare states and have helped to suppress the incidence and impact of poverty. They furnish earnings-related benefits – typically financed through contributions from employers, employees, and the state – replacing a portion of the income lost by workers who have temporarily or permanently left the paid labor market. Protection from various risks and other unexpected contingencies and circumstances is purchased through the pooling of contributions. Social insurance programs redistribute resources from workers who are not currently in need to those who are in need, and they do so more effectively and efficiently than is possible in the private sector.[15] Unemployment, old age and sickness insurance, disability benefits, and workers' compensation are among the most familiar and popular forms of social insurance. These programs help people avoid poverty by redistributing income "horizontally," over a recipient's lifetime – from periods of participation in the paid labor force to periods of unemployment, injury, or retirement – thus addressing the "life cycle" of poverty.[16] Nations with institutional welfare states have more social insurance programs, covering more risks, and provide greater support than liberal regime welfare states. The social democratic welfare states have been particularly successful in reducing the level and depth of poverty by combining generous universal demogrants with a second tier of earnings-related social insurance programs (Kangas, 1991; Kangas & Palme, 2005; Nordic Statistical Committee, 2017; Palme, 1990, 1999).

Although the Anglo nations have fewer and less generous social insurance programs than nations with institutional welfare states, the ones that exist have helped to reduce rates and severity of poverty. In the United States, for example, Social Security (Old Age, Survivors, and Disability Insurance, or OASDI) was more effective in reducing the poverty rate between 2008 and 2013 than five of the largest means-tested programs – the Supplemental Security Income (SSI), the Supplemental Nutrition Assistance Program, the Earned Income Tax Credit (EITC), and public assistance and housing assistance – combined (Meyer & Wu, 2018). However, social insurance programs typically exclude people who have been outside the paid labor force, or in it for short periods, because eligibility for social insurance programs and the level of benefits received are determined on the basis of employment records and contributions. Thus, when income levels decline, social insurance benefits follow. Moreover, some states have been withdrawing from or reducing their contributions to public programs, rendering them more like their private insurance counterparts.[17] In some key areas, the Anglo nations have not provided adequate social insurance coverage. Time-limited sickness benefits have been available in Canada via Employment Insurance (EI), but benefit levels have been relatively low and have declined in tandem with EI benefit levels. The United States does not have a universal sickness insurance program.

Social assistance (or "public assistance" in the United States) – often pejoratively referred to as "welfare" – refers to income security payments that are typically directly targeted at poor households with inadequate means of support. Although they are designed to provide some level of security and to redistribute income "vertically" (from those with higher income to those at the bottom), the level of support they furnish is generally meager and the conditions for eligibility are often stringent and punitive. They usually require a test to determine eligibility, and they stigmatize beneficiaries, undermine their reputations and dignity, and discourage others in need from seeking aid.[18] Social assistance includes social allowances, housing allowances, supplementary income benefits, subsidies, vouchers, food stamps, and implicit forms of cash support, such as income-related rents.[19]

Social assistance transfers have been more central to the liberal welfare states of the Anglo nations than to those of most other developed nations, and they have become more prominent over the past few decades, displacing demogrants. In the United States, given the demise, noted previously, of other social supports for poor and low-income families, the number of SNAP recipients rose dramatically. But its provisions fall far short of what people need to subsist. "Workfare" ("welfare-to-work") measures, pioneered in the US and soon replicated in Canada, the UK, and elsewhere, have also become more common in the neoliberal period. They require people to work in order to receive benefits, conscripting poor and unemployed victims of structural, institutional, and political change and reinscribing their subordination. They use taxpayers' money to subsidize employers, who pay workfare recipients very low wages or none at all, undermining minimum wage laws and "re-commodifying" workers (Schram, 2006). Means-tested programs in the three Anglo nations can play an important role in preventing, reducing, and alleviating poverty, even in the United States (Edelman, 2012; Meyer & Wu, 2018; Shaefer & Edin, 2013). But both the overemphasis on social assistance and the retrenchment, restructuring, and elimination of many income programs for poor and low-income families help to explain the sustained rates and deep levels of poverty (especially child poverty) found in the Anglo nations – and the variation across them – identified in the previous chapter.

The wide assortment of tax credits, allowances, exemptions, and preferences collectively referred to as "*fiscal welfare*" is an often neglected but increasingly central facet of the income supports pillar in the Anglo world. In the United States, the role of the Earned Income Tax Credit, a benefit restricted to wage earners, has become more prominent since its introduction in 1975, but it provides little support for the nonworking poor. In recent decades, the Anglo nations have increasingly promoted tax measures that benefit income earners. At the affluent end of the income scale, reductions in marginal tax rates for the wealthy, the elimination or easy avoidance of inheritance taxes, and the slashing of corporate tax rates have greatly reduced the resources available to fund social programs. These measures also helped to foster the dramatic rise in income and wealth inequality so thoroughly documented in numerous recent studies, as well as the growth of corporate giants that put small enterprises and farms out of business. They also subsidize the export of capital and jobs abroad, leaving unemployment and poverty in their wake. Yet the far greater levels of state spending on subsidies, grants, and tax breaks and exemptions for the wealthiest members of society and large corporations – and on bailouts when large corporations fail – are not widely viewed as state "dependence" and do not typically generate much outrage. Indeed, these practices are widely accepted as "normal" or inevitable (Broadway & Cuff, 2014; Farnsworth,

Table 4.1. Impact of Welfare States on Poverty Rates (%) in Nine Nations in 2016 (poverty = under 50% of median income)

Nation	Social Expenditure Rate (% of GDP)	Total Poverty Rate *before* Taxes and Transfers	Total Poverty Rate *after* Taxes and Transfers	Poverty Reduction Percentage	Poverty Gap (mean) *after* Taxes and Transfers
Canada	17.4	24.5	12.4	49.0	30.4
United Kingdom	21.2	29.5	11.1	63.4	35.5
United States	18.9	6.6	17.8	33.1	39.8
Denmark	28.7	24.9	5.8	76.7	29.9
Finland	29.8	34.3	5.8	83.1	22.5
France	32.0	37.0	8.3	77.6	23.9
Germany	25.1	33.5	10.4	68.2	26.5
Norway	25.7	25.6	8.2	67.9	35.3
Sweden	26.4	24.9	9.1	63.4	22.5

Sources: OECD (2020a); OECD (2020b)

2012; Himelfarb & Himelfarb, 2014; Myles, 2015; Newman & O'Brien, 2011).

A nation's expenditures on direct and indirect income measures and social services, expressed as a percentage of gross domestic product (GDP), is one measure of its commitment to well-being. Table 4.1 (column 1) shows that spending is much higher in nations with institutional welfare states (25 percent to 32 percent of GDP) than in the Anglo nations (17 percent to 21 percent of GDP). It is true that an exclusive focus on this as an indicator of commitment can be misleading; spending can take a variety of forms, and high levels may reflect the prevalence of social problems. But "virtually all studies conclude that poverty reduction, in particular among families with children, is closely related to levels of social expenditure" (Esping-Andersen & Myles, 2009, p. 665).

THE IMPACT OF TRANSFERS AND TAXES

Table 4.1 indicates that market poverty rates were high in all nine nations *before* the introduction of taxes and transfers, and especially high in France, Finland, Germany, and the United Kingdom, nations representing each of the three welfare regimes examined earlier (column 3).

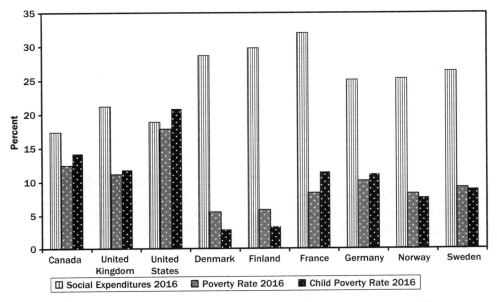

Figure 4.2. Social Expenditures (% of GDP), Total Poverty Rates (< 50% of median, after taxes and transfers), and Child Poverty Rates (< 50% of median, after taxes and transfers) in Nine Nations, 2016

However, there is significant variation in poverty levels *after* income transfers and fiscal measures have been implemented. Nations with institutional welfare states – and social democratic Denmark and Finland in particular – have much lower poverty rates than those in Canada, the United Kingdom, and, especially, the United States, the nation with the archetypal liberal welfare state (column 4). These differences are even greater when child poverty is examined. Child poverty is around 3 percent in Denmark and Finland, but reaches double-digit levels in the United Kingdom (11.8 percent) and Canada (14.2 percent) and almost 21 percent in the United States, as illustrated in Figure 4.2. The efficacy of taxes and transfers in these nine nations can be seen in Table 4.1: poverty reduction in Finland, Denmark, France, and Germany was far greater than that in the UK, Canada, and the US in 2016 (column 5). Poverty was also deeper in the liberal regime Anglo nations than in the five nations with institutional welfare states, especially Finland and Sweden (column 6, mean poverty gap).[20] The impact of taxes and transfers on child poverty is particularly noteworthy in Denmark and Finland (Figure 4.2).

The Social Services Pillar

The second pillar of welfare states – social services – furnishes care, facilities, and other "in-kind" benefits, rather than monetary transfers. It is a vast and diverse constellation of publicly provided and/or publicly funded social provisions to promote the well-being of families and communities. These measures are essential to reducing and containing poverty and addressing its consequences. The social services pillar comprises an extensive network of provisions, including healthcare and dental care; preschools and childcare centers; primary, secondary, and tertiary education; job training, job creation, and other active labor market programs; elder care; personal care, long-term care, training, and transportation services for people with disabilities; mental health centers; remedial and preventive counseling and other forms of social assistance for people with substance abuse problems; youth centers and services; centers for battered women and for neglected and abused children; transitional housing; foster homes, group homes, and other residential services; prenatal care, well-baby clinics, and other forms of assistance for new parents and for families in crisis; day programs, shelters, and social or public housing for the homeless; language training and settlement services for immigrants and refugees; legal aid; and public transportation, among many others.[21] Social services also include a multiplicity of other service-related, "in-kind" benefits and goods such as eyeglasses, prescription drugs, prosthetics, wheelchairs and other mobility aids, "talking books" and braille books for the visually impaired, and nutritious hot meals provided in schools and childcare centers. As with income programs, access to services may be universal, limited to people covered by insurance, or determined by need via a means test or needs test. Services may be offered in the public sector or in the private sector (nonprofit or profit) and subsidized by states (Alber, 1995; Bambra, 2005; Olsen, 2019a; Sipilä, 1998).[22]

Liberal welfare states provide a restricted range of social services and fewer still that are provided to everyone as a right. Healthcare is one of the most prominent forms of social services provided. Like the United Kingdom, Canada provides healthcare for everyone, including its poorest residents, but its healthcare system has never been as comprehensive as the National Health Service (NHS) in the UK. It does not include home care or prescription drugs, which have become increasingly critical over the past few decades as the nature of healthcare has shifted away from hospital and physician services. The United States is the only rich capitalist nation without a universal, public healthcare system, but it has provisions for its elderly population (Medicare) and for part of its low-income population (Medicaid). The orientation of healthcare in the Anglo nations remains largely reactive and curative rather than proactive and preventative. Public primary and secondary education is a universal service commonly provided as a right across virtually all developed nations. But neither Canada nor the United States has a public postsecondary education system, and England ended its provision of universal, public tertiary education in 1997.[23]

Few nations provide the full complement of measures listed in the extensive social services inventory above. But social democratic welfare states, to varying degrees, more closely approximate full provision, proactively addressing many of the conditions that can trigger and sustain poverty, and these social services have had an especially positive impact on the early crucial period of child development and growth.[24] Like generous family allowances and parental leave programs, social services that help to "degenderize" caring responsibilities in the home (especially childcare and elder care) can also promote higher rates of female participation in the paid labor force, helping to reduce poverty rates among women, especially among single mothers, a particularly vulnerable group in the Anglo nations.[25]

The Protective Legislation Pillar

Protective legislation constitutes a third central policy pillar, a foundational yet often neglected component of all welfare states with deep historical roots (Olsen, 2019b). Factory acts, workers' compensation laws, and compulsory primary education legislation are among its earliest and most familiar building blocks. Sometimes referred to as "legal welfare," this pillar encompasses numerous statutory rights and entitlements, as well as a dense web of regulatory, preventive, and proactive legislation, ordinances, rules, protections, and safeguards that can, directly or indirectly, help to prevent poverty and mitigate its impact.[26] In the labor market policy domain, for example, minimum wage and "living wage" laws, equal pay for equal work legislation, job protection laws, and antidiscrimination laws can help prevent poverty due to low income, unemployment, and underemployment. In the health field, legislation regulating air and water quality, food and drug safety, standards for housing and workplaces and myriad other products and services can help people from falling into poverty, or being sustained there, by preventing injury and illness and promoting good health, while reducing the strain on healthcare and other services. In the housing domain, tenancy regulations, rent control laws, eviction protection laws, and rights to housing legislation can help ensure that low-income families have decent shelter that will protect them and keep them safe (Gerull, 2014).[27] Laws can also stop large equity firms, corporate landlords, and real estate companies from buying up apartment complexes and letting them sit vacant ("warehousing" them) until they can reap greater profits later. They can also discourage large-scale luxury development and gentrification that make renting or buying homes impossible for many families and push others who are housed onto the street. These measures can be as consequential to our well-being as generous housing allowances and the provision of social housing.

Rights and legislation are particularly important in preventing homelessness. The Nordic nations have a quasi-right to housing for some vulnerable groups (such as families with children) embedded in their constitutions and other acts and have had stronger rent controls, protections against evictions, and other laws to help prevent tenants and homeowners from losing their homes. In the United States, millions of families are evicted from their homes every year, and many of them end up homeless (Desmond, 2016). But, like the measures associated with the other pillars, the capacity of protective legislation to promote our welfare depends on how laws are drafted, implemented, and enforced. Income programs and social services can be highly supportive, generous, and inclusive or notoriously stingy, difficult to access, and stigmatizing. Similarly, third pillar measures can protect us and promote our welfare by preventing problems from emerging, or they can be punitive. In the Anglo nations, a flood of anti-vagrancy laws and other legislation and related practices have been introduced that criminalize many acts in which homeless people must engage just to survive on the streets. These harsh laws bear the distinct, formative stamp of much earlier legislation introduced to address poverty during the prehistory of the welfare state. This early legislation's emphasis upon individualism and independence would provide a template, and set a trajectory, for the development of liberal welfare states in the Anglo nations.

POVERTY AND POOR LAWS: THE HISTORICAL ROOTS OF ANGLO WELFARE STATES

During the Middle Ages, the church assumed primary responsibility for the poor, establishing almshouses for the hungry, infirmaries for the sick and diseased, and temporary shelters for vagabonds, but the assistance it provided was typically paltry, doing little to diminish the numbers of the indigent or their misery. The church did not call for an end to poverty or dispute the steeply asymmetrical distribution of wealth; indeed, ecclesiastical altruism was central to the preservation of existing social hierarchies. Wealthy lords, merchants, and burghers enriched the church through charitable donations to parish coffers, which, in turn, allowed them to purchase their personal salvation and legitimated their opulent lifestyles amidst widespread abject destitution.[28] However, poverty became an increasingly urgent concern when the profound economic and social upheaval generated through the gradual dissolution of feudal systems and the enrooting of capitalism across Europe began to threaten the social order. The severe social dislocation, bourgeoning numbers of homeless vagrants, and widespread unrest would prompt greater state intervention, including the enactment of poor laws in the United Kingdom and its North American colonies, which became increasingly brutal over time. These welfare state antecedents would leave an indelible imprint in the Anglo lands, profoundly shaping the character of their social policy (de Schweinitz, 1943; Geremek, 1997; Jütte, 1994; Kahl, 2005; Lis & Soly, 1979; Mollat, 1986; Woloch, 1994).

The Prehistory of a Liberal Welfare State: Poor Relief in the United Kingdom

By the end of the seventeenth century, some form of public support for the poor was in place across much of Europe. France created one of the continent's first central public relief offices, the Grand Bureau des Pauvres, in the middle of the sixteenth century. England's system of poor relief can be traced back to late sixteenth century acts of Parliament.[29] But its Poor Relief Act of 1601 – popularly known as the Elizabethan Poor Law – is considered the most definitive social policy of the era (Elton, 1953; Leichter, 1979; Quigley, 1996/1997).[30] Rather than prohibiting poor relief, the Elizabethan Poor Law imposed a legal obligation upon local church authorities to furnish aid to those members of their parishes who were unable to support themselves. While ultimately the responsibility of the state and financed through compulsory taxation, this early form of public assistance was locally administered. Parishes also provided work for the able-bodied unemployed and apportioned punishment for those deemed able but unwilling to work.

The Elizabethan Poor Law proposed different strategies to address different "categories" of the poor. The elderly, sick, and disabled were to be provided with "outdoor relief" (groceries, fuel, and small amounts of cash) and cared for in their own homes. "Indoor relief" would be furnished through the creation of dedicated institutions or "houses": orphans, the incapacitated, and others without familial or alternative supports would be placed in *abiding houses*; the able-bodied poor would be sent to *workhouses* to inculcate the habits of industry and offset the costs of their keep; and those who refused to work would be consigned to *houses of correction* and, if still unaccommodating, sent to prison for longer terms of more brutal treatment. The argument advanced at the time was that, through rehabilitation, reform, and discipline, these institutions would greatly improve the moral character of the poor. Their "character" was underscored as the central cause of their poverty – not the land enclosures, famines, shortages of work, or uncertainty and inadequacy of their wages – a belief that remains popular today. But in practice, the state was not prepared to finance separately administered facilities for different divisions of the poor. Rather, children, the elderly, the infirm, the unemployed, and criminals were often tightly crammed together in notorious *poorhouses*, where hard labor was mandatory for anyone who was not too sick or too feeble to work.

By 1662, the British state was already extricating itself from its strictly circumscribed and conditional commitment to assisting the poor. Its Law of Settlement and Removal allowed local authorities to evict poor vagrant families and individuals who had become dependent on public support and force them to return to the town or parish where they were originally settled. The state's most severe treatment was reserved for "sturdy" vagrants; they might be whipped, branded, placed in pillories, stoned, have appendages cut off, or even executed. Similar poor law ordinances and practices, based upon the notion that the poor were lazy and that social assistance undermined the work ethic, were instituted across Europe, but they could be somewhat less repressive in some nations (Checkland & Checkland, 1974; Kusmer, 2002).[31]

By the early nineteenth century, residual charitable notions of public responsibility for the poor were largely displaced by a greater emphasis upon personal accountability, initiating the second and considerably more punitive social policy phase in Britain. Poor laws and other social supports were charged with promoting indolence, improvidence, intemperance, and immorality – undermining the habits of industry and interfering with labor markets. This prompted a series of policy amendments, culminating in a radical overhaul of the Elizabethan Poor Law, which had been in place for over 230 years. If the old Poor Law mirrored the medieval notion of noblesse oblige, instructing churches to take care of their poor parishioners, the new Poor Law clearly reflected the doctrine of capitalist accumulation (Furniss & Tilton, 1979 p. 97; Rimlinger, 1966, 1971). Introduced in 1834, it was explicitly designed to curb idleness, foster and enforce a strong work ethic, and diminish the costs of caring for the poor – goals expressly espoused by neoliberal governments today. Public expenditures for the poor were reduced, all forms of outdoor relief were terminated, and social control was emphasized. The main avenue for poor families to receive financial support became laboring in penal workhouses. Moreover, according to the "principle of less eligibility," the conditions of work and the level of assistance provided in the workhouses had to be significantly inferior to that available in the labor market in order to ensure that it was disadvantageous to avoid employment – another familiar policy trait today. The new Poor Law also exhibited a strong gender bias: it "took for granted the universality of the stable two-parent family, primarily dependent upon the father's wage, and the primacy of the family as a source of welfare" (Thane, 1978, p. 30). Women were often deemed ineligible for social support because their reliance upon a father or husband was assumed. Abandoned wives and mothers might also be denied social support if they were considered responsible for their plight.

The horrific conditions endured by the poor in the new poor-law institutions could be even bleaker than those depicted in the literary works and journalism of writers such as Charles Dickens and Victor Hugo. Family members were separated, and women were often put on starvation diets to discourage childbirth. House supervisors routinely pocketed the earnings of children as young as six years of age sent out to work as chimney sweeps or sold into employment to work sixteen-hour days in factories, mills, and mines where they were routinely beaten and often died of malnutrition. Grocers, merchants, and tavern keepers could be employed as "overseers" and suppliers, allowing them to profit by overcharging for the goods that they sold to the poor. Sidney and Beatrice Webb, members of the influential Fabian Society – a political organization that sought to gradually reform capitalism through the piecemeal installment of social policies – aptly described the web of poor relief measures in Britain during this period as a system of relief within a larger framework of repression (Webb & Webb, 1927). Few people would freely "choose" to live in these poorhouses – where they were denied basic amenities, civil liberties, and human dignity – if they had any alternative (Katz, 1986; Trattner, 1999). The large destitute population – comprising laborers thrown out of work during periods of economic contraction and other vulnerable groups, such as single parents, families with young children, and the elderly – desperately needed greater support, not repressive disciplinary laws. But the idea that poverty reflected the moral shortcomings of the poor had gained a firm hold, an issue more fully explored in the next chapter.

Poor Relief in Canada and the United States during the Colonial Period

The situation of the poor was equally grim in Britain's North American colonies. According to abiding myths and popular folklore, life in the "New World" provided boundless opportunity for all – land aplenty and employment for anyone willing to work. But these accounts do not fit the stark reality. Seeking refuge from deprivation and economic uncertainty in their homelands, large numbers of emigrants to North America were far from affluent, often exhausting all their life savings just to gain passage there, and "only a tiny fraction brought with them a competence with which to begin life anew" (McNaught, 1988, p. 78). Moreover, seasonal employment, long-term unemployment, illness, injury, the early death of family breadwinners, low wages and a consequent inability to save money for prolonged periods of hardship, and old age were some of the conditions ensuring that poverty was a momentous and sustained problem in the colonies. Living conditions were particularly arduous for women, whose wages were especially low, when they could find work. Parents were legally and financially responsible for their children, and when they grew up, children were held responsible for their parents and their grandparents. Social policy in the colonies largely reflected the presumptions, precedents, practices, and legislation in Britain (Finkel, 2006; Guest, 1997).[32]

The first colonial poor law in "British North America" was introduced in Rhode Island in 1647 patterned on the Elizabethan Poor Law. It allowed town councils to remove children from poor parents and force them to live with and work for other families – a practice that was soon targeted at Black children (Loiacono, 2013). Following the American Revolution, similar legislation was enacted in New Brunswick and Nova Scotia, while Upper Canada (Ontario) favored a greater reliance upon family support, private charities, and local jails, which were proliferating in this period. The poor in these regions might also have their care contracted out or publicly auctioned, or they might be placed in private homes at public expense, where they often endured neglect and abuse, occasionally resulting in death (Katz, 1986; Reid, 1946; Trattner, 1999). The groups particularly vulnerable to poverty and mistreatment in the British colonies – including women, children, Black people, immigrants, and Indigenous peoples, all of the subpopulations that remain overrepresented among the poor in the three Anglo nations today – could receive harsher treatment and be entirely bereft of social supports. "Needless to say," US social historian Walter Trattner (1999) observed, "there was little social welfare for native Americans during the colonial period – or later on, for that matter"; Black people too were "excluded from the social welfare system" and denied basic rights (p. 23). Similar racist and sexist poverty laws and programs were in place across Canada (Shewell, 2004).

The idea that poverty was largely a reflection of personal weakness or moral defect, which had animated the overhaul of the Poor Law in the United Kingdom in 1834, gained a particularly strong hold in the United States because people viewed it as the Promised Land, with abundant resources and greater employment opportunities than in overpopulated England. But "[t]hey failed to recognize that even in America some people could not find jobs, that even in the best of times some branches of industry were depressed and opportunities were limited or below-standard wages prevailed, that seasonal and technological unemployment was inevitable, and that nothing could be done about these ills" (Trattner, 1999, p. 54). In Canada, poverty policy closely followed the spirit of that in the mother country, with the creation of poorhouses and workhouses in larger towns, but the state also provided subsidies to private charities (Finkel, 2006).

Many other nations had networks of poor laws and supports similar to those emplaced in Britain and its North American colonies, partly reflecting an ongoing cross-border interchange of policy ideas and initiatives (King & Stewart, 2007). The Nordic nations in particular shared a broadly similar policy approach to addressing poverty, in part reflecting several commonalities, including their relatively small populations, the dominance of Lutheranism, long-standing cultural and political bonds, and historical roots as part of the same kingdom. Although there was no common "master plan" to address poverty across these lands, there was less consensus that poverty was the fault of the individual than in the Anglo nations, and a greater appreciation of the role of rapid urbanization, industrialization, famines, and other exogenous shocks. Denmark was a forerunner in the early establishment of social rights, introducing a universal, tax-financed, and citizenship-based program for its elderly with its Act on Relief in Old Age in 1891 (Petersen & Petersen, 2007); Sweden introduced "the world's first truly universal pension scheme" in 1913 (Esping-Andersen, 1992, p. 41). Finland and Sweden combined humanitarian concerns and relatively generous supports with their distinct concern for social order and control (Kouri, 1997; Markkola, 2007; Trydegård, 2000; Wilson, 1979).[33] The Norwegian poor law system also took a somewhat different path from Britain's (Seip, 2007). The early development of bureaucracies in these nations also encouraged a more embracing and somewhat less brutal form of state paternalism.[34] These different social conditions and approaches may have opened channels for the development of a very different kind of welfare state than that in the Anglo nations (Bendixsen et al., 2018).

The Legacy of Poor Relief and the Poor Laws in the Anglo Nations

The poverty measures introduced in Britain and its colonies were characterized by (1) an uncompromising distinction between those poor people who were viewed as "truly" needy and deemed "worthy" of assistance, one the one hand, and the lazy, "unworthy," "professional beggars" who simply refused to labor, on the other; (2) an emphasis upon repression over restitution; (3) the provision of meager and stigmatizing benefits; and, most crucially, (4) a fixation on the alleged weaknesses, deficiencies, and failings of poor individuals. These measures' consequent and virtually total obscuring of the structural and institutional causes of poverty would have a lasting legacy, coloring the character of modern Anglo welfare states. Today's social and public assistance programs (requiring means tests, needs tests, or income tests), the work incentives and imperatives associated with modern unemployment insurance programs, and workfare measures in the Anglo nations loudly echo the poor laws and programs introduced during the welfare state's prehistory. So too do other beliefs and practices: the contemporary suspicion and castigation of the "able-bodied" unemployed, the exclusion and stigmatization of female beneficiaries (especially single mothers), and the widespread belief that social supports undermine the work ethic and morality. These features are not absent from the poverty policy approach in any modern capitalist welfare state, but they are much more prominent and definitive in the Anglo lands today, and especially in the United States, where claiming benefits has been more strongly bound to ideas of conditionality, punitive sanctions, and stigma. However, the treatment of the poor today – and its deep roots in these early policies of the Anglo nations – is often neglected or minified in current poverty research.

The Limitations of Welfare States

Poverty cannot be adequately addressed by residual, liberal welfare states with few and relatively stingy measures. An integrated network of supports is required, along with a much greater emphasis on prevention. However, even highly developed welfare states have problems and limitations that inhibit them from eliminating poverty. Universal, comprehensive, and "free" (at point of delivery) public healthcare, for example, can be very difficult to access for many poor people. Given their transience or isolation in distant and deprived urban and rural areas, many homeless people cannot easily get to a doctor or register with a medical practice. The accident and emergency departments and hospitals that admit and treat them routinely discharge them back into the same environments responsible for their poor health. Universal healthcare systems can also become outmoded over time (see Box 4.1). These problems indicate that welfare states need to be habitually updated, improved, extended, and reinforced – not cut back (Anderson et al., 2006; Lester, 2001; Masson & Lester, 2003; Riley et al., 2003).

Another major problem with relying solely upon welfare states – even comprehensive, institutional welfare states like those in the Nordic nations – is that they cannot address many of the problems that emerge with the ongoing development of capitalism. Increasing the level of "human capital" in society through education and training has long been viewed as *the* panacea for poverty and unemployment. But it may be unrealistic to expect everyone in society to obtain postsecondary education, and, even if they could, the value of their degrees would soon decline, as that of high school diplomas has done. It is also unrealistic to assume that postindustrial economies will create only jobs that require high levels of training and pay well. Laborsaving technological changes and the outsourcing of work have resulted in the loss of a multitude of better-paid white-collar and blue-collar jobs, depressing or flatlining wages. At the same time, the number of poorly paid and insecure personal-service-sector jobs – which, by definition, cannot be exported or automated – has continued to expand. Promoting the attainment of higher education can increase the "quality" of workers but not the quantity of jobs, and recent research suggests that the demand for skilled, educated labor has been declining in the United States (Beaudry et al., 2013; Marsh, 2011).

Countless studies have confirmed that economic inequality has become much more extreme over the past few decades with the income and wealth levels of those at the very top exploding into the stratosphere. This development is especially evident in the Anglo nations, where tax and transfer systems have become much less progressive and high-ranking corporate executives can more easily set their own levels of remuneration without answering to anyone. While the incomes

BOX 4.1 THE LIMITS OF HEALTHCARE: HOMELESSNESS IN CANADA

Despite the existence of a universal, public healthcare system in Canada, a study of homelessness in Toronto indicated that, compared with the general population, homeless people were twice as likely to have diabetes, 3.5 times as likely to have asthma, 4 times as likely to have cancer, 5 times as likely to have heart disease, 20 times as likely to have epilepsy, and 29 times as likely to have hepatitis C (Street Health, 2007). A central problem is that universal healthcare systems, like many other social policy measures and programs, are still largely reactive and remedial rather than preventive.

Over the past few decades, increased emphasis has been placed upon more "proactive" healthcare measures and routines, which can be divided into two categories: (1) educational initiatives promoting health and (2) better health services and access to them. In the first category are policies encouraging healthier diets, daily exercise, the use of bicycle helmets, seat belts, and sunscreen; initiatives providing education on preventable injuries; and programs discouraging smoking, substance abuse, and other unhealthy "lifestyle choices." In the second are the promotion and provision of examinations, immunizations, and screening for a wide range of health problems and diseases – a biomedical strategy largely centered on "germs and genes." Yet however valuable these measures, they largely address factors that account for a relatively small proportion of illness and health issues in poor and low-income families. They also largely fail to alter, or even acknowledge, the broader structural sources of poverty, such as the severe deprivations of unhealthy and insecure living conditions, unemployment, poor working conditions, stresses and strains, unsafe neighborhoods, and social exclusion that are endured by the poor in wealthy capitalist nations. These neglected aspects of health are far more important than behavioral risk and biomedical factors in explaining the notably higher rates of health problems, diseases, and mortality rates among the poor, and their significantly lower rates of life expectancy. Moreover, the unhealthy "choices, habits, and lifestyles" of the poor – eating less nutritional foods, exercising less, and smoking heavily, for example – are closely associated with low income, unemployment, and stress.

The focus on behavioral and lifestyle "choices" made by the poor also does not consider who promotes and gains from these "choices." Relatively little attention is focused on the production, marketing, and distribution of highly processed, high-fat, and unhealthy fast foods; the encouragement of smoking and alcohol consumption; the growth of mind-numbing, stress-ful, competitive, insecure, and alienating minimum-wage jobs; the myriad new chemicals released into our environments every year; and our encouraged reliance upon automobiles rather than walking, cycling, public transport, and other healthier and more environmentally friendly measures. Social programs need to be more directly focused upon primary prevention; they need to go much further "upstream" than their current emphasis on risky behaviors, genetic predispositions, and remedial healthcare in order to eradicate and avert poverty by addressing the socio-economic conditions that foster and sustain it (Chernomas & Hudson, 2013; CSDH, 2008; Raphael, 2012).

of the extremely wealthy have increased tenfold, the income levels of everyone outside this group have been stagnating or declining, despite the fact that the current generation of workers is more highly educated than all previous generations.[35] All welfare states have limited ability to redistribute income and wealth; none of them has been able to elim-inate poverty or fully address its root causes. But, compared to their liberal counterparts, institutional welfare states (especially the social democratic variant) have been far more successful at reducing poverty and inequality, fostering better living conditions, and protecting people from what economic historian Karl Polanyi (1944/2001) aptly refers to as the "perils inherent in a self-regulating market system" (p. 80). The next two chapters evaluate the two dominant theoretical accounts of poverty in light of the data and discussion presented in the previous chapters. The individual-centered tradition, focusing on the alleged deficiencies of poor people themselves that animated and advanced the development of poor relief during the prehistory of the welfare state, is examined in Chapter 5. Societal explanations, focusing on the development of capitalism and the balance of power, are explored in Chapter 6.

NOTES

1 This chapter provides an overview of the welfare state and contrasts some key aspects of its character from a comparative perspective, with a particular focus on Canada, the UK, and the US. For more detailed historical and contemporary accounts of welfare states in the Anglo nations, many of which also offer a comparative perspective, see Barr (2020), Boyer (2019), Finkel (2006, 2019), Garfinkel et al. (2010), Garland (2016), Ginsburg (1992), Gould (1993), Olsen (2002), Pierson (2006), Trattner (1999), and Van Kersbergen and Vis (2014). Other invaluable sources that cover a range of social policy issues include *The Oxford Handbook of the Welfare State* (Castles et al., 2010) and *The Routledge Handbook of the Welfare State* (Greve, 2019).

2 John J. Heagerty, director of public health services in the federal Department of Pensions and National Health, chaired an interdepartmental advisory committee on health insurance that released its report in 1943. The Subcommittee on Housing and Community Planning, chaired by Queen's University economist C.A. Curtis, issued its report the following year.

3 Asa Briggs (1961, p. 228) provided an early classic definition of the welfare state as an effort to "modify the play of market forces" by guaranteeing individuals and families a minimum income, addressing social contingencies such as sickness and old age, and providing a range of social services. The *Merriam-Webster Dictionary* defines the welfare state as "a social system based on the assumption by a political state of primary responsibility for the individual and social welfare of its citizens"; The *Encyclopaedia Britannica* similarly identifies it as a "concept of government in which the state or a well-established network of social institutions plays a key role in the protection and promotion of the economic and social well-being of citizens."

4 The "welfare regimes" approach, developed by Danish social policy researcher Gøsta Esping-Andersen (1990), is the most widely employed typology today. Following Richard Titmuss (1974), who also identified three distinct welfare state models (the residual, industrial achievement-performance, and institutional redistributive models), Esping-Andersen set out three "regimes" or "worlds" of welfare, highlighting some different dimensions, such as their ability to decommodify people and their impact on social inequality.

His approach has been critically assessed from several different perspectives (Abrahamson, 1999; Arts & Gelissen, 2002; Bambra, 2004, 2005; Ellison, 2006; Lewis, 1992; Olsen, 1994, 2002; Orloff, 1993; Powell & Barrientos, 2011). Yet, however valid and useful these critical insights have proven to be, Esping-Andersen's welfare regime model remains an invaluable social policy research tool in cross-national research.

5   Numerous typologies and models of welfare provision have been developed by welfare state researchers over the past few decades (e.g., Castles, 1993; Esping-Andersen, 1990; Furniss & Tilton, 1979; Korpi, 1983; Korpi & Palme, 1998; Mishra, 1977, 1990; Pierson, 2006; Titmuss, 1974; Wilensky, 1975; Wilensky & Lebeaux, 1965).

6   While beyond the focus of this study, variation also exists in the levels of poverty and inequality across subnational jurisdictions in federal nations such as Canada and the United States, and in their social policy approaches (e.g., Béland & Daignault, 2015; Fishback, 2020; Haddow, 2014; Haddow & Klassen, 2006). The Canadian province of Québec, for example, is a notable outlier that has often more closely resembled its successful European counterparts, with lower poverty and inequality rates and more supportive social supports than in the rest of Canada (e.g., Fortin, 2010; Haddow, 2015; van den Berg et al., 2017).

7   Other Anglo nations, such as Australia, New Zealand, and Ireland, are also commonly assigned to the liberal welfare world by most comparative social policy researchers. However, their designation as liberal is disputed (e.g., Castles, 1985, 1993).

8   However, within the United Kingdom, Scotland still provides tuition-free tertiary education. The province of Québec has subsidized childcare and often outperforms the rest of Canada in addressing poverty and inequality and in the provision of social supports (e.g., Fortin, 2010; Haddow, 2014, 2015; Torjman, 2010; van den Berg et al., 2017).

9   Although Canada and the United Kingdom are classified as liberal welfare regimes, the UK's National Health Service (NHS) and, to a lesser extent, the Canadian healthcare system have been more closely aligned with the social democratic welfare state approach in the healthcare policy domain. But the fit of these healthcare systems in the social democratic world has become somewhat less secure with policy drift and restructuring (Olsen, 1994, 2007; Powell & Miller, 2016).

10 *Conservative* welfare states – also referred to as *corporatist* welfare states – tend to reproduce ("conserve") existing forms of stratification and inequality. Founded upon contributory social insurance programs, they provide different entitlements, benefits, and privileges to different groups of people. They do not have the same commitment to greater equality through redistribution that characterizes *social democratic* welfare states. However, because their expenditure levels are relatively high, and they

include most people, they have lower rates of poverty than *liberal* welfare states.

11 Of course, as in the other welfare worlds, there can be considerable variation across the nations within the social democratic model (Kvist et al., 2012). Welfare states change over time. Indeed, as noted in the previous chapter, poverty rates have been rising in Sweden over the past two decades, which is partly related to the restructuring of its welfare state (Olsen, 2013).

12 In Sweden, the emphasis is on minimizing the risk of defaults on housing loans rather than on helping families evade eviction *after* they have defaulted (Haber, 2015).

13 They also help to explain the higher rates of female participation in parliament in Sweden (43 percent), Finland (41 percent), Norway (41 percent), and Denmark (37 percent) than in Canada (27 percent), the United Kingdom (32 percent), and the United States (24 percent) in 2019 (Inter-Parliamentary Union, 2019). Women have long formed a "critical mass" in the parliaments and governments in the Nordic lands, allowing them to promote further progressive change and gender equality.

14 Introduced in 1945 to support larger families, the Family Allowance was "near-universal," providing benefits to families for every child *after* the first one.

15 Eligibility and benefit levels in *private* plans are more strictly related to an individual worker's record of contributions and likelihood of making a claim. *Public* social insurance is more "collective"; risks are pooled across the entire working population; eligibility is not strictly related to the chances of an individual becoming a beneficiary, so the payment of premiums is more like a form of taxation; benefit levels are typically based upon socioeconomic adequacy, rather than just actuarial considerations; and benefit levels can be higher because states make contributions as well. Moreover, unlike private insurance, which is voluntary and contractual, social insurance is typically statutory, based upon rights (Armitage, 2003; Lightman, 2003).

16 Social insurance programs, to a limited extent, may also redistribute income "vertically," from those with higher incomes to those with lower incomes, because there is typically a ceiling or limit on the level of income they provide; people with incomes that greatly exceed the ceiling receive less as a percentage of their total income. But because benefit levels are income related, social insurance programs generally tend to maintain class and income differences.

17 In 1990, the Canadian government stopped contributing to its unemployment insurance program (now called employment insurance or EI) and, as in many other nations, it tightened benefit rules making it harder to access support.

18 *Needs-tested* benefits determine eligibility on the basis of a person's needs (and those of their dependents), typically involving considerable investigation into their lives. *Means-tested* benefits focus on people's resources, such as income and fixed assets, to assess whether they qualify for a benefit. Access to *income-tested* benefits is based on income alone. Eligibility is based upon having an income below a certain threshold; as the recipient's income rises, the benefit is cut back and ends entirely when that individual's income reaches a certain designated amount – the "cutoff point" (Battle & Torjman, 2001). The specific terms of access of these forms of benefit eligibility may vary by nation or by regions within a nation.

19 Eligibility for means-tested benefits, such as the Supplemental Security Income program (SSI) in the United States is based upon an assessment of an applicant's resources (income and assets). Needs-tested programs, such as student aid and public housing in Canada, also assess resources but place greater emphasis upon an applicant's circumstances, requirements, and ability to meet their needs and are therefore more intrusive. However, some targeted benefits for low-income and poor households, such as the Earned Income Tax Credit (EITC) in the United States and the Guaranteed Income Supplement (GIS) for elderly poor in Canada, use "income tests" to determine eligibility for support. Income tests are less intrusive because they rely upon tax returns to assess need and avoid the surveillance, humiliation, and stigma so often associated with most means-tested social assistance programs (Armitage, 2003; Myles, 1998; Olsen, 2002).

20 The OECD poverty gap – a measure of the depth of poverty – indicates how far, on average (using the mean), poor people are below the poverty line. In the United States, the poverty gap is 39.8 percent; so, on average, the incomes of the poor are close to 40 percent below the poverty line income. In Finland and Sweden, the poverty gap is 22.5 percent.

21 In 2020, Luxembourg, one of Europe's smallest nations, became the first country to provide free public transportation to allow people to get around more easily, alleviate the heavy traffic on its roads, and reduce pollution. Some subnational-level regions, cities, or municipal districts in other countries have introduced or experimented with "zero-fare" public transport routes for some forms of transit, but Luxembourg is the first country to do so for its trains, trams, and buses on a national scale.

22 Although not part of the welfare state as traditionally defined, other essential public services furnished by the state include libraries, parks, public broadcasting, telecommunications, the provision of water and energy, police and fire protection services, and refuse collection. These measures, like public primary and secondary education, are no less "socialist" than the public healthcare, pharmacare, childcare, and other programs decried by neoliberal think tanks and organizations.

23 In Scotland, Scottish students do not pay for their first undergraduate degree but tuition is charged for postgraduate studies, while UK

students from outside of Scotland pay undergraduate tuition in Scotland.

24 Some studies suggest that the similarities across the Nordic nations and the distinction in social provision between social democratic and conservative welfare regimes are not as notable as they used to be – at least in the areas of childcare and eldercare (e.g., Rauch, 2007).

25 "Women-friendly" family policy measures are often said to "de-familialize" social programs. However, while some social programs, such as high quality universal childcare, shift some caring responsibilities into the public sphere, others, such as generous parental leave programs could encourage more care (and equality) *within* the family and home setting (Saxonberg, 2013).

26 Laws specifying the terms of the income programs and social services that are provided are not technically part of the "third pillar" because they ultimately promote greater well-being via the other pillars. The Canadian Health Act (1984), for example, sets out the conditions and criteria that Canada's thirteen provincial and territorial healthcare systems must comply with in order to receive federal funding: they must be comprehensive, universal, accessible, publicly provided, and portable (available to Canadians as they move among the provinces and territories of the nation).

27 Third pillar legislation also includes family violence laws; child safety laws, child welfare acts, and corporal punishment bans; laws protecting the elderly from abuse and neglect; legislation supporting people with disabilities; immigration and refugee protection acts; and a multitude of other measures that can be more indirectly related to poverty.

28 Church relief, provided through almshouses and other means, often emphasized the giver over the recipient. As Hugh Heclo (1974, p. 48) notes, "the word *alms* was itself derived from the Greek word for pity, and charity was a moral imperative believed to play a vital part in building up a credit of heavenly rewards and dispensations."

29 However, England had introduced a range of laws to control workers and beggars much earlier, including the Ordinance of Labourers (1349), the Statute of Labourers (1351), the Statute of Cambridge (1388), and the Vagabond and Beggars Act (1495), which made work compulsory (and quitting illegal), fixed or reduced wage levels, tightly restricted migration, and prohibited the provision of relief to "sturdy beggars" deemed fit to work. These laws also imposed fines, imprisonment, and severe corporal punishment for those who did not comply. Comparable legislation was enacted across much of Europe with similar intent and impact. "Thus with a stroke of the pen states attempted to crush the hopes of the poor for better living conditions" (Lis & Soly, 1979, p. 50; see also de Schweinitz, 1943; Woloch, 1994).

30 The Poor Relief Act was a modified version of the comprehensive Poor Law of 1598, which had been redrafted in an attempt to integrate earlier legislation pertaining to poverty.

31 In Sweden, for example, parishes were divided into smaller districts that were required to take turns caring for the poor, and they would sometimes attempt to finance the emigration of poor families to North America or elsewhere in Europe. There was also greater emphasis on the idea of a statutory right to receive relief and to appeal decisions denying support to poor families, although these laws were continually under attack as liberalism took hold (Forsberg, 1986; Koblik, 1975; Kouri, 1997; Markkola, 2007; Samuelsson, 1975; Scott, 1988; Skoglund, 1992).

32 In New France (called subsequently Lower Canada and then Québec), Acadia (the Maritime provinces), and other areas along the Atlantic coast colonized by France, charities, missions, almshouses, refuges, and hospitals (such as the hôtels-dieu) were established and administered by religious orders to tend to the destitute and the sick. The Catholic Church continued to play a more central role in poor relief than the government did until France surrendered its colonial possessions in North America to the British in 1763 through the Treaty of Paris at the end of the Seven Years' War and the arrival of the United Empire Loyalists from the United States in 1783 after the American Revolution (Finkel, 2006; Guest, 1997).

33 The centralized state institutions of nations such as Finland and Sweden allowed them to more closely approximate the ideal of separate houses for the elderly, orphanages for poor children, and hospitals for the ill, even if the latter sometimes served as almshouses and nursing homes as well. In Catholic nations, separate but non-secular accommodations were provided for the poor (Forsberg, 1986; Kahl, 2005; Kouri, 1997; Scott, 1988).

34 In Sweden, where the king had formed alliances with the land-owning peasantry to limit the power of the nobility, centralized public support for the poor was established earlier than in other Lutheran nations (Olsen, 2002).

35 Numerous studies have found this pattern, especially across the Anglo nations (e.g., Broadbent Institute, 2014; Davies et al., 2008; Dorling, 2014, 2015; Piketty, 2014; Saez & Veall, 2007; Sayer, 2015; Veall, 2012; Wolff, 2012; Yalnizyan, 2010).

FURTHER READINGS

The Character and Impact of Welfare States

Brady, D. (2005). The welfare state and poverty in rich western democracies, 1967–1997. *Social Forces, 83*(4), 1329–1364.

Castles, F.G., Leibfried, S., Lewis, J., Obinger, H., & Pierson, C. (Eds.). (2010). *The Oxford handbook of the welfare state.* Oxford University Press.

Esping-Andersen, G. (1990). *The three worlds of welfare capitalism.* Princeton University Press.

Esping-Andersen, G. (2015). Welfare regimes and social stratification. *Journal of European Social Policy, 25*(1), 124–134.

Greve, B. (Ed.). (2019). *Routledge handbook of the welfare state* (2nd ed.). Routledge.

Kenworthy, L. (2020). *Social democratic capitalism.* Oxford University Press.

Lewis, J. (1992). Gender and the development of welfare regimes. *Journal of European Social Policy, 2*(3), 159–173.

Olsen, G.M. (2002). *The politics of the welfare state: Canada, Sweden, and the United States.* Oxford University Press.

Olsen, G.M. (2019). Protective legislation: The "third pillar" of the welfare state. *Social Policy and Administration, 53*(3), 478–492.

Orloff, A.S. (1993). Gender and the social rights of citizenship: The comparative analysis of state policies and gender relations. *American Sociological Review, 58*(3), 303–328.

Quadagno, J. (1994). *The color of welfare: How racism undermined the war on poverty.* Oxford University Press.

Scruggs, L., & Allan, J.P. (2006). The material consequences of welfare states: Benefit generosity and absolute poverty in 16 OECD countries. *Comparative Political Studies, 39*(7), 880–904.

van den Berg, A., Plante, C., Raïq, H., Proulx, C., & Faustmann, S. (2017). *Combating poverty: Quebec's pursuit of a distinctive welfare state.* University of Toronto Press.

THE HISTORICAL DEVELOPMENT OF WELFARE STATES

Alston, L.J., & Ferrie, J.P. (1999). *Southern paternalism and the American welfare state.* Cambridge University Press.

Finkel, A. (2006). *Social policy and practice in Canada: A history.* Wilfrid Laurier University Press.

Finkel, A. (2019). *Compassion: A global history of social policy.* Red Globe Press.

Fraser, D. (2009). *The evolution of the British welfare state* (4th ed.). Palgrave Macmillan.

Guest, D. (1997). *The emergence of social security in Canada.* UBC Press.

Katz, M.B. (1986). *In the shadow of the poorhouse: A social history of welfare in America.* Basic Books.

Thane, P. (1978). Women and the poor law in Victorian and Edwardian England. *History Workshop: A Journal of Socialist Historians, 6*(Autumn), 9–51.

Thane, P. (1996). *Foundations of the welfare state.* Routledge.

Trattner, W.I. (1999). *From poor law to welfare state: A history of social welfare in America* (3rd ed.). The Free Press.

Wagner, D. (2005). *The poorhouse: America's forgotten institution.* Rowman and Littlefield.

PART THREE

Explaining Poverty:
Theoretical Approaches

Individual-Centered Explanations for Poverty: Biogenetic and "Culture of Poverty" Accounts

> Of all the preposterous assumptions of humanity over humanity, nothing exceeds most of the criticisms made on the habits of the poor by the well-housed, well-warmed, and well-fed.
>
> – *Herman Melville (1854/1997)*

The previous chapters have illustrated that the gravity of poverty in Canada, the United Kingdom, and the United States cannot be seriously contested. But many residents of these nations who readily acknowledge its magnitude, intensity, and consequences do not necessarily view poverty as an urgent problem or a reflection of any form of injustice. From their perspective, the primary causes of poverty can be largely attributed to the poor themselves; consequently, there is no need for alarm or for states to rush in to support them. This view of poverty, most prominent in the Anglo nations – and especially in the United States, where it is firmly entrenched – highlights the attributes of *individuals*. It asserts that poverty is a reflection of poor people's (1) inherent biological flaws, such as low cognitive ability, and/or (2) acquired "cultural" deficiencies, such as deviant sociocultural values, norms, and practices.[1] Firmly anchored in nineteenth-century thought and social policy, these ideas have endured and have often been invoked in some manifestation to explain the overrepresentation of women, Black people, Indigenous people, and immigrants living in poverty in Anglo nations and, in turn, to legitimate the denial or restriction of their access

Table 5.1. Theories of Poverty

Site of Explanation	Focus of Explanation
Individual	Biological
	Cultural: The Culture or Subculture of Poverty
Societal	Character of Capitalist System
	Sociopolitical or Balance of Power

to social programs. It is the first of two central theoretical traditions or schools of thought, each highlighting different sites and levels of analysis in order to explain the origins and persistence of poverty. The second school (addressed in the next chapter) focuses on a range of *societal* conditions and issues, including the "balance of power"; the character of the social institutions, policies, and legislation that it fosters; and the capitalist system itself. Given their starkly different accounts of how poverty is generated and sustained, the proponents of each of these traditions (and of the variants within them) also propose very different means to address poverty (Table 5.1).[2]

INDIVIDUALIST EXPLANATIONS FOR POVERTY: BIOLOGY AND THE "CULTURE OF POVERTY"

Although they have experienced intermittent periods of reproach, explanations locating the causes of poverty in the shortfalls of individuals are tenacious. They are seductive and durably popular for several reasons: they legitimate wide and burgeoning disparities in income and wealth; they can be wielded to justify the retrenchment of public supports for poor and low-income families, ensuring their dependence upon, and vulnerability to, market forces; they are routinely promoted by many political parties, organizations, think tanks, and the media; and they have an entrenched history. These narratives are associated with principles of "classical liberalism," such as the sanctity of private property, competition, free markets, equal opportunity, and meritocracy. However, they often exhibit strong conservative biases and tendencies too, including the embrace of steep socioeconomic hierarchies as "natural," just, and resistant to modification.[3]

Despite their differing emphases, the "biological" and "cultural" variants of this tradition are strikingly similar in key respects: both maintain that it is deficits among the poor themselves that render them incapable of competing successfully in otherwise fair education systems and labor markets, and both approaches have typically vehemently opposed most forms of state intervention. These affinities reflect their common roots in the work of Thomas Malthus, Herbert Spencer, and William Graham Sumner who were writing during a period of rapidly expanding industrial capitalism, which needed an industrial labor force with no alternative means of supporting itself. These scholars were among the first to forthrightly blame the poor for their plight and champion the idea that social measures to help them are both ineffective and highly detrimental to social progress, and they helped to legitimize a new laissez-faire regime that compelled workers to accept working conditions and wages dictated by capital – a strategy reprised in the service of neoliberal austerity today. While the popularity of these accounts of poverty has oscillated, they routinely recur, in softer or harsher forms, brandishing new propositions and neologisms (e.g., "poverty traps," "cognitive underclass," "welfare dependency," "behavioral pathologies," "culture of entitlement," and "troubled families") that personalize poverty and stigmatize poor people, profoundly shaping the character and orientation of social policy in Anglo nations (Macnicol, 2017; Streib et al., 2016).

The Historical Roots of Individualistic Accounts of Poverty

In the late eighteenth century, when British economist and clergyman Thomas Malthus (1798/2008) was writing his influential treatise, *An Essay on the Principle of Population,* industrialization was well underway in England, and poverty was acute and pervasive. Amid this bleak and tumultuous socioeconomic context, he set out to refute arguments advanced by Enlightenment philosophers and political writers, such as William Godwin, the Marquis de Condorcet, and Jean-Jacques Rousseau, that conveyed a considerably more optimistic belief in progress and the perfectibility of human society. Malthus's central claim was that there was a natural tendency for population growth to increase faster than the resources that people needed to live. Population growth, he maintained, could only be contained within resource limits by "positive checks" that increased the death rate, such as malnutrition, sickness, disease, famines, epidemics, and war, and by voluntary measures that lowered the birth rate, which he referred to as "preventive checks."[4]

Malthus viewed population growth as a natural reflection of innate biological drives, but he maintained that the desperately poor masses were largely responsible for their grim predicament. The moral superiority of the upper classes – and their strong desire to avoid dissipating their property among numerous heirs – both allowed and encouraged them to restrict the size of their families. The poor, however, lacked such restraint, irresponsibly reproducing beyond their means to sustain themselves and, consequently, were "the cause of their own poverty" (Malthus, 1803/1890, p. 458). His "population principle" foreclosed hope for a more equitable society and a brighter future for the masses. Efforts to address poverty by increasing the output of the land or redistributing income through wage increases would be self-defeating, invariably leading to reproductive profligacy and further population growth. The greater numbers of the poor, in turn, would lower the demand for labor, decreasing wage levels, and increase the demand for food and other goods, inflating their prices and ultimately fostering greater privation, misery, and starvation.[5] Social assistance and protection would also promote fecundity and greater destitution. The Poor Law was not a solution to the problem of poverty but central to its perpetuation. Malthus viewed "dependent poverty" as "disgraceful" and favored the use of workhouses for those experiencing extreme economic distress.

Malthus was not the first or the most famous writer to resolutely condemn the provision of statutory aid to the poor. In a series of articles written between 1753 and 1789, Benjamin Franklin – celebrated inventor and one of the Founding Fathers of the United States – also argued vociferously that public and charitable support in England and the United States were destroying industry and independence among the poor (Williams, 1944). But Malthus's ideas were especially impactful. They profoundly influenced the Royal Commission's recommendation to replace the Old English Poor Law with more punitive legislation in 1834 and markedly shaped public views on poverty and social support in the Anglo world. Indeed, as one study of his influence affirms, Malthus "became the beacon against which all proposals for solving the growing problem of poverty in early industrial society had to be measured" and the many influential adherents to his principles in Whig circles and among the gentry and aristocracy "ensured the legislative triumph of his ideas" (Huzel, 2006, pp. 1–2).[6]

Malthus's theory hinged on his firm, if largely unsubstantiated, belief in an abiding iron law of population growth.[7] His account of poverty as solely the result of population pressure on the food supply concealed its systemic roots. As the influential German social theorist and revolutionary Karl Marx trenchantly observed, the existence of a "surplus" population living in poverty is dependent upon the availability of jobs; "the quantity of grain available is completely irrelevant to the worker if he has no *employment*" (Marx, 1845–1846/1973, p. 607). Marx argued that capitalists and capitalism greatly benefit from the existence of a large pool of poor, dispossessed, unemployed or underemployed workers who are forced to compete with each other for jobs. Workers were poor because they were exploited in the labor market; the unemployed were poorer still because they were excluded from it. Malthus was reviled by Marx as "a shameless sycophant of the ruling classes" whose work supported their economic interests (Marx, 1863/1969, p. 120). But Malthusian theory provided a sturdy theoretical foundation for the "Social Darwinists," Herbert Spencer and William Graham Sumner, whose ideas purporting the profoundly detrimental impacts of social protections and support for the poor would take root, especially in the United Kingdom and the United States.

Like Malthus, British sociologist Herbert Spencer pointed to flaws among the poor to account for their impoverishment. However, while Malthus focused on quantity – the increasing numbers of the poor – Spencer was concerned with the quality or caliber of the population in society. Unlike Malthus, he maintained that social progress was the innate, default trend in society, and his central concern was that this progress not be impeded or sidetracked by state interference. Spencer believed that evolutionary societal development toward "higher stages" was natural, driven by a healthy competitive struggle for existence in which the poor, the weak, the sick, those with physical or mental impairments, and other less capable members of society were systematically rooted out. He believed that this "purifying process" reflected "the decrees of a large, far-seeing benevolence" (Spencer, 1851/1969, p. 323).[8] Social supports for those at the bottom would divert this development, not only halting the elimination of society's most reckless, incompetent members but enabling their multiplication, which he viewed as a great "curse to posterity" that would deter social progress (Spencer, 1873/1929, p. 314).

In the United States, sociologist and clergyman William Graham Sumner closely followed Spencer's lead, combining evolutionary thought with classical liberalism. He maintained that people were hierarchically stationed exactly where they should be in society, justly sorted into classes through the crucible of fair competition. The fervor of his belief in this natural justice, including his resistance to any form of political interference that would compromise the position of the elites or preserve society's most deficient members, exceeded that of Spencer, his mentor. Those at the bottom of society, he argued, "constantly neutralize and destroy the finest efforts of the wise and industrious, and are a dead-weight on the society in all its struggles to realize any better things" (Sumner, 1883/1974, p. 19). Social supports for the poor would only ensure the survival of society's weakest members – those who had failed to compete successfully. The people at the top of society were also "a product of natural selection"; it picks out "those who can meet the requirements of certain work to be done," and wealth, thereby, "aggregates under their hands" (Sumner, 1963, p. 157). A staunch advocate of the free market, Sumner argued that tampering with the natural order, and encouraging freeloading via social supports, was irresponsible and immoral.

Not surprisingly, the "Social Darwinist" perspective was ardently embraced by the wealthy, powerful elites of the period, including John D. Rockefeller and Andrew Carnegie.[9] After all, it legitimated the enormous fortunes they had amassed through their unscrupulous and exploitative practices, and those of other industrial and financial titans in the late nineteenth and early twentieth centuries, such as John Pierpont Morgan, Cornelius Vanderbilt, Leland Stanford, Jay Gould, James J. Hill, and other "robber barons" whose names remain familiar today.[10] Despite their vigorous public endorsement of unfettered free markets, competition, and minimal state intervention, they built their fortunes by creating monopolies or oligopolies – typically with the collaboration and malfeasance of federal, state, and local governments and courts – and they often promoted their interests by bribing state officials (Beatty, 2008; Josephson, 1962; Myers, 1936; Zinn, 2003). Rockefeller clandestinely negotiated preferential rates from the railroad companies that transported oil to put his competitors out of business and establish his industrial behemoth, Standard Oil. Carnegie achieved dominance in the steel industry by gaining control over the chain of production, buying up mines that produced the iron ore and coal required to make steel in his factories and mills as well as the railroad and shipping companies needed to transport it. The Carnegie Steel Company was later sold to financier John Pierpont Morgan, a transaction that made Carnegie the wealthiest person in the world. It also allowed Morgan to establish the world's largest corporation (United States Steel) by merging his new acquisition with two other steel giants.

The Social Darwinists championed free enterprise and considered the harsh living and working conditions of the poor, and the countless casualties they generated, part of the steady march of progress. They legitimated the stark income and wealth disparities and poverty generated in the market and through graft and political corruption during the "Gilded Age" in the United States (Beatty, 2008; Nace, 2003; Zinn, 2003).[11] They failed to consider the role of inheritance and the wide range of advantages and opportunities enjoyed by those with great wealth and power – or the myriad obstacles, disadvantages, and hardships overburdening poor and low-income families in society. They also provided little empirical evidence to support their contentions that the poor lacked the intelligence, talent, skills, motivation, and discipline necessary to succeed in society, or that those at the top possessed these traits.[12] But their ideas laid the foundation for subsequent "biogenetic" and "cultural" accounts of poverty, two widely embraced explanations often perpetuated in the mainstream media that continue to stigmatize victims of systemic poverty today.[13] Given their common pedigree, these two approaches are highly compatible and have been frequently combined to account for the existence of poverty and sustain the notion that social programs to help the poor are ineffectual and harmful to both their recipients and to society.[14]

POVERTY AS A REFLECTION OF BIOGENETIC DEFICIENCIES

While Spencer and Sumner simply asserted that poverty was necessarily a product of the biological makeup and weak moral character of poor people – pointing to their positions at the bottom of society as incontestable evidence of their inherent flaws and inferiorities – contemporary advocates of a refurbished "biogenetic" approach seek to demonstrate scientifically that poverty can be largely explained by genetically determined characteristics and traits, such as intelligence, which can be quantified and measured through the use of standardized tests. First developed by psychologist Alfred Binet in France and revised by Stanford University eugenicist and psychologist Lewis Terman in the United States, intelligence tests soon became central to the discipline of psychology. They also "became the newest 'objective' method of proving Black intellectual inferiority and justifying discrimination" (Kendi, 2016, p. 311).[15] Decades later, the prominent and highly influential educational psychologist Arthur Jensen (1969) promoted and reinforced the idea that intelligence was a highly heritable trait, and his contention that differences in intelligence across "races" could be genetic ignited the "Great IQ Debate" in the late 1960s and early 1970s. Echoing Spencer and Sumner, he further maintained that remedial educational measures and other programs designed to help the poor were bound to fail because they were targeted at people whose potential was strictly limited by their lower levels of largely immutable, inborn intelligence. Jensen's framework, arguments, and data were endorsed and further elaborated upon by several others, including two of the most well-known and influential exponents of this view, Richard Herrnstein and Charles Murray (1994; see also Herrnstein, 1971).[16]

In their popular and inflammatory study, *The Bell Curve: Intelligence and Class Structure in American Life*, Herrnstein and Murray (1994) focused on people's intelligence quotients (IQs) in the United States. Contemporary US society, they argued, is a meritocracy in which class background, inherited wealth, and social connections had become much less important than intelligence for gaining access to the best schools and top positions in society. According to Herrnstein and Murray, cognitive ability has become *the* decisive driving force in society, resulting in more "cognitively based" class divisions today. Occupying the top rungs in the socioeconomic hierarchy is a bright, cognitive elite; the poor and low-income families at the bottom of society constitute a "cognitive underclass" comprised of people with below-average intelligence. The moderately intelligent members of society, in turn, take their rightful place between these two poles, constituting the middle classes. "Putting it all together," they concluded, "success and failure in the American economy, and all that goes with it, are increasingly a matter of the genes that people inherit.... Social class remains the vehicle of social life, but intelligence now pulls the train" (Herrnstein & Murray, 1994, pp. 91, 25). Like the Social Darwinists, they explicitly argued that public social supports would only promote the proliferation of members of the "cognitive underclass." They further warned that this could greatly undermine the nation's competitive position in the world.

Although *The Bell Curve* received favorable coverage in the media when it was first published, it was subsequently censured on numerous fronts across several academic disciplines (e.g., Arrow et al., 2000; Devlin et al., 1997; Fischer et al., 1996; Fraser, 1995; Gould, 1994; Jacoby & Glauberman, 1995). Many critics pointed to problems with the conventional IQ tests that Herrnstein and Murray relied upon. Some of them noted that IQ scores were generated by heavily biased tests reflecting white middle- and upper-class Anglo-American values and culture. IQ tests do not simply measure a person's relative ability in a specific area of intelligence. They also measure levels of exposure to particular sociocultural settings, and they rarely acknowledge the strengths and abilities fostered and acquired in other sociocultural and class environments. Other critics went much further, questioning the general validity of *any* IQ test, and the credibility of a single score to represent a concept as complex as human intelligence. A person's IQ is a score derived from a battery of standardized tests. Although the tests may use different methods and measures, they assess a relatively narrow range of aptitudes, such as abstract reasoning, logic, comprehension, problem solving, memory, reading, vocabulary, and general knowledge. All of these cognitive abilities, assessed through various tests, are said to be closely correlated, reflecting a common underlying factor ("g") that succinctly summarizes a person's general intelligence.[17] However, the "g" reflects a very restricted concept of intelligence because the tests it is based upon address a circumscribed range of scholastic abilities most useful in classroom settings. Research suggests that intelligence is "contextual" and indicates that many people perform better "on the job" than they do on written or verbal tests (Lave, 1988). Moreover, as Andrew Hacker (1995) notes, IQ test results reflect skills that often have "little relation or relevance to most human endeavors" (p. 100).

Psychologists such as Robert Sternberg and Howard Gardner – supported by a large and steadily growing body of cognitive research – argue that intelligence is a considerably more complicated and multidimensional concept than most standardized IQ tests suggest. They point to many important dimensions of intelligence that are not typically assessed through standard intelligence tests. Sternberg (1985), for example, emphasizes analytical, creative/synthetic, and practical forms of intelligence and "giftedness." He also highlights people's varied abilities to adapt to and shape their social environments. Gardner (1983, 1999) also identifies nontraditional dimensions of intelligence, such as bodily kinesthetic, spatial, musical, interpersonal, and intrapersonal intelligence, that are not addressed by traditional IQ tests.

Biogenetic arguments invert cause and effect. They fail to consider seriously how social conditions associated with poverty, such as hunger, poor nutrition, inadequate housing, poor health, inferior schools, and myriad other deprivations and hardships, can influence "intelligence," ability, and academic performance, however these are defined. Herrnstein and Murray's discussion of "racial" differences in intelligence also ignores the legacy of a wide range of socioeconomic disadvantages. These include the oppressively heavy weight of centuries of slavery, Jim Crow practices, racism, segregation, and discrimination endured by Black people in the United States (Fischer et al., 1996; Kendi, 2016).

The conclusions reached by Herrnstein and Murray are further contradicted by myriad cross-temporal and cross-national studies of poverty, including the data presented earlier in this volume. Poverty rates can fluctuate over time with socioeconomic change, including booms and busts, levels of unemployment, and the availability and character of social supports. Moreover, research indicates that, apart from a relatively small core of the chronically poor, who are often very seriously disadvantaged on several fronts, the individuals and families living in poverty are not the same people over time. Longitudinal studies suggest that poverty is characterized by a great deal of fluidity, with individuals and families continually moving in and out of poverty (Hacker, 2008; Jäntti, 2009; Rank, 2005; Sandoval et al., 2009).[18] These observations and trends challenge the idea of a genetically inferior cognitive underclass stuck at the bottom.

Similarly, biogenetic arguments cannot explain the marked variation in poverty rates among the Anglo nations or, more starkly, between the Anglo and Nordic nations observed across myriad studies. Are people in the Nordic nations simply more intelligent than their

Anglo counterparts? If so, how do we explain the higher poverty rates seen in those nations in the late 1800s and early 1900s? How do we account for the dramatic decline of poverty in these nations and elsewhere (including in the United States) with rising unionization rates and the establishment of supportive welfare states in the post–WWII period? How can we explain the increasing poverty rates seen virtually everywhere in the current era of global integration and retrenchment? Biogenetic theories of the origins and persistence of poverty are unable to adequately account for cross-national variation or developments and trends over time and place. The rapidly growing body of research on extreme and rising concentrations of income, wealth, and power today – evident across the developed capitalist world, but with notable cross-national variation – further undermines the biogenetic defense of meritocratic hierarchy in contemporary capitalist societies (e.g., Dorling, 2014; Piketty, 2014; Sayer, 2015; Stiglitz, 2013).

Although Herrnstein and Murray's work has been widely and roundly critiqued over the past few decades, biogenetic arguments have proven decidedly resilient. They persistently emerge in new incarnations, often underscoring gender, racial, or ethnic differences and positing distinct genetically determined social behaviors (e.g., Lynn, 2015; Lynn & Becker, 2019; Wade, 2015). They are also invariably reflected in policy prescriptions stressing the futility of offering support to poor people and advocating the redirection of public financing to other people and groups that will make better use of it. Like the Social Darwinists, Charles Murray (1984, 2006, 2012) strenuously insists that social programs are counterproductive and a gross misuse of limited resources.[19] In his recent work – *Human Diversity: The Biology of Gender, Race, and Class* – Murray (2020) reaffirms his contentions about gender and race and defends his view that class is not a function of privilege; people's genes largely explain where they are stationed in socioeconomic hierarchies. Although it may be tempting to take comfort in the notion that these ideas were comprehensively and conclusively discredited long ago, debates about the validity of approaches linking IQ, race, and social position in society are continually generated in research, the media, and on policy blogs, websites, and podcasts (e.g., Ball, 2020; Holmes, 2018; Klein, 2018; Lynn, 2015; Lynn & Becker, 2019; Reich, 2018a, 2018b, 2019; Robinson, 2017; Shepherd, 2020; Sullivan, 2018; Turkheimer et al., 2017; Verbruggen, 2020; Wade, 2015).[20] In a period when mobs of white supremacists openly march on US streets across the nation and prominent leaders issue statements suggesting that some immigrant groups are inferior undesirables, it cannot be assumed that biogenetic views are irrelevant curiosities now; few anticipated they would resurface and gain traction again after the Holocaust. But, however tenacious and insidious, these accounts of poverty do not typically overtly blame poor people for their alleged inherited genetic deficits; after all, from this perspective, their trajectory was largely predetermined at birth. "Culture of poverty" accounts, in contrast, more readily hold poor people directly accountable for their poverty, fomenting vitriolic attacks on public programs created to support them.

THE "CULTURE OF POVERTY"

The contention that the poor possess deviant and deficient values and morals and an inadequate work ethic was central to the theories of Malthus and the Social Darwinists, but the idea that the poor had a distinct identifiable "culture" was developed by the American social anthropologist Oscar Lewis. He originally focused on poverty in Mexico and Puerto Rico, later suggesting that his observations about the poor there might be applied in the United States (Lewis, 1959, 1966a, 1966b, 1968).[21] His "culture of poverty" thesis suggested that poor people had a unique subculture that differed markedly from mainstream culture at three interconnected levels – individual, family, and community. At the *individual level*, the poor were fatalistic and resigned to their circumstances because of their strong feelings of marginality; apathetic rather than goal directed; present-time oriented, with little ability to defer gratification or plan for the future; unable to recognize or seize opportunities when they arose; unable to control their impulses; and disposed toward authoritarianism. At the *family level* the poor rejected long-term commitments and commonly engaged in free unions or consensual marriages; had a relatively high incidence of mother- or female-headed families due to men's abandonment of their wives and children; and typically experienced shorter periods of childhood. At the *community level* there was an almost complete absence of any stable organization or participation in major societal institutions, apart from the criminal justice and social welfare systems. Together, Lewis maintained, these characteristics constituted a distinct "way of life" – a "design for living" that sustained poverty and perpetuated it over time as new generations were socialized into this subculture.

For Lewis, the "culture of poverty" was deeply rooted in institutional and structural contexts that cultivated greatly reduced life chances, social exclusion, and social stigma. Poverty originated in these conditions and was perpetuated by them. The poor, he argued, pragmatically developed an alternative problem-solving style that allowed them to exploit their dire situation. Apathy, resignation, low aspirations, and "living for the moment" with little thought of the future were deliberate responses to the blocked opportunities, frustration, disappointment, and hopelessness of daily life. This "subculture" was a rational reaction to circumstances that allowed the poor to survive in an extremely hostile environment. It reflected their creative abilities to endure and accommodate to a situation in which conformity to dominant values and behaviors was not possible. But it would disappear when it was no longer required, when the societal root causes of poverty were eliminated (Lewis, 1966a, 1968).[22]

Lewis's culture of poverty theory was soon appropriated and rerouted by neoliberals and neoconservatives, most notably by the political right in the United States. Proponents of this new orientation argued that poverty *originated* in the poor's subculture. For them, the subculture became the central *cause* of poverty, rather than an adaptive *response* to its harsh quotidian conditions. Unlike Lewis, these theorists argued that the poverty subculture was entirely pathological, with a life of its own, and largely independent of the conditions that generated it. From this perspective, the poor were primarily responsible for their poverty (Jencks, 1992; Kelso, 1994; Magnet, 1987, 1993; McLanahan, 2009; Mead, 1986, 1992). Defective personality traits, preferences, morals, behaviors, and practices – held to be profoundly different from those embraced by mainstream society – were deeply embedded in the poor themselves and transmitted to their children. Consequently, it was the poor themselves who must "shape up"; they must alter their flawed values, attitudes, and behaviors to conform to those of wider mainstream society if their poverty was to be eliminated.[23] Simply creating greater opportunities for the poor cannot help them because they are not culturally equipped to take advantage of these opportunities.

These views, widely disseminated by the media, have been popularly embraced over the past few decades, and they have proven especially useful in legitimating rising poverty levels and the disproportionately higher rates of poverty seen among particularly vulnerable groups. The values and habits of the poor – said to be reflected in single parenthood, unemployment, school failure, welfare dependency, drug and alcohol abuse, and chronic lawlessness – are targeted as the central problem, the real root of poverty. It is stressed that these conditions must be addressed by poor people themselves, not by the state. Even if the poor could be lifted out of poverty through social programs, they would not be capable of maintaining their new socioeconomic position; their low aspirations, poor work habits, spontaneous indulgence of impulses, inability to sacrifice or save for the future, weak family structures, frayed connections to society, and other aberrant values and behaviors ensure that they would soon sink back into poverty (Banfield, 1974; Mead, 1986).[24] The poor people that are trapped at the bottom due to their behavior, culture, and other related pathologies are said to constitute an "underclass."[25] This argument has been often wielded against Black families in the United States (Steinberg, 2015).

Charles Murray (1984), whose work with Herrnstein on the biological roots of poverty was examined earlier, has pushed this line of thinking well beyond the idea of the simple futility of compensatory social and educational programs. Like Spencer and Sumner in the nineteenth century, Murray and several others in the reformulated "culture of poverty" tradition suggest that policy measures such as the "War on Poverty" and other social programs in the United States were not simply an entirely unsuccessful waste of resources; they were also exceptionally harmful to society because they nurtured the dysfunctional values and behaviors prevalent among the poor, greatly reducing their incentives to work while fostering their dependency on the state (Gilder, 1981; Magnet, 1987, 1993; Marsland, 1995; Mead, 1986, 1992; Murray, 1984, 2006, 2012). They argued that social programs and supports encourage people to remain unemployed; sustain and further family breakdown by enabling mothers to stay single or get divorced; foster dependency and laziness; shield people from the befittingly adverse consequences of abusing drugs and alcohol, dropping out of school, and having children "out of wedlock"; and give too much and ask for too little in return.

The prevailing discourse today routinely targets social policy as a central reason for the emergence and perpetuation of the "culture of poverty," and welfare reform is considered central to reforming the character and habits of the poor. Some alloy of these "culture of poverty" views and neoliberal thought has promoted the erosion and reconstitution of welfare states underway across many nations in the developed capitalist world over the past few decades, rendering them less generous and accessible. A foundational goal of "welfare reform" in the Anglo nations has been the reduction of public spending and welfare dependency (Beatty & Fothergill, 2018; Daguerre, 2008). This goal is epitomized in the United States by the elimination of the long-standing Aid to Families with Dependent Children Program (AFDC), achieved through the passage into law of the Personal Responsibility and Work Opportunity Reconciliation Act (PRWORA) in 1996, which replaced AFDC with the Temporary Assistance to Needy Families program (TANF). In the United Kingdom, the Universal Credit program, enabled through the Welfare Reform Act of 2012, was similarly motivated.[26] Like biogenetic explanations of poverty, approaches that root poverty in the poor's "culture" have been thoroughly assailed from several angles. Some critics, more faithful to the original cultural approach set out by Oscar Lewis, argue that the values and behaviors of the poor should be seen as an adaptive response to their situation and not a deviant rejection of mainstream culture or a preference for an alternative one. These critics argue that poor families do not have differing values and norms; they embrace the dominant values but simply do not possess the means of realizing them. Consequently, they lower their expectations and may act in ways that sometimes deviate from the norm.[27]

Anthropologist Elliot Liebow's (1967) classic ethnographic study of "streetcorner men" in Washington, DC, *Tally's Corner*, suggests that men without regular jobs and stable families may devise a "shadow system of values" to shield themselves from a profound sense of personal failure. Their immediate exhaustion of the few resources they possessed reflects their acute awareness of their foreclosed futures and the limitations of their means – not a present-time orientation or the inability to defer gratification. Similarly, sociologist Hylan Lewis (1967, p. 11) refers to the "broad spectrum of pragmatic adjustments to external and internal stresses and deprivations" that poor families must make. Like Oscar Lewis, both Elliot Liebow and Hylan Lewis viewed the "aberrant"

behaviors exhibited by poor people as logical adaptations to their situation.[28] But, unlike Oscar Lewis, they did not view them as anchored
in a new set of adaptive values and morals that differ from those of
dominant society. Rather, poor people's restricted circumstances and
limited resources discourage them from adhering to the mainstream
values they embrace. For example, while low-income parents accept
the importance of their children's education, it is their involvement in
night work or shift work – without paid leave, affordable childcare, or
accessible transportation – that often prevents them from becoming
involved in school functions and organizations (Dill, 1998; Edwards et
al., 2001; Gorski, 2008; Iversen & Farber, 1996; Lichter & Crowely, 2002;
Rank, 1994; Seccombe, 1999).

Other critics of the culture of poverty theory underscore striking
similarities in the behaviors of poor and middle-class people. Although
often stereotyped as unemployed and lazy, most poor people work, and
many of them hold multiple jobs. Many of these critics also stress that
there is no single, homogeneous, or monolithic culture embraced by all
individuals or families in any class. While often portrayed as "apathetic,"
many poor people are active in the welfare and civil rights movements
and highly involved in their communities and in politics. People from
the middle class also exhibit traits and behaviors typically invoked to
characterize and stigmatize the poor. They often avoid involvement in
political issues and social organizations. They may act "irresponsibly"
and may be just as "present-time oriented," overusing credit cards, ac-
cumulating large debts, and paying exorbitant interest rates. Members
of middle- and upper-class families engage in crime, cheat on taxes,
and smuggle purchases across national borders. Divorce, cohabita-
tion, and single-parent families are not uncommon among the middle
classes either. While drug and alcohol use and abuse may be most visible in poor neighborhoods in media reports, these social ills are also
common across all classes (Gould et al., 2015; Little, 1965/1971; Piven
& Cloward, 1971, 1979; Valentine, 1968; Wright & Rogers, 2015).

Still other critics point to the implicit ethnocentrism of the culture
of poverty approach, which idealizes middle-class values, morals, aspirations, and behaviors and assumes that alternative "cultures" and strategies
adopted by poor families are always inferior, disorganized, dysfunctional, irresponsible, and self-destructive. Anthropologist Carol Stack
(1974/1997), for example, challenged the stereotypes of single-parent

families in her ethnographic study of poverty in a Black community in the United States, highlighting their use of creative and cooperative strategies to cope with extreme adversity. These included the development of extended, informal networks of social and economic support comprising members of extended families (kin) as well as friends, neighbors, and others not related by blood or marriage ("fictive kin") who could provide advice and help with childcare, transportation, and paying bills and engage in trading or recirculating clothing, furniture, and other household goods. These systems of support, mutual assistance, and sharing proved invaluable, often furnishing greater sustenance than a typical, more isolated nuclear family model could provide. Middle-class values and concerns, for example, keeping money issues private and not telling lies, were irrelevant to the lives of many poor families struggling to get by; indeed, deception might be required to defend family interests when dealing with caseworkers or demeaning surveillance (Fraser, 1989; Gordon, 1990; Ladner, 1971; Seccombe, 1999).

As with biogenetic accounts of poverty, the central assertions of the culture of poverty approach are quickly undone by comparative studies (e.g., Biegert, 2017; Brady et al., 2017; Rothwell & McEwen, 2017). It cannot account for marked cross-national variation in poverty rates or their rise and fall over time. The emphasis placed on the negative impacts of social programs by proponents of the neoliberal version of the cultural approach is entirely contradicted by cross-national research. Single mothers in Sweden and other nations, for example, are furnished with a denser and far more generous web of income programs, social services, and other supports than in most other nations, and, consequently, their poverty rates are significantly lower. The culture of poverty approach assumes a shared, uniform, and negative set of attitudes, values, morals, aspirations, goals, and behaviors among poor individuals and families. What they actually share is a "deficit" in their living conditions, life chances, opportunities, basic rights, and level of inclusion, as well as the stigma and discrimination they endure.[29]

The Persistence of "Culture of Poverty" Explanations

The idea that poor people constitute a distinct group whose "cultural disposition" is clearly different from that of everyone else and largely responsible for their poverty has a long and deeply entrenched history in the Anglo nations. Some version of the culture of poverty approach, variously identifying poor people as members of a "residuum," a "social problem group," an "underclass," or "troubled families," has been engaged for nearly two centuries (Macnicol, 2017; Streib et al., 2016; Welshman, 2002, 2006). As detailed in Chapter 4, the early Poor Laws in the United Kingdom and its colonies sharply distinguished from the outset the "deserving" poor and the "undeserving" poor in order to determine eligibility for social support. The Poor Law reform of 1834 inaugurated an even harsher view that overshadowed the existing limited concerns for the worthy poor and their need for assistance. This view has persistently shaped the character of social programs addressing poverty in the Anglo nations, which, in turn, have helped to animate and sustain it. The minimal assistance they provide has been recurrently deemed too "generous" and too "easily accessed," thereby abetting the poor's defective traits and habits and encouraging them to avoid work whenever possible.

The culture of poverty perspective still has wide currency today (e.g., McLanahan, 2009; Sawhill, 2003).[30] This is evident in the interminable and often sensationalized accounts of "makers vs. takers" or "strivers vs. skivers" in the media – the starkly contrasting portrayals of productive, hardworking, moral people who pay taxes and contribute to society versus the lazy, unemployed, immoral, untrustworthy, and dependent welfare scroungers who take advantage of them. Accounts that personalize poverty as a reflection of a deviant subculture have had greater resonance in the Anglo nations than in most European countries, and this alleged deviance has been used to justify the limited supports provided to poor families and the recent retrenchment of what supports remain (Alesina & Angeletos, 2005; Gans, 1995; Gilens, 1999; Shildrick, 2012, 2018; Swanson, 2001). Conservative think tanks and foundations – such as the American Enterprise Institute, the Cato Institute, the Heritage Foundation, and the Manhattan Institute for Policy Research in the US; the Centre for Social Justice in the UK; and the Fraser Institute in Canada, for example – have dense networks of connections to large corporations, wealthy elites, and conservative political parties. These foundations have routinely highlighted behavioral pathways to poverty and promoted greater work incentives and the urgent need to make social assistance less attractive by reducing benefit levels, tightening eligibility rules, and introducing more punitive sanctions (e.g., Centre for Social Justice, 2007a, 2007b; Tanner & Hughes, 2013; Sarlo, 2019).

The strikingly similar stereotypical and stigmatizing depictions of poor people in the Anglo nations – referred to as "poor bashing" in Canada (Swanson, 2001), "poverty propaganda" in the United Kingdom (Shildrick, 2018, p. 2), and a "war against the poor" in the United States (Gans, 1995) – are more widespread and more firmly embraced there than in the Nordic nations (Larsen, 2008, 2013; Larsen & Dejgaard, 2013). This, in part, reflects the different character of the welfare states in each group of nations and how they address poverty. In the Anglo nations, potential benefit recipients must be in desperate need to qualify for support, and they come to be viewed as a distinct group – them, not us (Hills, 2015). Within the Anglo world, there is a greater tendency to blame the poor, especially in the United States, the nation where the welfare state is the least developed, unions are the weakest, and the poor's reliance upon targeted social policy measures is the greatest. Emphasizing universal supports for all citizens, social democratic welfare states generate very different public perceptions of benefit recipients.[31] Their provision of supports and services to everyone as a right, and the generosity and quality of those benefits, foster a greater sense of unity and solidarity. State assistance with finding employment through active labor market policies, the provision of public childcare and education (including at the tertiary level), and the reliance upon unions and union confederations to improve wages and job security ensure that poverty is unlikely to be viewed as a sign of personal failure. Moreover, universal measures generate greater support for increasing social spending and extending social supports (Korpi & Palme, 1998; Larsen, 2008). The dominance of the "culture of poverty" discourse forecloses discussion of national cultures and ideologies but is itself a reflection of the emphasis upon individualism, the veneration of independence, and the general distrust of the state that are greater in the liberal Anglo nations than in the Nordic nations and most other European countries.

FROM "CULTURE OF POVERTY" TO CROSS-NATIONAL ACCOUNTS OF CULTURE AND POVERTY

Culture has been a pivotal focal point in many comparative accounts of poverty, social inequality, and social policy, but it is a notoriously complex and slippery concept to apprehend, especially across nations.

Although there is no standard definition of "culture," it is generally understood to encompass the totality of broadly shared meanings, attitudes, beliefs, values, and ideologies in a society and the allied network of norms, behaviors, practices, traditions, and institutions, all of which is socially transmitted over time across generations. The creation and availability of a range of cross-national and longitudinal surveys and data sets over the past few decades – such as the EU Eurobarometer, European Social Survey (EES), European Values Study (EVS), International Social Survey Program (ISSP), and World Values Survey (WVS) – have allowed researchers to explore some dimensions of culture by closely examining public opinion toward various indicators of social inequality (including poverty, income disparities, and pay differentials) and support for redistribution and social protection across time and place (e.g., Bonoli, 2000; Hadler, 2009; Oorschot & Halman, 2000; Osberg & Smeeding, 2006; Roex et al., 2019; Svallfors, 1997). These surveys have been employed to explore the popular view that marked variation in levels of poverty and inequality across nations and, relatedly, in the character of welfare states can be explained by variation in national cultures.

However valuable, social attitude surveys can be fraught with difficulties and limitations. In an attempt to be universally applicable across nations, they have sometimes relied on shallow, general questions concerning, for example, support for "the welfare state," concealing more complex, ambiguous, or conflicting opinions about specific social policies (such as healthcare) or about particular dimensions of these policies. Alternatively, they may ask narrow, targeted questions that are unable to adequately address larger, more complex issues. Questions about support for existing social assistance or other programs for poor and low-income families, for example, cannot ascertain the level of support for eradicating poverty in a nation. Attitude surveys are designed to capture people's views in varied social contexts, but the same questions can have very different meanings and connotations across nations and, consequently, may yield puzzling or misleading conclusions. For example, support for increased social spending to address poverty may be relatively low in nations that already have developed and effective networks of social programs. Finally, national surveys may conceal marked differences among classes, groups, or regions within countries (Chung et al., 2018; Gelissen, 2002; Olsen, 2002; Svallfors, 1991, 2003).

Table 5.2. Attitudes to Poverty, Inequality, and Redistribution in Seven Nations

Nation	The government should spend less on benefits for the poor[a] % agree (2009)	It is the government's responsibility to reduce income differences between the rich and the poor[b] % agree (2016)	It is the government's responsibility to provide a decent standard of living for the unemployed[b] % agree (2016)	Individualism[d] (scale 0–100)
Canada	n/a	67.8[c]	63.0[c]	80
United Kingdom	17.4	70.8	60.2	89
United States	18.0	56.0	56.6	91
Denmark	8.7	56.6	75.6	74
Finland	7.7	78.7	82.0	63
Norway	7.0	78.2	89.3	69
Sweden	10.0	66.9	76.5	71

Sources:
[a] International Social Survey Program (ISSP) Social Inequality IV 2009
[b] International Social Survey Program (ISSP) Role of Government V 2016
[c] International Social Survey Program (ISSP) Role of Government IV 2006
[d] Hofstede Insights (n.d.), Hofstede (2001), Hofstede et al. (2010)

For a variety of reasons, comparative studies examining the link between membership in a particular welfare regime and attitudes toward poverty, redistribution, and social protection do not always produce clear-cut patterns. Despite their broad similarities, nations within a regime can approximate the ideal type in different ways, which may be reflected in intra-regime attitudinal variation. And, while the welfare regimes themselves are stable as ideal types, the social policies of their member nations are constantly in flux, which may also influence public attitudes (Bonoli, 2000; Jæger, 2006; Larsen, 2006; Oorschot & Halman, 2000; Roosma et al., 2012; Svallfors, 1997). In general, however, "support for equality, redistribution, and state intervention is strongest in the social democratic regime, weaker in the conservative regime, and weakest in the liberal regime" (Svallfors, 2010, p. 245). This observation is supported by data contrasting attitudes in the Anglo and Nordic nations. As Table 5.2 shows, support for reducing benefits for the poor is twice as high in the United Kingdom and the United States as in the Nordic nations, and, on a scale of 0 to 100 measuring individualism, the Anglo nations obtain higher scores.[32]

It is commonly noted that, compared to most other advanced, wealthy capitalist countries, the Anglo nations are characterized by much more "individualistic" cultures. They emphasize the priority of private property and self-reliance in the market and – most resolutely in the United States – renounce and discourage personal dependency upon the state. Large corporations and financial institutions are supported through protective tariffs and sustained, rescued, or "bailed out" by governments through a wide range of generous subsidies, "incentives," and other expenditures with relatively little public antipathy toward these forms of "corporate welfare." Social supports for poor people, however – especially poor single mothers – are typically stingy, closely monitored, punitive, and highly stigmatized. Individuals are expected to be autonomous and independent and, when necessary, to rely upon support from their families. From a culturalist perspective, this individualist, anti-statist orientation goes some distance in explaining why the Anglo nations have relatively high levels of poverty and inequality and less developed, liberal welfare states. However, there is variation among the cultures of the Anglo nations; Canada and the United Kingdom have long been viewed as somewhat more communitarian and statist than the United States, where the notion of self-reliance is paramount (Harles, 2017; Hartz, 1955, 1964; Lipset, 1986, 1990; Olsen, 2002).[33]

In many other nations, there is a considerably stronger "collectivist," communitarian, and "statist" orientation than that found in Canada, the UK, and the US. This is particularly true of the Nordic nations, where there is far greater public support for social programs and the high taxation rates that finance them. It is also reflected in their folktales and literatures, and epitomized in the idea of society as "folkhemmet" (the "people's home") in Sweden. However, their strong collectivist values are tempered by liberal individualism. In the Anglo nations, "freedom" is widely interpreted as "freedom from the state," and people who rely upon it for support are more readily stigmatized with the label "dependent." In the Nordic nations, the welfare state is more fulsomely embraced. However, this is not simply a reflection of the prioritization of the community over the individual; it is also viewed as a central means of promoting individual freedom and autonomy (Daun, 1991; Kautto et al., 2001; Olsen, 2002; Simon, 2017;

Trägårdh, 1990; Witoszek & Midttun, 2018). As indicated in Table 5.2, while the Nordic nations are decidedly less individualistic than the Anglo nations, they are all well above the midpoint between collectivism and individualism on the scale.

Fascinating discussions and debates have long ensued over the impact of culture upon levels of social inequality and the character of social policy. The cross-national, comparative cultural approach provides valuable insights into why poverty rates are lower in the Nordic nations than in the Anglo nations. Unlike "culture of poverty" theory, which suggests that one particular subgroup (the poor) *within* society has adopted a deviant subculture that is largely responsible for its members' poverty and inability to escape this poverty, the cross-cultural approach highlights varying ways that poverty is understood and how successfully it is addressed *across* nations. However, in order to understand why some national cultures are more tolerant of high levels of poverty and inequality than others are, we must necessarily understand how these heightened levels are created and sustained over time – as well as their links to key historical institutions and traditions and the balance of power in society. The systemic, structural, and political roots of poverty are addressed in the next chapter.[34]

NOTES

1 *Human capital* theory is a third approach that views poverty as a reflection of deficiencies among poor individuals; low levels of education, skills, and training are its central focus. This theory does not overtly blame or denounce poor people, but there is typically great emphasis upon them becoming economically productive and autonomous workers who are independent. Proponents of this perspective often assume that good jobs will be available if people are better trained and educated. However, the nations that have been most successful with education and training programs have implemented them as part of an active labor market policy approach that includes programs to promote job creation as well as a network of other social supports (Hvid & Falkum, 2018; Kenworthy, 2008; Monday Morning, 2012; Olsen, 2008). For an overview and critique of human capital theory see Royce (2009), Steinberg (1985), and Woodbury (1993).

2 Of course, theories of poverty might be categorized in a variety of ways based upon the facets and dimensions that are in focus (e.g., Royce, 2009; Wright, 1995).

3 "Classical" conservatism emphasized the priority of the community and cooperation among the hierarchically arranged social orders in feudal societies, with the elites at the top holding some degree of responsibility for the strata at the bottom who were considered innately inferior – a concept referred to as "noblesse oblige," the obligation of the nobility. Under capitalism, the previous focus on noble birth and great wealth gave way to the idea of a "natural aristocracy of talent and virtue," but conservative governments and parties often maintained a paternalistic obligation toward poor and low-income families and other disadvantaged groups through state intervention ("Red Toryism"). Allied with "neoliberalism," the contemporary variant of conservatism – "neoconservatism" – in contrast, calls for austerity as the most appropriate and effective response to poverty. Unlike neoliberalism, however, it does not purport to have faith in market forces to remedy poverty, or to have any concern with doing so.

4 Published in 1798, the full title of the first edition of this book was *An Essay on the Principle of Population as It Affects the Future Improvement of Society, with Remarks on the Speculations of Mr. Godwin, M. Condorcet, and Other Writers* (Malthus 1798/2008). A greatly expanded and revised second edition was published five years later with an altered and even more impressively unwieldy title – *An Essay on the Principle of Population; or, a View of Its Past and Present Effects on Human Happiness; with an Inquiry into Our Prospects Respecting the Future Removal or Mitigation of the Evils which it Occasions* (Malthus 1803/1890). The second edition is sometimes viewed as less harsh because the previous emphasis upon wars, famine, and disease to bring the population back in line with the capacity to sustain it was softened by a greater emphasis on the potential role of preventive checks. However, this edition also placed greater stress on the lack of moral restraint among the poor and the futility of providing them with social support. Four more editions of the book, with relatively minor revisions, were published within Malthus's lifetime (Foster, 1998).

5 Conservative historian Gertrude Himmelfarb (1985) highlights the stark contrast between Adam Smith's faith in the free market and economic growth to end poverty with Malthus's "population principle," which condemned the poor to a ceaseless struggle for survival and a life of absolute misery.

6 However, Huzel (2006) also notes that Malthus's ideas generated intense opposition in the working-class press.

7 Like most of his contemporaries, Malthus could not anticipate the great gains in agricultural output or the decline in fertility rates of the nineteenth and twentieth centuries that would accompany industrialization. Although he is often considered an early ecological champion, Malthus was not directly concerned with the impact of "overpopulation" on the environment or the depletion of natural resources. Rather, he stressed that the inevitable and invariable population pressure on the food supply

precluded any hope for social change, condemning the masses to a life on the edge of subsistence and premature death.

8 Spencer's work centered on his idea of the "survival of the fittest," a phrase often misattributed to Charles Darwin. Darwin (1872/1958) argued that the evolution of a species occurred through a blind, random process animated by its "fit" with changing environments. A species, or member of a species, was only considered "superior" to another in terms of its ability to survive and thrive in a particular setting; the ones that were better suited to an environment would be naturally selected to flourish on the basis of this functional advantage – a process he referred to as "descent with modification." But they were considered "fitter" than other less adaptable forms of life only in that very restricted sense; they were not deemed more "advanced" or at a higher level of development. Focusing on the evolution of human society, rather than the evolution of species, Spencer's "Social Darwinist" perspective, in stark contrast, was built upon the idea of an inherent, unilineal, relentless, evolutionary "advance" toward a higher stage. However, the Social Darwinists also strenuously cautioned that this progress could be forestalled by state interference in the form of social programs, laws, and other protections that altered or interfered with this natural development (Baldus, 2016).

9 Andrew Carnegie was Spencer's most prominent disciple and an intimate friend who "showered him with favors" (Hofstadter, 1955, p. 45; White, 1979).

10 The term "robber barons" originally referred to European feudal lords who charged unauthorized tolls on people and ships using roads and rivers that traversed their estates – an activity that enhanced their private riches without creating public wealth. It was later applied to powerful nineteenth-century capitalists who engaged in graft, bribery, influence peddling, and other forms of political corruption, as well as in the abuse and hyper-exploitation of their workers.

11 In their novel, *The Gilded Age* (1873/2006), Mark Twain and Charles Dudley Warner satirized the greed, corruption, and plutocracy of the post–Civil War era in the United States. Inspired by Shakespeare's reference to gilding refined gold in *King John*, they used the term *gilded age* to capture the ostentatious and wasteful excess exhibited by immensely wealthy families during this period and the gross inequalities and deep, widespread poverty concealed below. Piketty (2014) provides a comparative account of the concentration of wealth during the "Gilded Age" in the United States and "La Belle Époque" in Europe. Bartels (2008) documents the growing gap between the rich and poor and the undermining of democracy in the "new gilded age."

12 Social Darwinism would also provide impetus for the eugenics movement in the twentieth century that took root in the United States, Canada, and Australia, among other former colonies of the British Empire, as well as

across continental Europe and the Nordic nations. See Bashford and Levine (2010), Broberg and Roll-Hansen (2005), Hansen and King (2013), and Ladd-Taylor (2020).

13 Social Darwinism encouraged the adoption of forced sterilization policies around the globe and fostered the creation of segregationist legislation and practices and state-sponsored genocide in some nations. Miscegenation laws designed to maintain "racial purity" by criminalizing "interracial" marriage and intimate relationships were also introduced in several nations, including the United States, South Africa under apartheid, and Nazi Germany. Although "race" is a social construct, the creation of racial categories and identities through "racialization" has had dire consequences, maintaining power, wealth, and privilege for the "races" at the top while fostering poverty, social exclusion, discrimination, and the denial of human rights for those at the bottom (Jacobson, 1998; Rattansi, 2007).

14 For an application of individualistic approaches applied to "inequality" more broadly, see Baldus (2016) and Olsen (2011).

15 Francis Galton, Darwin's cousin, was among the first to attempt to develop a measure of intelligence. However, the modern field of intelligence testing began with the work of Alfred Binet in 1905. The French government commissioned Binet to develop a test that would help to identify children with learning difficulties and determine the kind of educational programs for which they were best suited. This test, which assessed attention, memory, and verbal skills, was revised in the United States by Stanford University psychologist Lewis Terman in 1916, and several times since. Known as the "Stanford-Binet test" it is still widely employed today.

16 Jensen (1995) continued to publish studies on intelligence, race, and gender often working with British-born, Canadian psychologist Philippe Rushton, whose research was funded by the Pioneer Fund (e.g., Rushton, 1995; Rushton & Jensen, 2005). The Pioneer Fund provided funding for numerous studies on the connection between race and intelligence that informed Herrnstein and Murray's work (Tucker, 2002). Philippe Rushton was the head of the Pioneer Fund from 2002 until his death in 2012. The work of his successor, British psychologist Richard Lynn (2015; Lynn & Becker, 2019) – also financed by the Pioneer Fund – has a similar orientation, focusing on the relationships among race, gender, wealth, and IQ.

17 The British psychologist Charles Spearman was a pioneer of a statistical technique called factor analysis that is used in intelligence testing. Factor analysis is based upon a family of techniques used to find relationships among multiple measures, reducing them into one, or a few, factors. Spearman conducted the first formal factor analysis of IQ tests measuring different aspects of intelligence and concluded that they reflected a single underlying general factor he called the "g" factor. In measures of cognitive ability, "g" represents general intelligence.

18 As noted earlier, even the residual welfare states in the US and other Anglo nations are able to move some people out of poverty. However, nations that have more developed welfare states are much more effective at reducing both absolute and relative forms of poverty and at keeping people from falling back into poverty (Brady, 2005; Brady & Bostic, 2015; Marx et al., 2015; Scruggs & Allen, 2006; Smeeding, 2006a, 2006b).

19 The idea of ending public support for poor and low-income people has been the driving force behind Murray's work, reflecting his close connections to several prominent, moneyed neoliberal and conservative think tanks in the United States. These include the Manhattan Institute; the American Enterprise Institute, which gave him its Irving Kristol Award in 2015; and the Bradley Foundation, which provided grants to work on the *Bell Curve* and awarded him its Bradley Prize in 2016. His first notable publication in 1984, *Losing Ground: American Social Policy, 1950–1980*, gained popularity with the Reagan administration and greatly shaped the welfare reform debate in the United States. His subsequent work – like that of Malthus and the Social Darwinists – continues to legitimate deep welfare cuts, generating both support and revulsion. The Southern Poverty Law Center (SPLC) – an organization based in Montgomery, Alabama, that was founded in 1971 to protect and promote civil rights – acknowledges on its website that, despite his use of "racist pseudoscience and misleading statistics," Murray is "one of the most influential social scientists in America" (SPLC, n.d.).

20 Some of this work, such as that by Harvard geneticist David Reich (2018a, 2018b, 2019) seeks to undermine insidious racial stereotypes. However, while acknowledging that "race" is a social construct – "a way of categorizing people that changes over time and across countries" – Reich also contends that "differences in genetic ancestry that happen to correlate to many of today's social constructs are real" (2018a).

21 Although not a US state, Puerto Rico has been an unincorporated territory of the United States since 1898 under the terms of the Treaty of Paris that ended the Spanish-American War. People born in Puerto Rico are US citizens.

22 A somewhat similar perspective was taken by American sociologist Michael Harrington (1962/1981). He placed greater emphasis on the mechanics of capitalism than Lewis did in his account of poverty, but he also viewed the "culture of poverty" as the "institutionalization of the poor's misery." Both of them argued that, under the right conditions, this cultural orientation might be forged into an instrument of self-emancipation (Greenbaum, 2015; Harrington, 1984; Harvey & Reed, 1996).

23 Senator Daniel Patrick Moynihan's (1965) contentious landmark report, *The Negro Family: The Case for National Action*, acknowledged that widespread poverty among Black people in the United States was the legacy

of slavery and of centuries of discrimination and was linked to urbanization and high levels of unemployment. But these conditions, he stressed,
culminated in broken homes and in the fragmentation of families, high
numbers of illegitimate births, the replacement of traditional families by
matrifocal families, and dependence upon public welfare. This "tangle
of pathology" became the prime mover, trapping Black families in cycles
of poverty and deviance (Greenbaum, 2015; O'Connor, 2001; Steinberg,
2015).

24 Some theorists or social scientists (e.g., Petersen, 1985; Wilson, 1987) attempt to explain poverty by pointing to the interaction of cultural factors
(such as broken families, welfare dependency, and drug dependency) with
broader structural concerns, such as deindustrialization, unemployment,
and discrimination.

25 An interesting historical overview of the term "underclass" is provided by
Gans (1996).

26 First announced by Work and Pensions Secretary Iain Duncan Smith,
the Universal Credit (UC) program was introduced in 2012 and mobi-
lized the following year. However, it ran into many problems, and the
gradual rollout of the program was delayed for several years. The UC
program was designed to replace six means-tested, income-related benefits and tax credits (Job Seeker's Allowance, Employment and Support
Allowance, Income Support, Working Tax Credit, Child Tax Credit, and
Housing Benefit); to emphasize personal responsibility; and to incentivize work.

27 Focusing on Black Americans, the eminent Harvard sociologist William J.
Wilson (1978, 1987, 1996; Wacquant & Wilson, 1989), for example, argues
that a network of interrelated structural factors, such as deindustrialization, widespread unemployment, economic deprivation, marginalization
and segregation in ghettos where there are few opportunities ("spatial
mismatch"), and a lack of the education and skills needed to do well in a
postindustrial society are among the most important factors contributing
to the concentration and endurance of poverty. However, his views have
garnered criticism (e.g., Steinberg 1997, 2007; Willie, 1978), especially
his views that race and racism are of declining significance and that certain "cultural traits" among the poor (habits, styles, skills, and micro-level
processes of meaning making and decision making) may limit social mobility and "contribute to the perpetuation of poverty" (Wilson, 2010, p.
203–204).

28 The idea of adaptation has a functionalist cast; poor people develop new
values and behaviors that allow them to survive. However, American sociologist Herbert Gans (1962, 2012) refocuses functionalism to show more
critically how poverty benefits the dominant class and other nonpoor
groups in capitalist society. He identifies several functions that the poor
serve by (1) generating new middle-class professions and services to help

the poor and shield the population from them, including criminology, social work, public health, homeless shelters, and charitable organizations; (2) taking on low-wage, menial, and often high-risk work that others refuse; (3) creating a subeconomy of pawn shops, dollar stores, secondhand clothing stores, rental furniture outlets, fringe banks, and check-cashing outlets; (4) serving as a warning to others and making them feel better about themselves; and (5) maintaining the status quo by not participating in elections and other political activities. On poor industries, see Caplovitz (1963), Caskey (1996), Soderberg (2018), and Williams (1977). Gans's functionalist account of *poverty* is very different from functionalist explanations for *inequality* (Olsen, 2011) and the origins of social policy (Olsen, 2002).

29 There are several useful critical overviews of various forms and dimensions of the "culture of poverty" perspective, including Greenbaum (2015), Rank (2005, 2011), Royce (2009), and Steinberg (2011, 2015).

30 This perspective is most ardently held in the United States, but the idea that poor people have their own inferior culture is also prominent in the United Kingdom, where poor working-class people in public housing are often referred to as CHAVs ("council housing and violent").

31 However, negative attitudes toward the poor and suspicion of people on social assistance are not entirely absent in these nations (Lindqvist et al., 2017; Svallfors, 2011).

32 The collectivist-individualist scale runs from 0 to 100, with 50 as a midpoint. The higher the score, the greater the level of individualism – understood as the belief that individuals are expected to take care of only themselves and their immediate families (Hofstede et al., 2010).

33 A fascinating and expansive literature explores why socialism, unions, welfare states, and other manifestations of collectivism have been more acceptable in Canada and the UK than in the "exceptional" US (e.g., Bevir, 2011; Horowitz, 1968; Lipset, 1986, 1990, 1996; Lipset & Marks, 2000; McKay, 2005; McKibbon, 1984; Naylor, 2016; Pierson, 1990; Shalev & Korpi, 1980; Voss, 1993).

34 There is a rich literature on the links between the character of welfare states and attitudes toward the poor, poverty, inequality, and state intervention (e.g., Baumberg, 2016; Blekesaune & Quadagno, 2003; Coughlin, 1979; Korpi & Palme, 1998; Larsen, 2006, 2008; Lepianka et al., 2009; Pantazis, 2016; Pemberton et al., 2016; Spicker, 1984; Svallfors, 1997, 2003, 2011, 2012; Taylor-Gooby & Leruth, 2018).

FURTHER READINGS

Baldus, B. (2016). *Origins of inequality in human societies*. Routledge.

Brady, D. (2019). Theories of the causes of poverty. *American Review of Sociology, 45*, 155–175.

Katz, M.B. (2013). *The undeserving poor: America's enduring confrontation with poverty* (2nd ed.). Oxford University Press.

Royce, E. (2009). *Poverty and power: The problem of structural inequality*. Rowman and Littlefield.

Shildrick, T. (2018). *Poverty propaganda: Exploring the myths*. Bristol University Press.

Swanson, J. (2001). *Poor-bashing: The politics of exclusion*. Between the Lines.

Wright, E.O. (1995). The class analysis of poverty. *International Journal of Health Services, 25*(1), 85–100.

CHAPTER SIX

Society-Centered Explanations for Poverty: Systemic and Sociopolitical Accounts

> For one very rich man, there must be at least five hundred poor,
> and the affluence of the few supposes the indigence of the many.
> – *Adam Smith (1776/2003)*

Individual-centered theories contend that poverty is largely the result of alleged deficiencies, character flaws, and deviancies of poor people themselves while ignoring the social forces and contexts that generate and sustain it. As a result, these theories have difficulty accounting for significant variation in the level and severity of poverty across nations, and with fluctuations within nations over time. Nor can they easily explain the continual turnover among the members of destitute populations in most nations. Their insistence that social programs and supports for poor people only encourage them to act irresponsibly is also effectively routed by comparative research. Nations that provide the most social support – prioritizing people's interdependence as a natural part of the human condition rather than castigating it as a sign of individual failings – have lower rates and less severe forms of poverty. The theoretical approaches examined in this chapter take an entirely different tack, headlining *society-centered* causes of poverty.

As in the individualistic tradition, there are two principal variants in the society-centered theoretical school – *systemic* and *sociopolitical.* The first one highlights the imperatives of capitalist systems. Consequently, it is concerned with identifying *common* forces at work in *all* wealthy capitalist nations and explaining why, despite the great prosperity of these nations, none of them has eliminated poverty. From this system-focused perspective, poverty is inherent to capitalism, routinely generated through the normal functioning of markets, and sustained by networks of institutions and laws. The systemic approach provides valuable insights into the causes of poverty and the conditions and trends that are similar across all of the rich capitalist nations, including sustained or rising levels of poverty and social policy retrenchment (e.g., Offe, 1985; Peet, 1975; Wright, 1995). But it has difficulty explaining the strikingly lower rates of poverty in some rich capitalist nations, which are especially notable among children and other vulnerable groups. Its strongest proponents are inclined to dismiss, or at least fail to fully appreciate, the meaningful and impactful gains achieved in many nations, including the various and extensive income measures, social services, and protective laws that have been championed and entrenched. The second approach focuses on other sociopolitical factors, such as the balance of power among key social actors in society. Pronounced cross-national *variation* in the levels and severity of poverty and in the character and impact of welfare states is better explained through a close examination of the mobilization of social actors, class-based "power resources," and the "balance of power in society" – and how these vary across nations, shifting over time (e.g., Brady, 2003b; Korpi, 1980; Moller et al., 2003; O'Connor & Olsen, 1998).

SYSTEMIC EXPLANATIONS FOR POVERTY

The systemic approach is centered on the operation of capitalism, a socioeconomic system based on the private ownership of property and private profit, as well as on the use of markets as the central means of allocating resources. From this perspective, the political-legal frameworks that maintain and protect capitalism – despite the often marked architectural variation apparent across capitalist nations – necessarily reflect and enforce starkly unequal relations of power among classes and among other groups in society.[1] Challenging dominant eighteenth-century declarations and mainstream beliefs concerning "freedom," the "rights of man," and "equality before the law," the influential German political theorist Karl Marx was among the first to argue that laws, practices, and institutions derive from "commerce" – an insight he would continue to sharpen and deepen throughout his life's work.[2] Many contemporary legal scholars have further explicated how power is embedded in the legal system, and how this has steadily enhanced the dominance of corporations in capitalist society today (e.g., Bakan, 2004, 2020; Glasbeek, 2002, 2018a, 2018b; Mandel, 1986; Winkler, 2018a, 2018b). From this perspective, the often-invoked "structural" causes of poverty – such as rising unemployment rates, globalization, and neoliberalism – are themselves generated through the constitution and instinctual dynamics of the capitalist system itself (Harriss-White, 2006; Parenti, 1995; Snider, 1993; Wolff, 2012; Wright, 1994, 1995, 2019).

From the Structural to the Systemic Roots of Poverty

Rejecting individual-centered theories, some approaches have usefully highlighted the role of *structural* change to explain how poverty is generated. Rising rates of unemployment and the proliferation of precarious nonstandard contract work associated with deindustrialization, the decline of relatively highly paid jobs, the retrenchment of social supports, and "globalization" are often cited as among the key catalysts for higher and more severe forms of poverty over the past few decades (e.g., Kalleberg, 2011, 2018; Rank, 2005, 2011; Ross et al., 2000; Stiglitz, 2013; Waldfogel, 2010, 2013). These changes have stranded many people in segregated communities with few opportunities for escape. Black people, Indigenous people, and immigrants are among the vulnerable groups particularly negatively affected by these structural developments (UN HRC, 2014, 2017; Wilson, 1987, 1996). Dual-labor market theory, another structural approach, highlights the segmentation of the labor market into two parts: (1) a "primary sector" characterized by stable employment, relatively good wages and benefits, and opportunities for advancement and (2) a growing "secondary sector" characterized by low-wage, insecure, and dead-end jobs associated with poverty, and one in which women, visible minorities, and immigrants are greatly overrepresented (Gordon et al., 1982; Harrison & Sum, 1979; Kalleberg et al., 1981).[3]

Despite their valuable insights, theories emphasizing structural changes often treat them as accidental or blind developments rather than as endemic; they are not typically acknowledged as *systemically* generated by markets, the profit motive, and competition (Harriss-White,

2006; Wright, 1995). Consequently, the targeted solutions to which these approaches lead – promoting economic growth and increasing "human capital" – will have a limited impact on poverty. From a structural perspective, the best way to address poverty is through the promotion of economic growth. But continuous economic growth can be generated through the proliferation of bad jobs, fewer jobs, and part-time work, which sustain or increase poverty rates and have a negative impact on communities. In an economy characterized by the rapid proliferation of low-wage, precarious employment and freelance jobs, people with higher levels of education and new skills can find themselves "all dressed up with nowhere nice to go" while structural changes continue apace (Bernstein, 2007, p. 17; Marsh, 2011; Standing, 2011).[4] Moreover, as shown in myriad recent studies, new wealth created through economic growth may largely accrue to the very few at the top, as we have witnessed across the Anglo nations over the past few decades (e.g., Collins, 2018; Dorling, 2018; Heisz, 2016; Osberg, 2018; Piketty, 2014).[5]

The structural view fails to fully appreciate "what" and "who" animate and engineer these structural changes. Some changes are inherent to the system; some – including the loss of good jobs through the ongoing introduction of new "laborsaving" technologies and capital flight, union busting, and the retrenchment of social programs and supports – ultimately reflect conscious, self-serving, calculated choices made by an economic elite to increase its wealth and power, with flagrant disregard for the consequences of these choices. The systemic approach identifies forces that activate structural changes and the impact of these changes on the degree, depth, and duration of poverty, including the degradation of the neighborhoods, communities, and environments where poor families live.

Systemically Generated and Sustained Poverty

> Pauperism forms a condition of capitalist production, and of the capitalist development of wealth.
>
> – *Karl Marx (1867/1977)*

Capitalism's predominant and definitive form of labor is "free" wage labor.[6] Unlike slaves or feudal serfs, workers in capitalist societies are formally free to enter into labor contracts with owners of productive property (e.g., businesses, industries, corporations). But they are also compelled to do so in order to survive because they do not own productive property. Consequently, they are largely dependent upon capitalists to set the terms of exchange that play a central role in shaping their work environments, living conditions, and life chances. The law assumes that workers are as sovereign and free as capitalists, *voluntarily* entering into work-for-wages contracts. However, as the Australian barrister and solicitor of the Supreme Court of Victoria and Canadian law professor Harry Glasbeek (2018b) notes, capitalists "can choose not to invest their property" whereas workers "have no freedom not to sell their assets, their minds and bodies" (p. 21). States have typically reinforced this dependency on capitalists by providing social supports that are difficult to access, temporary, and minimal. The retrenchment and austerity prevalent across most of the capitalist world today – ensuring that workers have few viable alternative forms of livelihood – have been central market-enforcing strategies implemented and sustained throughout capitalism's history from the outset. Even in nations where strong labor movements have allowed for the creation of more generous social supports provided as a right of citizenship, eligibility is often contingent upon long-term, full-time participation in the paid labor force. From this perspective, poverty and homelessness are products of capitalism that escalate and intensify much more rapidly when capitalism is left alone and unsupervised.

Capitalist markets are often overlooked as poverty generators because they are taken for granted. But, while they appear natural and immutable – the assumed or default form of social organization – they are social constructs. So too are the corporations that dominate within them. Like markets, corporations are not simply *subject* to state regulation; they are legally constituted, empowered, and enforced through dense networks of legislation including property rights, contract rights, regulatory law, tax laws, labor law, and free trade agreements. Since their creation, modern corporations have steadily expanded their rights and profoundly augmented their privileged position in society, most notably in the Anglo nations (Bakan, 2004; Dimick, 2019; Glasbeek, 2018a, 2018b; Winkler, 2018b).

Although elements of it can be found in some organizations much earlier, the modern mega-business corporation is largely a creation of the nineteenth century.[7] During that period of rapid industrialization, the enormous amounts of capital required to build and operate the burgeoning railroad companies, oil refineries, iron and steel industries, and other large-scale enterprises encouraged the corporation's development in the United States, where it would serve as a model for Canada, the United Kingdom, and many other nations. These new corporations were built on three central principles that clearly distinguished them from unincorporated companies and earlier corporate entities: (1) they raised capital by selling shares or stocks to investors who were issued certificates of ownership and became part owners or shareholders (*the joint stock principle*); (2) their shareholders were liable for the company's debts only up to the value they had invested in the company (*the limited liability principle*); and, perhaps most momentously, (3) they would be considered "legal persons" with many of the rights held by natural persons (*the corporate personhood principle*). In concert, these three principles have endowed corporations with unparalleled influence and furnished them with a solid foundation to further increase their wealth and power (Barak, 2017; Cerri, 2018; Glasbeek, 2002, 2017).

Although they are aggregations of great amounts of "collectivized" capital from numerous sources, corporations are legally separated from their actual owners, and each is treated as if it were just one person. This pooling of people and resources is widely viewed very positively. But it furnishes corporations with several forms of leverage, unavailable to other social actors, with which to influence the state directly – through proffering bribes, incentives, or threats of capital flight or investment strikes – ensuring favorable treatment for themselves, increasing income and wealth disparities, and undermining democracy. In the United States, the reckless predatory lending that triggered the subprime mortgage scandal in 2008 hit low-income households hardest, culminating in foreclosures, devalued homes, and impoverishment for many families, but the corporations that played a central role in this disaster were deemed "too big to fail" and were promptly bailed out at public expense.[8] Indeed, corporate bailouts (like those of the "Big Three" automakers) through taxpayer funds, loans, capital injections, and measures such as the Troubled Asset Relief Program (TARP) are commonplace, complementing the equally routine admonishment of poor families for their dependence on the state and the ongoing retrenchment of public support for them. Workers – particularly in the Anglo nations – face considerably more objection and resistance when they attempt to pool their resources through the formation of unions or engage in collective actions such as striking and picketing to defend their interests (Aalbers, 2016; Dimick, 2019; Frege & Kelly, 2003; Glasbeek, 2017, 2018a, 2018b; Mitchnick & Etherington, 2006; Panitch & Swartz, 1984).

The owners of capital, through limited liability, gain another power – a kind of immunity that few other market actors possess. Since shareholders are only liable for the amount that they have invested, they cannot be held personally responsible for any further losses or obligations incurred by the corporation. Although often touted as great "risk takers" and hence deserving of the exorbitant gains they may reap, investors are protected in that their personal wealth is not available to anyone the corporation owes money to, even if the corporation cannot meet its obligations because of its efforts to return profits to them. Limited liability encourages shareholder indifference to the creation of risk to others by their corporation. Focused on short-term increases in the value of their shares, investors are more willing to endorse or overlook corporate actions that produce harm-inflicting goods and services, eliminate jobs and reduce wages, displace people from their homes and neighborhoods, exhaust nonrenewable resources and destroy the environment, and exploit poor workers in developing nations. The real risks of the corporation's actions are shifted to others (Bakan, 2004; Barak, 2017; Glasbeek, 2002, 2017, 2018b; Whyte, 2020).

Corporations are legally authorized to pursue their own self-interests above those of their workers, the community, and the nation. In fact, the directors and managers who run the corporations have a fiduciary duty to serve the interests of the shareholders who collectively constitute corporations. These directors and managers also enjoy a form of limited responsibility; they are "exempted from the norms of personal responsibility by corporate law" (Glasbeek, 2002, p. 12). Moreover, they are handsomely rewarded by shareholders when they increase share value. Lawyer and law professor Joel Bakan (2004) suggests that the constitution of the corporation and the web of laws it operates within have created an organization unlike any other – a kind of psychopath that is *required* to promote its own interests above all others – and one that consistently engages in reckless and irresponsible behavior to do so. Consequently, the idea of corporate "social responsibility" is somewhat of an oxymoron: a legally hobbled nonstarter.

Another source of power is conferred upon corporations through their status as legal persons. "Corporate personhood" means that corporations have many of the same rights enjoyed by citizens, but, as noted above, they have been exempted from many of the responsibilities to which people and other organizations in society are held. Recipients of social assistance and unemployment insurance benefits are routinely chided and disciplined for what is deemed "irresponsible" behavior (however minor), but corporations enjoy impunity for legally proscribed or encouraged acts of irresponsibility that are far more consequential and often violate human rights (Barak, 2017; Glasbeek, 2002, 2017; Whyte, 2020). This is not, as commonly thought, simply a matter of corporations being under-regulated or deregulated. Rather, they are legally licensed and emboldened to act recklessly with relatively little fear of repercussion. As the United Nations High Commissioner for Human Rights (2016) noted,

> Business enterprises can be involved with human rights abuses in many different ways.... At present, accountability and remedy in such cases is often elusive. (p. 3)

Incorporation provided companies with new capacities and advantages, including limited liability, easy transferability of shares, and perpetual existence. Corporations exist independently of their owners (surviving their death). Like individuals, they can buy, sell, and lease property, but corporations can do so forever (Cerri, 2018; Glasbeek, 2002, 2017). Initially, the rights of corporations in the United States were strictly circumscribed, and centered on upholding their contracts.[9] However, throughout the nineteenth century, as corporations grew larger and wealthier during the Gilded Age, they steadily increased their rights through a barrage of aggressive, successive, and successful court challenges, culminating in a Supreme Court decision in 1868 that would lead to their personhood status. As a result, they accumulated rights that had been created to protect people, including the right to free speech (allowing generous corporate contributions to political candidates, campaigns, and parties) and the right to privacy (which can be used to conceal corporate actions and keep out regulators). This expanding body of rights concentrates and amplifies corporations' power, undermining the protection of people and the environment (Hartmann, 2002; Winkler, 2018a, 2018b).[10] By examining the systemic roots of power, we can see beyond the popular idea that poverty and inequality are simply the unfortunate but innocent outcome of ongoing social change and development.

Even some of capitalism's most insightful and harshest detractors, including Marx, have readily acknowledged that capitalism is a revolutionary and dynamic socioeconomic system, unleashing productive capacities and opportunities that were unattainable and unimaginable under earlier stable but stagnant socioeconomic systems such as feudalism.[11] Capitalism emancipated people from their formal socio-legal bondage and dependence upon aristocratic feudal lords, and it promoted many technological advances, inventions, and innovations – from railroads, automobiles, steamships, and jets to indoor plumbing, electricity, computers, and modern medicine. It dramatically improved living standards and life expectancies for many people while fostering greater possibilities for the general development of human potential. But, because it is a system that is based upon the domination of capital, competition, and the pursuit of profits above everything else – with all of its aims and efforts to address human needs necessarily ancillary to this central goal – it also aggressively promotes the introduction of new technologies and forms of social organization that generate new waves and forms of insecurity, inequality, and poverty wherever it takes root. It has spawned innovations that have improved daily life for many people, even if the greatest benefits have disproportionately accrued to the developed world and been enjoyed by its most well-off members. It has gradually and often markedly reduced the prices we pay for the dizzying array of products it perpetually introduces, mass-produces, and vigorously markets. But, through the creation of monopolies in many markets, it has artificially and dramatically increased the price of many essential products. Giant pharmaceutical and health corporations, for example, reap enormous profits from patients held hostage for the drugs they need to improve and save their lives.[12] System-generated incentives and laws allow corporations to raise and sustain prices for drugs and other essential products and services, which, in turn, are intimately related to higher and deeper poverty levels. In the United States, the cost of life-saving drugs and healthcare is a major cause of bankruptcy (e.g., Greene & Riggs, 2015; Himmelstein et al., 2009; Ramsey et al., 2013).

Corporations' calculated focus on growth, competition, and enlarging market shares routinely generates contradictory developments, creating great insecurity for countless families. "Flexible" work regimes have eroded traditional job security and reduced wages while often placing greater emphasis upon social control, discipline, and surveillance across many workplaces. Hundreds of thousands of relatively good-paying jobs in rich developed nations have been steadily eliminated through the continual development of new forms of automation, robotics, computers, and other technologies, while the introduction of satellite communications, fiber optics, the internet, container ships, and other innovations in the field of transportation have made it much easier for corporations to outsource assembly work or relocate industries to domestic or offshore locations with significantly lower operating costs and fewer regulations and restrictions protecting workers, including children (ILO, 2017; Standing, 2011). Manufacturers of clothing, toys, food, cell phones, computers, and myriad other products employ workers in developing nations where they are paid low wages and are often required to labor in dangerous factories with long workdays and few rights – and where paramilitary groups may be employed to intimidate union leaders and others who focus attention on the deplorable conditions and destitution workers experience (Karim, 2020; International Trade Union Confederation, 2020; Solidarity Center, 2006; Thomas, 2009). These conditions are all too familiar to historians of industrialization in the nations of the developed world (see Box 6.1). Moreover, the popular defense celebrating the benefits of injecting foreign investment in poor nations obfuscates the roots of their underdevelopment and impoverishment as exploited colonies and satellites of those in the wealthy capitalist world (Brooks, 2019; Lindio-McGovern & Wallimann, 2016).[13]

Within much of the developed world, this job relocation has led to higher levels of unemployment and poverty and a severely eroded tax base, with a consequent weakening of social supports for families and a marked decline in the quality of life for almost everyone but the wealthiest members of society. In such a sociopolitical climate, the industries opting to remain in these rich nations have often been able to intimidate domestic workers into accepting lower wages and substandard working conditions by merely threatening to relocate operations to more accommodating sites – while enjoying large subsidies, cheap loans, large tax breaks, and relaxed restrictions and laws from the state.

BOX 6.1 CHILD LABOR TODAY: REPLICATING NINETEENTH-CENTURY BRITAIN

Friedrich Engels (1845/2009), Karl Marx's close friend and collaborator, was among the first to document thoroughly the starkly oppressive working and living conditions of the working class in England, the first capitalist nation to industrialize. Many social reformers, including political philosophers and novelists such as William Godwin and Charles Dickens, and Romantic poets, including William Wordsworth, William Blake, and Elizabeth Barrett Browning, graphically depicted and condemned the wretched lives of the masses of working-class children in factories, fields, and mines. Historian E.P. Thompson (1968, p. 384) referred to the extensive and intensive "exploitation of little children" as one of the "most shameful" chapters of British history. But the British experience was hardly unique; indeed, it was largely replicated in the workplaces of its colonies and across all industrializing capitalist nations. In the United States, children worked in cotton and textile mills, mines, and glass factories; in Canada, they were employed in clothing and shoe industries, cigar factories, woodworking, and printing. Children often worked for twelve to sixteen hours a day in crowded, cramped, oppressively hot, poorly ventilated, and highly hazardous conditions, often without breaks. They were viewed as more docile, compliant, and easier to control than adults and could be subject to beatings and whippings or forced to wear heavy weights around their necks if they did not meet work quotas, did inferior work, arrived to work late, talked, or fell asleep (de Coninck-Smith et al., 1997; Hindman, 2002; Kealey, 1973; Parr, 1980, 1982; Pike, 1966).

The bleak living standards and appallingly cruel working environments that were widespread in the factories, mills, and mines during the Industrial Revolution were slowly but steadily improved through the massive and tireless efforts of organized labor in the nations that constitute the rich developed world today. At great cost, including the loss of countless lives, workers fought to regain some humanity by campaigning for and attaining safer workplace conditions; shorter working hours; better wages, health, and retirement benefits; labor rights; and the creation of a more just society for everyone. Yet in recent decades, market forces have provoked and hastened a replication of early abusive and hazardous capitalist workplaces, particularly through the export of jobs and industries to nations that are in desperate need of investment. The International Labour Organization's (ILO, 2017) most recent quadrennial report estimates that there were approximately 152 million child laborers in the world in 2016, with 73 million of them employed in hazardous work. Many of those children work in industries under conditions that were once prevalent in the rich nations of the developed world, providing cheap products for their populations today.

The expansion of the low-wage sector, in turn, makes it impossible for many families to survive without taking on huge debt (Gautie & Schmitt, 2010; Ross & Bateman, 2019; Valencia, 2018).

This "globalization" of work has not been confined to blue-collar labor. The shift to a service- and knowledge-based economy was supposed to provide an abundance of high-wage skilled and semiskilled replacement positions in the white-collar sector of wealthy nations. But the creation of new technologies has facilitated extensive job displacement and the redirection of new job growth in this sector too. White-collar work across diverse industry lines, including accounting, financial analysis, claims adjusting, biotechnology research, information technology (IT), telemarketing, and telecommunications has been increasingly exported abroad in recent years. Work has also been steadily "outsourced" to consumers via electronic gas pumps, internet banking, ATMs, online purchasing, and self-checkout scanners. These developments have markedly reduced costs for many companies, allowing them to lower consumer prices greatly and capture larger market shares in wealthy developed nations (Chandy, 2016; ILO, 2019; Janoski et al., 2014; Valencia, 2018). However, without a commensurate expansion of jobs that pay well and in the context of rapidly declining social supports and benefits, these innovations and trends also have encouraged higher levels of unemployment, significantly lower wages for those in the paid workforce, and greater numbers of people living in poverty in many of these nations.

These changes have also forced many one-salary families to send two income earners into the paid labor force – where they often take on two or more low-wage jobs – *and* to increase their household debt loads greatly just to make ends meet. According to the US Bureau of Labor Statistics almost 4 percent of the workforce was employed in contingent or temporary jobs in 2018, the equivalent of six million workers; the percentage of the US labor force with multiple jobs held steady at around 5 percent between 2010 and 2018 (US Department of Labor, 2019; see also Kalleberg, 2009, 2011).[14] But, like estimates of US homelessness, this figure almost certainly underestimates the percentage of people in the labor force working in multiple jobs. The Current Population Survey (CPS) data used by the Bureau of Labor Statistics (BLS) to determine how many people have multiple jobs relies on "in person" or landline telephone interviews, but people so employed are difficult to reach this way. Moreover, they may not realize that their self-employment or "moonlighting" in the gig economy counts as employment, or they may not report this additional work to avoid being taxed.

The departure of large numbers of better-paid white-collar jobs has undermined the role and promise of the education system as a primary means of social mobility. After mortgage debt, student debt is the second highest consumer debt category, ahead of both credit cards and auto loans in the United States. According to the US Federal Reserve, the average student debt in 2016 was over $37,000; cumulative student loan debt reached $1.56 trillion in 2018 (Friedman, 2018; Gebelhoff, 2018; Singletary, 2018). Apart from all of this, postsecondary education is a "supply-side" policy; it improves the qualifications of workers but does not ensure there will be jobs for them when they graduate, and postsecondary graduates increasingly leave university to take on unpaid internships, temporary work, or minimum-wage employment, which makes tackling their debt a challenge. With rising tuition and other costs of postsecondary education and with steeply declining public supports, students from middle-class families graduate from colleges and universities with far higher debt loads and far fewer job prospects than ever before while poor and lower-income families have far fewer resources and much less time to support the education of their children or to improve their children's chances of getting ahead (Bernstein, 2007; Hartlep et al., 2017; Marsh, 2011).[15]

The visions and promises of technological utopias advanced in the first decades of the post–WWII period failed to recognize that the problems that are identified, and the solutions that are embraced to address them, are necessarily driven by competition and the need for larger market shares, procurement of higher profits, and company growth. The development and introduction of new technologies and innovations have been largely guided by compulsions to lower labor and other costs, not by humanitarian interest in eliminating exhausting, monotonous, alienating, or dangerous jobs; creating secure and fulfilling lives for families and healthy vibrant communities; or ending poverty. Indeed, many innovations and inventions – including some that could extend or save human lives – have often been shelved or suppressed when they threatened corporate profitability (Saunders & Levine, 2004).[16] New technologies have also been introduced with astonishingly little consideration of how consumer demand for new products and services would be generated among people who have lost their jobs, had their wages slashed, or fallen into poverty.[17] The primary response to the problem of "under-consumption" has been to devise new ways to encourage families to borrow more money, increase their debt loads, and become more reliant upon banks and other financial institutions. The long-standing defense that capitalism bestows enormous riches on a small minority but also necessarily increases prosperity and opportunities overall is forcefully contradicted by increasingly asymmetrical distributions of wealth and income, higher levels of unemployment, and steadily climbing rates and deeper levels of poverty across the developed capitalist world over the past few decades – developments greatly facilitated by deregulation and neoliberal austerity (e.g., Brown, 2017; Collins, 2018; Dorling, 2014, 2018; Heisz, 2016; Piketty, 2014).

Capitalism's relentless drive for profits and market expansion, and its promotion of ceaseless consumption, has also ablated social and environmental landscapes. Capitalist systems are premised upon the idea of unlimited growth, but they operate in a world with strict social and ecological limits and finite resources. Just as they impulsively foster a reduction of jobs, lower wages, and higher levels of poverty – which dampen demand for the commodities that they ceaselessly conjure – they also recklessly vitiate and exhaust the nonrenewable natural resources and raw materials required for manufacturing, undermining the very foundation of production and accumulation and irreparably damaging the environment (Barak, 2017; Bradshaw, 2018; Magdoff & Foster, 2011; O'Connor, 1998; Whyte, 2020).[18] The most brutally adverse effects of this environmental degradation have the heaviest impact upon the poorest, most vulnerable members of society. The rural poor, farmers living on the margins, and Indigenous communities are heavily and directly reliant upon the cheap, easily accessible sources of clean water, food, energy, and shelter that ecosystems furnish, and on the opportunities that these ecosystems provide for people reliant on the land to earn a modest income. But the plunder and desecration of the environment has severely undermined their ability to support themselves, led to a deterioration of their health, and reduced their longevity. Environmental destruction has been accompanied by repeated violations of the sovereignty and rights of Indigenous peoples around the globe, including those found in very wealthy countries such as Canada and the United States. Much environmental damage has been wrought by the use of coal and petroleum, the lifeblood and prime energy sources of global capitalism. Diminishing petroleum supplies have encouraged the development of "alternative" energy sources that can be even more harmful. The creation of ethanol, for example, diverts supplies of corn, grains, and cropland – urgently needed to address widespread poverty and hunger in the world – toward fuel production. The oil created from tar sands releases even greater amounts of harmful greenhouse gases than conventional oil extraction (Foster, 2008; Klare, 2004; Shiva, 2008).

New technologies and other innovations and practices that lower production costs while concurrently wreaking havoc on families, communities, and ecosystems are systemically generated within and by capitalism. The dense foundation of legislation on which capitalism rests ensures that the rights of private property supersede those of individuals, families, and communities; capitalist enterprises are increasingly free to relocate, automate, and decimate. "The corporation's legally defined mandate," as legal scholar Joel Bakan (2004) underscores, "is to pursue, relentlessly and without exception, its own self-interest, regardless of the often harmful consequences it might cause to others" (pp. 1–2).

A hauntingly similar indictment of capitalism was voiced by renowned physicist Albert Einstein (1949/2009), over half a century ago:

> The economic anarchy of capitalist society as it exists today is, in my opinion, the real source of the evil. We see before us a huge community of producers the members of which are unceasingly striving to deprive each other of the fruits of their collective labor – not by force, but on the whole in faithful compliance with legally established rules. (p. 59).

A system predicated upon interminable growth and which promotes the notion that corporations and individuals are entitled to as much of the world's resources, assets, and wealth as they can seize is unjust, unethical, and entirely unsustainable. The system-focused perspective usefully reminds us that simply replacing the top layers of corporate executives, industrialists, financiers, and bankers will not fundamentally address these problems and issues because their replacements will be inclined, enticed, compelled, empowered, and rewarded to perform in a very similar manner. They are just "playing the game": doing what must be done to survive and prosper in the global market and engaging the state to enforce their claims to the resources they garner in the market. This does not absolve them of responsibility for their actions. They have played central roles in setting, shaping, and continually revising the rules, regulations, laws, institutions, and ideas that constitute the sociopolitical environment in which they operate, acting to safeguard and advance their own interests at great expense to society and our world. The way these inherent systemic pressures and restrictions are manifest is partly contingent on the shifting balance of power among classes and other key actors in society, which has varied substantially across nations and time. This dimension of power has received considerable attention in cross-national poverty research and has yielded invaluable insights but is missed if we focus only on the systemic context of capitalism.

THE SOCIOPOLITICAL ROOTS OF POVERTY: THE BALANCE OF POWER

Although the two societal-level perspectives are closely related, explanations that emphasize the "balance of power" in society highlight "human agency" rather than systemic determinants. These explanations focus on *who* holds great power and how they wield it in order to account for the existence and growth of poverty and inequality. Some of them set their sights on the upper echelons – the capitalist class or "power elite" that controls key economic, normative, and political resources in society. Although the primary focus of this body of research is on power rather than on poverty and homelessness, it helps to elucidate how the powerful dominate and shape the lives of people with far more limited means, including the most resource-deprived members of society. By virtue of its control over the economy, its ownership of most of the popular mainstream media, and its direct and indirect influence on the state, a numerically small group of people is able to wield an enormous level of power, allowing it to manipulate the distribution of wealth and income, thereby increasing the level and depth of poverty. This powerful elite also influences the way poor people are viewed by the public, and the forms of state assistance they receive (e.g., Carroll, 2010; Carroll & Sapinski, 2018; Domhoff, 1990, 2014; Miliband, 1974, 1977). However, other researchers in this tradition emphasize the fluidity of power relationships, highlighting how poverty can be greatly attenuated when the balance of power in society is altered (e.g., Esping-Andersen, 1985a; Korpi, 1983; Stephens, 1980).

Power from Above

Most people would agree that an unmatched level of power is conferred upon the numerically tiny group controlling the world's largest corporations. The members of this group hold vast personal and family fortunes that approach or exceed $100 billion. With virtually unlimited economic resources, elites can commit immense sums to fund political candidates, campaigns, and lobby groups that promote views and policies that secure and further aggrandize their wealth and power. These include a range of fiscal measures that tax income from labor more heavily than income from wealth, as well as policies that promote low minimum wage levels, the retrenchment of social programs and supports, and the enervation of legislation and agencies that protect people, communities, and the environment. This outsized political influence is further bolstered by "billionaire activism" through tax-exempt "philanthropic" mega foundations. In the United States, the early twentieth century's large, affluent philanthropic foundations, such as the Russell Sage Foundation, the Carnegie Corporation, and the Rockefeller Foundation – touting grand but often open-ended, ill-defined missions to "improve the human condition" and "promote the well-being of mankind" – were typically run by boards of trustees who operated at some distance from the affluent families that endowed them. They were largely public relations entities, designed to restore the reputations of unscrupulous business moguls who had amassed huge family fortunes during the Gilded Age. The twenty-first century's foundations are much more focused, strategic, and impact oriented – adopting an approach sometimes referred to as "venture philanthropy" or "philanthrocapitalism." They openly promote neoliberal and conservative values, including championing free markets, private schools, low minimum wages, privatization of the public sector, and welfare state retrenchment (Barkan, 2013; McFadden, 2014; Nichols & McChesney, 2013; Rothkopf, 2008; West, 2014).[19] Of course, Canada and the United Kingdom have their own foundations and think tanks. Some of the most influential ones in the UK, such as the Adam Smith Institute, the Centre for Policy Studies, the Institute of Economic Affairs, and Policy Exchange, receive substantial donations from wealthy benefactors in the US (Evans et al., 2019; *The Week* Staff, 2019). Right-wing think tanks are closely connected to conservative political parties and to the corporations, foundations, and wealthy elites that help to fund them. Not surprisingly, the conclusions reached in their studies are routinely recounted in the corporate media.

In the United States, the most influential newspapers and media outlets comprise media networks that are often central components of larger conglomerates and reflect the interests, orientations, and biases of the billionaire moguls who own them (Chomsky, 2011; McChesney, 1998, 2008; Noam, 2015; Vinton, 2016). Media in the UK and Canada are also highly concentrated and closely linked to a small number of very large corporations (e.g., CMCRP, 2019; Media Reform Coalition, 2019; Noam, 2015). But the influence and impact of these huge, like-minded media conglomerates is transnational. Giant mixed media conglomerates, such as AT&T/WarnerMedia, Disney/21st Century Fox, News Corp (Fox Entertainment Group), Verizon, Comcast, Netflix, and Sony, are often closely tied to financial, oil, pharmaceutical, manufacturing, retailing, and distributing industries through vertical integration (ownership), interlocking directorates across their boards of directors and dependence upon them for advertising dollars. These dense connections ensure that members of the elite have the incentives, opportunities, and power to shape dominant views. Critical appraisals of capitalism, including any notion that it has any responsibility for poverty or homelessness, are virtually nonexistent in the popular mainstream media that most people rely on for information and entertainment.

Poverty and homelessness themselves are rarely and usually only superficially covered in the media. Stereotypical, unflattering portrayals of the working class, the poor, and homeless people in newspaper reports, television programs, and films denigrate them and serve to legitimate their position at the bottom of society – especially in the case of racialized groups (Clawson & Trice, 2000; Gilens, 1999; Larsen & Dejgaard, 2013; Shildrick, 2018; Swanson, 2001). Media coverage of poverty typically highlights the "bad choices" or "bad luck" of particular individuals, and it emphasizes that the only way for them to transcend their unenviable circumstances is through education, training, employment, and hard work – and through reducing their dependence upon state supports. Other reasons for poverty and homelessness are rarely seriously broached as central causes, including the increasing commodification and financialization of housing as large private equity firms and hedge funds amass foreclosed homes, rental housing, and other properties; the gentrification of working-class neighborhoods; the reluctance of states to foster the provision of affordable public or private housing and protect tenants from eviction; the retrenchment of housing allowances and other social supports and services; the rising cost of drugs and healthcare; stagnant wages; and the elimination of jobs due to automation and capital flight. The corporations that own the media are the ones often largely responsible for these very developments and conditions (Doyle, 2002; McChesney, 1997, 2008; Noam, 2015; Steven, 2004).

In the Anglo nations, we seldom see programs or articles in the popular media about countries that have been more successful in addressing poverty, homelessness, and inequality. Media accounts critical of capitalism and the free market almost never appear unless the people who subscribe to these views are marginalized or derided as eccentric or heretical. The media typically present the narrow, particular interests of the economic elite – such as low taxes, low minimum wages, and the retrenchment of welfare states – as universal interests that will benefit all and the existing social reality as the best or only credible option possible. Critiques of the status quo are rarely brooked, and even relatively moderate proposals that have worked well in other nations – such as strong unions, comprehensive and generous social programs and services, and universal healthcare, still lacking in the United States – are often discredited as "unworkable" or targeted as a cause of unemployment and poverty, not a solution.[20] People are encouraged to accept poverty and inequality as inevitable, and to hold those at the bottom of society accountable for their station.

Of course, the super-wealthy members of society also have greater *direct* influence over the government – beyond shaping public ideas and values through the media and endorsing and funding political candidates and campaigns. Many studies have documented the considerable overlap between state and economic elites in the Anglo nations and across the capitalist world (e.g., Carroll, 2010; Carroll & Sapinski, 2018; Clement, 1977; Domhoff, 1990, 2014; Phillips, 2018; Useem, 1986). This is particularly striking in the United States. In 2009, less than 1 percent of the American people were millionaires, but 66 percent of the members of the Senate and 41 percent of the members of the House of Representatives were millionaires. By 2012, a majority of the members of Congress were millionaires. The most powerful people in the US government have typically been super wealthy, but Donald Trump, the first billionaire president in the United States, and the roster of billionaire and multimillionaire friends and donors that comprised his cabinet and network of top advisors were the richest governing group in US history.[21] Studies of the US executive from the late nineteenth century to the present indicate that the overwhelming majority of presidential cabinet members have come from the economic elite and the corporate world, whatever their political party orientation. In capitalist societies, the people who hold command positions within the state tend to have views and promote policies that reflect their origins in the world of business and property. Alternative viewpoints, experiences, and proposals – such as those of working people, the poor, and the homeless – are largely absent, or dismissed as uninformed (Freitag, 1975; Gill, 2018; Miliband, 1977; Peterson-Withorn, 2017; Swank, 1998).

Wealth and power have allowed those who wield them to alter the rules and regulations of the game continually and in myriad ways – to seize *greater* wealth and power – increasing inequality and weakening the fabric of society, most notably in the United States. Intellectual property rights (e.g., patents, trademarks, copyrights, industrial design rights) have been enlarged and extended, creating longer periods of monopoly and higher prices for consumers, and they have become a central means of corporate tax avoidance through interfirm royalty payment schemes. Bankruptcy laws create economic opportunities for large corporations to renegotiate or abrogate labor contracts by threatening to declare bankruptcy and close operations if they do not receive significant wage, benefit, and work rule concessions from their workers. New fiscal legislation has reduced corporate taxes, marginal tax rates on the highest incomes, and estate taxes on great wealth. Antitrust laws and financial regulations have been weakened, and the use of legal and illegal offshore tax evasion schemes and havens have, in effect, been broadly endorsed.[22] New free-trade agreements make it easier for corporations to outsource jobs to low-wage nations with lax labor and environmental laws. Restrictions on the corporate funding of political campaigns have been weakened in the name of "free speech." If all else fails, or if a government is elected that is viewed as hostile to their goals, economic elites can simply threaten to move their industries abroad, or actually engage in capital flight. No other actors in society even remotely approximate the economic, ideological, and political clout wielded by wealthy corporate elites in capitalist societies. Holding few assets and facing a complex of compounding deprivations and difficulties, poor families are easily marginalized and excluded and, if they are dependent upon public social supports, held in disdain (Reich, 2012, 2016, 2020; Stiglitz, 2013).

Power from Below

In capitalist societies, the people with the greatest power, by definition and default, are those who own and control substantial capital. But power is also a function of organization. An overwhelming body of research accumulated over the past four decades has demonstrated that the prevalence and severity of poverty, and many other forms of inequality, are much lower in countries where the working class is well organized and politically represented. Power-centered sociopolitical theories, such as "power resources theory" (PRT), focus upon the "balance of power" among classes (and other groups) in society and the sociopolitical outcomes this engenders, drawing our attention, in particular, to the strength of organized working classes. These theories document how the balance of power can vary markedly over time and place. Where and when the working class has greater power, poverty and inequality are notably lower and less severe (e.g., Esping-Andersen, 1985a, 1985b; Korpi, 1980, 1983; Stephens, 1980).

In the socioeconomic sphere, people can gain power by organizing. A substantial body of research indicates that countries with high levels of unionization, such as the Nordic nations, have markedly lower rates of poverty and inequality than those with low levels of unionization, such as the Anglo nations. Unions can have a *direct* impact on poverty rates by raising wages and an *indirect* impact by supporting more generous welfare states. High levels of union density are associated with fewer low-paid jobs in the economy and higher earnings for all workers, not just those who are unionized – including those who are less skilled, contingently employed, and most vulnerable to poverty (Denice & Rosenfeld, 2018; Kalleberg et al., 1981; Rosenfeld & Denice, 2019; Rosenfeld & Laird, 2016). Unions promote networks of rules, regulations, and laws that secure greater protections, rights, and benefits; raise minimum wage levels; and foster more redistributive social and fiscal policies (Bradley et al., 2003; Brady, 2009; Kristal, 2010; Moller et al., 2003). Declines in union density are associated with higher income shares for the top 1 percent and higher CEO compensation levels (Gomez & Tzioumis, 2006; Huang et al., 2017; Huber et al., 2017; Volscho & Kelley, 2012). In the Nordic nations, where levels of unionization are high *and* where union federations are organized into confederations that coordinate union strategies and efforts, the impact of the labor movement on poverty and inequality is striking.[23]

In the sociopolitical sphere, poverty can be reduced via the existence and incumbency of leftist parties (labor, social democratic, socialist, and communist parties). Their impact on poverty rates and inequality is specially marked when they have held power, alone or in coalitions, for significant periods (Brady, 2003b, 2009; Huber & Stephens, 2001; Moller et al., 2003). PRT explains why some countries, like the Nordic nations, have much lower rates and less severe forms of poverty and inequality than others. But it also helps to explain why there is variation across the liberal-regime Anglo nations. Canada and the UK have had notably higher levels of unionization than the US in the post–WWII period, and leftist parties that have held power at the national (UK) or subnational (Canada) level. This has fostered a somewhat more collectivist culture and, in turn, more developed welfare states. In the United States, where labor has been less organized and less represented in the political sphere, poor people and other marginalized groups have engaged in various forms of spontaneous disruptive politics, including marches, protests, rallies, riots, sit-ins, strikes, and other forms of civil disorder and insurgency to bring about change. But the social programs and other responses they have triggered have been less supportive, comprehensive, and universally accessible – and often linked to greater social control (Eidlin, 2018; Harles, 2017; Olsen, 2002, 2011; Piven & Cloward, 1971, 1979; Piven & Minnite, 2016; Zuberi, 2006).

An expansive and diverse body of research has attempted to account for the relatively high levels of poverty and inequality in the United States – even among the Anglo nations – and its notably more limited efforts to address both through social policy and the welfare state by exploring the relative weakness of socialism there.[24] While some arguments, such as the notion that capitalism in the United States was more successful and provided greater opportunities for social mobility than in most European nations, have always been empirically weak and are even less compelling today, many of the other arguments focusing on national "cultures" have greater explanatory power when considered conjointly and when related to the balance of power across classes. The UK, unlike the US, had a long entrenched feudal tradition built on community and cooperation across hierarchical social orders. With the Declaration of Independence and victory in the Revolutionary War of Independence, the United States severed its ties to Britain; Canada remained a British colony and became home for tens of thousands of British Loyalists who migrated there from the US, conveying and firmly transplanting their more traditional values. Consequently, it is suggested, the US developed purer forms of liberalism and individualism than in the UK and Canada, ideological strains that were more resistant to socialism and state support (Horowitz, 1968; Lipset, 1990, 1996; Lipset & Marks, 2000; McNaught, 1988).[25]

The US labor movement was also more divided than in the UK and Canada. Rather than "industrial unionism," which organizes workers by industry, regardless of skill, the dominant American Federation of Labor

(AFL) embraced "craft unionism," a model of trade unionism that organized workers on the basis of skill. Consequently, it excluded people who were not skilled craft workers, including large numbers of women, African Americans, and immigrants. Some historians argue that the US labor movement was not so different from that in the UK; its Knights of Labor federation was the equivalent of the UK's inclusive "new unions." But US employers were much more hostile to working-class organization and, partly due to high levels of economic concentration, had greater resources to more thoroughly crush class-based unionism and solidarity before they could become institutionalized (Eidlin, 2018; Fantasia & Voss, 2004; Kennedy, 1996; Olsen, 2002; Voss, 1993). Racism also played a significant role in dividing and weakening the working class in the United States. White workers often aligned themselves with white elites against Black workers, who were generally excluded from trade unions and, given their more desperate living conditions, were often called upon by employers as strikebreakers, deepening this division (Arnesen, 2007; Leiman, 2010). Consequently, "when the working classes of Europe were building durable and resilient socialist movements, the American working class was hopelessly split along racial lines" (Pope, 2016, p. 1590; Shalev & Korpi, 1980). Preeminent sociologist and activist William Edward Burghardt Du Bois (1933) highlighted the gravity of this division:

> ... while Negro labor in America suffers because of the fundamental inequities of the whole capitalistic system, the lowest and most fatal degree of its suffering comes not from the capitalists but from fellow white laborers. It is white labor that deprives the Negro of his right to vote, denies him education, denies him affiliation with trade unions, expels him from decent houses and neighborhoods, and heaps upon him the public insults of open color discrimination. (p. 104)

In the United Kingdom, industrial unionism gained ground in the 1890s, and the labor movement launched the Independent Labour Party (ILP) in 1893 and the Labour Party in 1900, which would play a significant role in the development of the UK's welfare state, reducing inequality and poverty (Pelling, 1991; Saville, 1988). The AFL, in contrast, embraced "business unionism" with a narrow, economistic agenda centered on wage bargaining rather than the "social movement unionism" more common in many European nations and geared toward broad social change and political activity. The AFL was intolerant of socialist doctrine, viewed public social programs as a sign that unions could not take care of their workers, and rejected the idea of creating a labor or socialist party. Rather it acted as a lobby group, putting its electoral might behind whichever mainstream party provided the greatest support for its members (Goldfield, 1989; Moody, 1988). In Canada, a left-wing social democratic/labor party, the Co-operative Commonwealth Federation (CCF) was created in 1932 and formed an alliance with the Canadian Labour Congress (CLC) in 1961, leading to the emergence of the New Democratic Party (NDP). Neither the NDP nor its predecessor has ever held power at the federal level, but the party's incumbency at the provincial level and its periods of rising popularity at the national level have played a crucial role in the more supportive character of the Canadian welfare state, and in Canada's lower rates of poverty and inequality relative to those found in the United States (Eidlin, 2018; Lexier et al., 2018; Naylor, 2016; Olsen, 2002).

The balance of power between economic elites and organized working classes can have a significant impact on poverty and inequality by reshaping the laws, rules, regulations, and institutions in capitalist society. But the character of state structures can also promote or hinder the adoption of policies addressing poverty. In Canada, for example, the federal structure of the state allowed the CCF/NDP to assume power at the provincial level where it introduced and "auditioned" measures – most notably healthcare – that would later spread across the nation and be embraced by the federal government. In the United States, the nature of the electoral system in the national arena has inhibited the formation of viable "third" parties outside the entrenched two-party system (Olsen, 2002).[26] Moreover, because each of the fifty US states, regardless of the size of their populations, elects two representatives to the Senate, largely rural states with relatively low population densities are significantly overrepresented in Congress's upper chamber. As a result, large swaths of significant urban poverty in larger states often fail to receive the attention and resources they require when the senators determine which issues are most pressing and how they will be resolved.[27] Like rules, regulations, and laws, state structures are the "residue" of past conflicts and represent a congealed, earlier representation of the balance of power among classes and other groups (Esping-Andersen et al., 1976; Olsen, 2002; Pierson, 2004).

The markedly higher rates of unionization and the lengthy incumbency of left-wing parties in some countries, most notably Sweden and the Nordic nations, have generally generated more progressive social, economic, and fiscal policies and legislation, and instituted more developed, comprehensive, generous, and accessible welfare states, culminating in much lower and less severe poverty than in the Anglo nations (Brady, 2009; Brady et al., 2016; Olsen, 2002). Within the Anglo world, the greater power resources of labor in Canada and the United Kingdom have led to lower poverty levels and greater social supports than in the United States. The gains achieved in these nations are not illusory; rather they reflect a "compromise" between opposing classes and groups in society and the balance of power among them at a particular juncture. Some adherents to the PRT approach view these compromises as a reflection of mutual "cooperation" among a society's classes and groups; proponents of this perspective accentuate the possibilities for steady gains for all. Others usefully remind us that the "balance of power" is fluid, shifting with structural change and developments, such as "globalization" and automation, which can undermine or erode compromise agreements and welfare states and lead to a return to higher rates of poverty and inequality, as in the current period, even in exemplary nations such as Sweden (e.g., Kananen, 2016; Olsen, 2013).[28] The erosion of labor strength and the consequent changes in the balance of power in the Anglo nations in recent decades are briefly reviewed next.

The Changing Balance of Power in Canada, the United Kingdom, and the United States

Capitalism has developed through several stages and assumed varied forms but has proven to be an extraordinarily crisis-prone system almost from the moment of inception, oscillating between periods of growth and downturn.[29] The ways that states have responded to these systemic crises – including how they have addressed poverty – have been partly shaped by the ability of people to organize and challenge powerful economic elites and promote the development of a range of institutional and social supports. In most nations of the advanced capitalist world, the greatest gains achieved by workers occurred in the first few post–WWII decades. Labor shortages, rising rates of unionization and organization, greater support for political parties on the left, the growing strength of socialist movements, and the existence of noncapitalist alternatives around the globe gave workers considerably more power and influence, even if they were never "in the driver's seat." Under this pressure, wages rose and states assumed greater responsibility for the well-being of their citizens, gradually building up networks of policy measures that provided some degree of insulation from some of the worst market excesses (e.g., Esping-Andersen, 1985a; Hicks, 1991; Hicks & Swank, 1984; Korpi, 1983; Stephens, 1980; Swank, 2002). These policy networks included restrictions on capital, regulations on banks and financial institutions, more progressive forms of taxation, the creation of key public enterprises, and varying blends of income supports, social services, legal protections, and rights that constitute modern welfare states.[30]

There was significant cross-national diversity in the character, scope, and impact of these more or less dense policy grids – with the most far-reaching, supportive, and effective measures generally found in those nations where labor movements were the strongest. With few measures provided as a right to everyone, the welfare states in the Anglo nations did not fully embrace all of their citizens. This has been most strikingly true in the United States, where there are fewer universal social programs and protections in place. Migrants and poor workers employed as domestics and farm laborers – areas where women and most Black men were employed – typically did not qualify for core social programs, including unemployment insurance, minimum wage protection, farm subsidies, and social security in old age (Brittain & Blackstock, 2015; Lieberman, 1998; Neubeck & Cazenave, 2001; Quadagno, 1994; Shewell, 2004; Trattner, 1999).[31] Yet despite significant variation in the generosity and inclusiveness of welfare states across nations, they all allowed for more equitable distributions of resources, promoted higher employment, decreased inequality, and reduced poverty.

However, while these policy packages led to significant gains for many working families, they also reflected the interests of those factions of the capitalist class and corporate community that were willing to reach a compromise. Capitalist systems everywhere remained firmly intact and, with the exception of some important, high-profile new public or state-owned companies and "Crown corporations," most enterprises remained securely under the control of capitalists and their managers in the private sector. Moreover, employers greatly benefitted from the healthier, higher-educated, and better-trained workforces, which had markedly greater capacities to purchase commodities and services. Even in their most advanced and supportive form, capitalist welfare states could be contradictory – both supportive and repressive. This is especially true in the Anglo nations, where discipline and control have been central (Domhoff, 1990, 2014; O'Connor, 1973; Offe, 1972, 1985).

By the late 1950s, industrial and financial capitalists in the Anglo nations were already pressuring states to eliminate or ease many regulations and protective measures that had been recently secured through the "historical compromises" between capital and labor brokered by the state. But it was in the 1970s, amid declining productivity and profitability, spiking energy prices, high unemployment and inflation rates, and great instability, that capitalists redoubled their efforts to undermine these historical accords and the related concessions they afforded workers, and to re-shift the balance of power and control more firmly to capital and the economic elite. The offensive capitalists launched against the working class at this time would gradually transform into neoliberal austerity. This shift in the Anglo nations is best symbolized by the elections of Prime Minister Margaret Thatcher in 1979 and President Ronald Reagan in 1980, as well as in the prominent public-sector labor defeats in the United Kingdom (the National Union of Mineworkers/NUM) and the United States (the Professional Air Traffic Controllers Union/PATCO) that these two leaders championed (Jackson & Saunders, 2012; McCartin, 2011; Milne, 2014; Round, 2013).

In the United States, it was considerably easier to ignite and propel the neoliberal revolution. The power of the US labor movement had already been undermined decades earlier through the Labor Management Relations Act of 1947, and the US welfare state was not nearly as developed or as closely embraced as that in the United Kingdom.[32] The United States lost its war on poverty, Reagan suggested, because social programs, regulations, and other "big government" intrusions were part of the problem, not the solution. Yet even a very cursory cross-national glance at social policy indicators clearly shows that the "big" US welfare state is underdeveloped and stingy compared to most of its counterparts in the rich capitalist world and that poverty rates are much lower in nations with more developed and generous social programs (e.g., Brady, 2009; Bradley et al., 2003; Scruggs & Allan, 2006; Smeeding, 2006a, 2006b). Along with the economic boom ignited by WWII, labor organizations, welfare states, and market regulations were actually among the developments that allowed capitalism to rebound from its collapse in the 1930s. Moreover, the level and severity of poverty in the United States would have been much worse without its frayed, patchy network of social supports. Ignoring all of this, Reagan proudly trumpeted the rolling back of the state as a new start that would provide great opportunity for all. Although already comparatively undeveloped, social supports in the United States were pared back and the conditions for poor families – already among the most distressing across the rich nations of the world – deteriorated further (e.g., Plotnick, 1992; Stoesz & Karger, 1993). Similar retrenchment was soon underway in the UK and Canada (Jackson & Saunders, 2012; Porter, 2012). In Canada, the neoliberal turn began with the election of the Conservative government under Prime Minister Brian Mulroney (1984–1993). Although not as far reaching as in the UK and the US, neoliberalism would be furthered by the Conservative government of Stephen Harper (2006–2015; Porter, 2012). Over the four decades between the economic crisis of the 1970s and the financial collapse of 2007–8, neoliberalism invaded and altered almost every corner of society in the Anglo nations and left a distinctive imprint across the globe. Top elites in large corporate enterprises today candidly admit that they have no real allegiance to their domestic middle and working classes and little sympathy for their plight. Workers in the United States earn ten times more than workers in developing nations, one CEO in the US noted, but they are not ten times as productive, so they must take a pay cut or lose their jobs; another CEO candidly stated that, while the outsourcing of work might be a problem for America, it is not necessarily a problem for American business (Freeland, 2012). Callous market calculations increasingly override social rights, standards of living, and a sense of community.

Poverty and at least some manifestations of inequality (income and wealth inequality in particular) were contained or even notably diminished in the first few decades after WWII across much of the developed capitalist world via broadly similar but nationally distinct aggregations of regulations, laws, and policies and related levels of labor organization and strength. However, a large and rapidly proliferating body of research has shown steadily rising levels of inequality in recent decades, in tandem with the enervation or elimination of these safeguards and protective measures. The past few decades of neoliberalism have witnessed surging income gaps between the wealthy and the middle and working classes; higher levels of unemployment, poverty, and homelessness; increasing misery among the most vulnerable members of society; and fewer opportunities for families across almost all nations in the developed capitalist world. The extent and gravity of these developments vary with how ardently and thoroughly nations have embraced market solutions. In 2015, the world's 62 richest people had the same level of wealth as the bottom 50 percent of the world's population (3.6 billion people); the richest 1 percent held half of all the assets in the world. The following year, just 8 billionaires had as much wealth as the 3.6 billion people that comprised the poorest 50 percent of humanity (Credit Suisse Research Institute, 2016; Oxfam, 2016, 2017). Inequality has been conspicuous in the Anglo nations – where it is now as pronounced as it was in the 1920s and approximates that of the notoriously class-ridden "Gilded Age" of the late nineteenth century – and these nations have sustained high rates and deep levels of poverty.[33]

Many solutions proposed to address poverty and inequality call for a return to the "golden age" of the historical compromises of the post–WWII period. Most of them would be difficult to pursue and implement in the current globalized environment. Relying on existing institutions and markets would also be challenging. And the forces and actors that were responsible for the tarnishing and decline of the "golden age" over the past few decades are still with us and retain the incentive and the capability to overturn any reclaimed achievements. The next chapter examines some proposals that directly or indirectly address poverty and inequality.

NOTES

1   The nations of the advanced capitalist world are all liberal democracies, but there can be striking differences in their structural design – even across the Anglo nations. Canada and the UK are constitutional monarchies (like Denmark, Norway, and Sweden); the US is a republic (like Finland, France, and Germany). Canada and the United States have written constitutions that entrench citizen rights through a Charter of Rights and Freedoms and a Bill of Rights, respectively. The United Kingdom is one of the relatively few nations in the world with a constitution that is not codified into a single document; its "unwritten constitution" comprises numerous separate instruments (laws, acts, conventions, treaties, and bills,

including a bill of rights). The three Anglo nations are all liberal democracies, but Canada and the UK have parliamentary systems of government while the US has a presidential system. The Anglo nations all have "first-past-the-post" electoral systems (with single-member plurality voting) that differ from those based upon proportional representation in the Nordic and other nations. But the United States employs another, separate "winner-take-all" institution – the Electoral College – to elect its president and vice president. The legal systems in the three Anglo nations are all based on common law, but the province of Québec in Canada and the state of Louisiana in the United States have been shaped by the tradition of civil law in France. Although they do not view these differences in the structural design of political systems as irrelevant, theories that focus on capitalist systems highlight how they all sustain power imbalances.

2 Marx inverted the German economist Adolph Wagner's notion that laws allow for the creation of commerce: "First there is commerce and then a legal system develops out of it" (quoted in Reiss, 1997, p. 78). Marx's (1859/1970) most well-known and classic elaboration of this idea is set out in the preface to *A Contribution to the Critique of Political Economy*, where he argues that the legal system, state, ideology, and culture that comprise the "superstructure" of society are generated and shaped by its economic foundation and will tend to bear its stamp and largely reflect its needs. This idea would be reassessed, refined, and developed further by many others, including Antonio Gramsci, Georg Lukács, and the Frankfurt school theorists (Hall, 1977; Jay, 1973; Jeffries, 2016; Williams, 1973).

3 The term "dual" labor market theory was eventually replaced by the term "segmented" labor market theory, acknowledging that there can be more than just two submarkets. Parallel feminist accounts of the "dual-stream" character of the US welfare state have been advanced to explain the perpetuation of high poverty levels among women and other vulnerable groups in the nation. They distinguish a "primary" stream of relatively generous social supports, which are provided as a right and typically accessed by white men, from a "secondary" stream of meager, means-tested benefits that have stringent eligibility rules and stigmatize their beneficiaries, who are typically women, visible minorities, and immigrants (Gordon, 1990; Nelson, 1990).

4 Sociologist Mark Rank (2005) aptly compares the operation of modern capitalist economies to a game of musical chairs. Since there are more players than chairs, losing is inherent to the game. It is not possible for everyone to win no matter how hard people try. The musical chairs metaphor effectively challenges and undermines both the conservative idea that the character flaws of individuals are responsible for their poverty and the less disparaging human capital notion that it is their lack of marketable skills, training, and education that is its cause.

5 See note 3 in Chapter 1 for a fuller list of recent income and wealth inequality studies.

6   However, several other forms of labor have been crucial to the genesis, development, and survival of capitalism throughout its relatively short history, including mass enslavement, debt peonage, indentured servitude, penal labor, child labor, and undocumented migrant and "guest" workers with severely curtailed rights, as well as women's unpaid domestic labor.

7   Created through the granting of state charters, the Dutch and English East India Companies are often considered to be among the world's first real corporations, and they exhibit many similarities to those that exist today. They limited the risk of private investors to just the amount that they invested – a right not enjoyed by individuals; they were permanent entities with an unlimited lifespan; and their ownership was separated from their control. However, the creation of mutual insurance arrangements by independent mills in France to pool common risks in the twelfth century and the establishment of share ownership in the thirteenth century can be seen as important intermediary forms of incorporation. As organizations of people authorized by the state to act as a single legal entity independent of its members and to own property, the cities, churches, universities, guilds, and numerous other public and private associations dating back to ancient times also share some characteristics of modern business corporations (Cerri, 2018; Pomeranz & Topik, 2012; Robbins, 1999; Sicard, 2015).

8   The popular phrase "too big too fail" contradicts the very premise of capitalism. By definition, in a competitive market system, businesses and companies should *never* be "too big" and *always* have the possibility of going under when they cannot compete. Moreover, being affirmed as "too big too fail" encourages corporations to engage in excessive risk taking (Stiglitz, 2010).

9   As in the United Kingdom, corporate charters were granted in the United States to enable activities that benefitted the public, such as the construction of roads and canals. But unlike in the UK (and elsewhere in Europe), American legislators did not originally protect the directors and managers of these chartered corporations, or their shareholders, from liability due to debts or harms they incurred. They could not own stock in other corporations or any property that was not essential to their chartered purpose, and they could not make political contributions (Hartmann 2002).

10 In the 1860s, when California lawmakers introduced a tax on robber baron Leland Stanford's highly profitable Southern Pacific Railroad, its corporate lawyers argued that the tax violated the 14th Amendment of the Constitution. Ratified in 1868, the 14th Amendment – which guaranteed every "person" equal protection under the law – was introduced to protect the rights of freed slaves. Without the backing of any solid evidence, the Southern Pacific Railroad's legal team argued that the 14th Amendment had been explicitly designed to protect all persons – natural and artificial (corporations) – so the new tax was unconstitutional (Hartmann, 2002; Winkler, 2018a, 2018b).

11 In their 1848 *Communist Manifesto*, Karl Marx and Friedrich Engels
    (1888/1967, p. 85) noted that "during its rule of scarce one hundred
    years" the capitalist class "has created more massive and more colossal
    productive forces than have all preceding generations together. Subjec-
    tion of Nature's forces to man, machinery, application of chemistry to
    industry and agriculture, steam navigation, railways, electric telegraphs,
    clearing of whole continents for cultivation, canalization of rivers, whole
    populations conjured out of the ground – what earlier century had even a
    presentiment that such productive forces slumbered in the lap of labour?"

12 Large pharmaceutical manufacturers in the United States exploit a cap-
    tive market of poor and low-income people by grossly inflating prices for
    medicines they need to survive in a "free market" that makes it difficult
    for companies to sell generic alternatives to "biologic" drugs (like insulin)
    and legally prevents Medicare from negotiating lower prices. Among their
    profiteering tactics is the "hard" or "forced" switch to evade or delay the
    production of cheaper, generic versions of their drugs. When the expira-
    tion of the patent for one of their products is on the horizon, they stop
    manufacturing it, introduce a new, slightly modified version (with a new
    patent) and run aggressive advertising campaigns marketing it to both
    doctors and consumers. Most people have adopted the new drug by the
    time the generic version of their original product is on the market and are
    unaware of its availability. Although the costs of some drugs are lower in
    Canada than in the United States because there is greater regulation on
    price increases for patented drugs, many poor families also have to choose
    between paying for life-saving drugs and paying the rent or buying food.
    Unlike the United Kingdom, New Zealand, and other nations with a na-
    tional healthcare system, Canada does not have a national pharmacare sys-
    tem allowing it to negotiate prices as a single purchaser for an established
    list of drugs (a national formulary) or to guarantee supplies (Hirschler,
    2015; Marwaha, 2016).

13 In the developed world, competition and the quest for greater profits and
    market share have also encouraged many corporations to conceal studies
    finding that their products were defective and even deadly, while they
    continued to manufacture them and sell them to the unsuspecting pub-
    lic – often after callously calculating that it would be more "cost effective"
    to deal with the expenses associated with potential injuries and the loss
    of human lives than to recall and repair their faulty products (American
    Association for Justice, n.d., 2018).

    There are myriad examples of such unethical corporate behavior in
    pursuit of profits, including the Ford Motor Company continuing to
    produce its first subcompact vehicle, the Pinto, when it knew from prepro-
    duction crash tests that its gas tank would explode if the car was involved
    in a rear-end collision. Its internal cost-benefit analysis suggested it would
    be cheaper to settle damage suits related to death and injury than to

retool the assembly-line machinery (or recall vehicles later), and Ford was facing stiff competition from Volkswagen in the lucrative small-car market (Dowie, 1977). More recently, Volkswagen was involved in its own highly publicized emissions scandal, known as the "diesel dupe." In an attempt to gain a larger share of the environmentally conscious green consumer market, it installed a "defeat device" in its vehicles that would deceive Environmental Protection Agency (EPA) emission tests in the United States by engaging greenhouse gas pollution controls only while its vehicles were being tested and disengaging them during normal driving. Similar defeat devices were also used by other automotive giants including Fiat Chrysler, Mercedes, Mitsubishi, Nissan, and Renault (Hotten, 2015; Whyte, 2020).

14 On precarious work in Canada, see Fanelli and Shields (2015) and Vosko and Closing the Enforcement Gap Research Group (2020).

15 On the increasingly neoliberal character of universities see Giroux (2013), Hartlep et al. (2017), Rustin (2006), and Waller et al. (2018).

16 Generic drugs, safer cigarettes, and vehicles that emit lower levels of pollutants are among the products that have been suppressed or delayed (Saunders & Levine, 2004).

17 Capitalism also perpetuates endless unnecessary consumption via design and marketing strategies associated with "planned obsolescence." This may involve (1) creating products contrived to break down after a certain period of time, and making it difficult or more expensive to repair than to replace them; (2) developing new products that are not compatible with older systems (e.g., computer software); and (3) continually introducing new cosmetic changes, designs, and styles, so products previously purchased are viewed as outdated and their discontented owners feel socially pressured to buy new ones (e.g., clothing, furniture, and automobiles) even if this means taking on more debt (see Packard, 1960; Slade, 2006).

18 Among countless indicators of capitalism's disregard for long-term human needs and its contradictory, crisis-generating tendencies are ocean acidification; diminution and degradation of freshwater supplies; depletion of forests, fish stocks, and fossil fuels; destruction of ecosystems and violation of wildlife habitats; extinction of species and loss of biodiversity; land and soil damage; air pollution; the destruction of the ozone; and global warming (Barak, 2017; Whyte, 2020).

19 It is often noted that plutocrats and big corporations commit, directly or indirectly, similar levels of support to candidates, campaigns, ballot initiatives, policies, and legislation associated with different parties not only to hedge their bets but because they can often greatly benefit from political gridlock in the legislature (Hasen, 2016; Nichols & McChesney, 2013).

20 This is especially true in the United States where even liberal Canada is often derided as "socialist" by right-wing politicians and in the media. Its close proximity and long-standing history with the United States has rendered it an important target for many in that country. For example, Wendell Potter,

a former US executive with Cigna health insurance recently acknowledged that he and other industry spokespeople routinely lied to the American public about Canada's universal public healthcare system, discrediting it as "socialized medicine." In the context of the COVID-19 pandemic, he acknowledged that it is superior to private medicine in the United States and has expressed great remorse for misleading Americans (Robinson, 2020).

21 According to the Center for Responsive Politics, a nonpartisan, nonprofit research group based in Washington, DC, the majority of members of the US Congress are millionaires. Although the median net worth of the members who filed disclosures in 2019 was just over $1 million, many of them in the Senate and the House of Representatives, from both parties, had far greater wealth, including Senator Rick Scott (Republican, $260 million), House Representative Greg Gianforte (Republican, $189 million), and House Leader Nancy Pelosi (Democrat, nearly $115 million). See Cody (2014), Condon (2012), and Evers-Hillstrom (2020).

22 In 2016, a trove of documents was leaked to a German newspaper (*Süddeutsche Zeitung*) and released to the International Consortium of Investigative Journalists (ICIJ) for examination. These documents, which came to be known as the "Panama Papers," disclosed the role played by a large Panamanian law firm and corporate service provider, Mossack Fonseca, in helping wealthy corporate leaders, politicians, celebrities, athletes, and other super-rich individuals use offshore jurisdictions to engage in tax avoidance and tax evasion. The following year, another much larger set of leaked documents – the "Paradise Papers" – unveiled the use of offshore jurisdictions by giant multinational corporations such as Allianz, Apple, Facebook, McDonald's, Nike, Siemens, Walmart, and Yahoo. However, despite the media attention they initially garnered, these recent disclosures had relatively minimal impact. Like earlier exposures – such as those by Offshore Leaks (June 2013), Lux Leaks (November 2014), and Swiss Leaks (February 2015) – they did not lead to real change (Bernstein, 2017; Collins, 2016; Montalban, 2017; Obermayer & Obermaier, 2017b). As award-winning German journalists Bastien Obermayer and Frederick Obermaier (2017a) note, investigations of these criminal activities are typically protracted processes that often lapse under statutes of limitations.

23 Legal scholar Matt Dimick (2019) identifies three regimes of labor law that parallel the three welfare regimes set out in Esping-Andersen's welfare state typology: an Anglophone model of *dependency*, a Scandinavian model of *self-regulation*, and a continental European model of *displacement*.

24 Foner (1984), Pierson (1990), and Rosenberg (1969) provide excellent short overviews of some key arguments proffered to explain why the United States is an "exceptional" outlier. See also Laslett and Lipset (1984) and Lipset and Marks (2000).

25 Several important left-wing political parties – such as the Socialist Labor Party, the Social Democratic Party of America (SDA) and its more

popular successor the Socialist Party of America (SPA); the Communist Party of the United States of America (CPUSA), which split from the SPA after the Russian Revolution; and the Communist Labor Party – emerged in the late nineteenth and early twentieth centuries, reflecting the values, traditions, and efforts of many working-class immigrants. But they never became as prominent, electorally viable, or deeply rooted as many of their European counterparts. The literature on the weakness of socialism in the United States is large and wide ranging (e.g., Devinatz, 2019; Foner, 1984; Fantasia & Voss, 2004; Griffin et al., 1986; Hope, 2016; Jacoby, 1991; Kennedy, 1996; Lipset & Marks, 2000; Pierson, 1990; Rosenberg, 1969; Shalev & Korpi, 1980; Voss, 1993; Zumoff, 2020).

26 The parliamentary systems of Canada and the United Kingdom do not have separate elections for the leaders of parties; the party that obtains a majority (or plurality) of seats forms the government, and its leader becomes the prime minister. In the presidential system in the United States, separate elections are held for the president and vice president at the national level and for governors at the state level. In this context, voters are more likely to perceive the electoral chances of a presidential candidate who is not a member of the Republican or Democratic Parties as highly remote and vote for the person from one of these established parties who most closely reflects their political position instead (see Olsen 2002, chapter 7).

27 The number of representatives elected to the House of Representatives – the second chamber of Congress, the nation's law-making bicameral body – in contrast, is proportional to the size of each state's population, with "apportionments" updated according to changing population size. This way of determining how many representatives each state would send to Congress was a compromise (the "Great Compromise" of 1787) brokered between smaller states, which wanted equal representation, and larger ones that favored proportional representation during the Constitutional Convention of 1787.

28 Many studies over the past five decades have highlighted the impact of the balance of power on lower poverty and inequality rates (e.g., Björn, 1979; Bradley et al., 2003; Brady, 2003b, 2009; Dryzek, 1978; Esping-Andersen, 1985a; Hewitt, 1977; Hicks, 1991, 1999; Huber & Stephens, 2014; Korpi, 1980, 1983; Olsen, 1992, 2013; Wright, 2000).

29 These endemic "business cycles" have been periodically punctuated by much larger and even full-scale breakdowns – the "Long Depression" in the late 1800s, the "Great Depression" of the 1930s, recessions in the 1970s and 1980s, and the "Great Recession" of 2007–8 – each of them fostering new socioeconomic relations and new forms of state intervention to enable the system to survive.

30 However, these gains for workers achieved through agreements ("historic compromises"), largely in the rich nations of Europe and North America,

were also based upon the extraction of resources and exploitation of workers in the poorer and developing regions of the world.

31 Individualistic accounts of poverty have often suggested or implied that Black people were genetically inferior or culturally deficient. Societal accounts that address "race," in contrast, highlight the impacts of "racialization" (the social construction of "race" as a structure), discrimination, and racism – and how they support capitalism (Carmichael & Hamilton, 1967; Steinberg, 2007, 2015).

32 Sponsored by Senator Robert Taft and House Representative Fred Hartley, and promoted by business lobbies such as the National Association of Manufacturers, the "Taft-Hartley Act" was expressly designed to undercut the gains that the labor movement had made through the introduction in 1935 of the National Labor Relations Act (NLRA), also known as the "Wagner Act" (sponsored by Senator Robert Wagner), which was a key part of President Roosevelt's "New Deal" reforms.

33 For example, see Broadbent Institute (2014), Dorling (2014, 2015), Lansley (2006, 2012), Mishel et al. (2012), Mishel and Davis (2014), Piketty (2014), Sayer (2015), Yalnizyan (2010), and Veall (2012). Ironically, the invaluable research that has focused upon rising *inequality* – especially the studies that focus upon the "social gradient" in health – has often overshadowed *poverty* as a pressing issue, obscuring the plight of poor and low-income families (including the extremely poor health outcomes associated with destitution).

FURTHER READINGS

Baldus, B. (2016). *Origins of inequality in human societies.* Routledge.

Brady, D. (2009). *Rich democracies, poor people: How politics explain poverty.* Oxford University Press.

Brady, D. (2019). Theories of the causes of poverty. *American Review of Sociology, 45,* 155–175.

Einstein, A. (2009). Why socialism? *Monthly Review: An Independent Socialist Magazine, 61*(1), 55–61. (Original work published 1949)

Royce, E. (2009). *Poverty and power: The problem of structural inequality.* Rowman and Littlefield.

Wright, E.O. (1995). The class analysis of poverty. *International Journal of Health Services, 25*(1), 85–100.

PART FOUR

Conclusion

CHAPTER SEVEN

What Can Be Done? Beyond the Welfare State

[O]vercoming poverty is not a gesture of charity. It is an act of justice. Like slavery and apartheid, poverty is not natural. It is man-made and it can be overcome and eradicated by the actions of human beings.

– Nelson Mandela (2005)

Poverty has a devastating impact on the individuals, families, and communities that it engulfs, and it critically abrades the fabric of society. Its extent, severity, and repercussions have intensified in recent decades, but it is not new. Poverty existed long before capitalism; it has also existed *with* capitalism since its inception four centuries ago. Poverty, homelessness, and a wide range of other manifestations of inequality have been more prominent and brutal during periods of unbridled capitalism. However, even in places and periods where they have been contained, and their impact attenuated, they have remained ready to surge when new conditions are unleashed by capitalism's innate growth and profit imperatives. The introduction of "laborsaving" technology, the expansion of the gig economy and jobs with zero-hour contracts, the movement of capital across the globe to take advantage of the lowest production costs, the undermining of unions, and an assemblage of related policy shifts – including deregulation, a shrinking public sector, welfare state restructuring, and massive tax cuts for corporations and the wealthy elites – have all ensured that poverty has been a constant, familiar fixture despite increasing prosperity in the wealthiest nations. This book's comparative overview of poverty and homelessness in Canada, the UK, and the US and the contrasts between these nations and other wealthy capitalist nations that it describes can help us understand the strengths and limitations of a range of existing and proposed strategies to confront these issues, including reformist measures and more far-reaching transformative ones promoting economic democracy.

REDUCING POVERTY AND ALLEVIATING ITS IMPACT: WELFARE STATES AND BASIC INCOME

Social policy and the creation of welfare states have been among the more fruitful means of addressing poverty in most nations, albeit to widely varying extents, as seen in earlier chapters.[1] Comprehensive, institutional social policy approaches – and especially those of the social democratic welfare states in the Nordic nations – have been much more successful in addressing some of the problems routinely generated in capitalist systems that can increase the rates and depth of poverty, including unemployment, shortages of affordable housing, and medical expenses. The three Anglo nations examined in this study have been on the frontline of neoliberal restructuring and austerity and are undisputed leaders in the growth of inequality, poverty, and homelessness. Most conspicuously, a web of legislation criminalizing homeless populations – restricting their access to public spaces and banning panhandling, homeless camps, and other survival strategies – has been introduced and strictly enforced in all three Anglo nations. In stark contrast, Finland has been able to reduce its homeless population from over 18,000 in 1987 to 4,600 in 2019 – despite the nation's long-standing use of a broader, more inclusive definition of homelessness and a concurrent increase in its total population size. It has also sustained relatively low rates of poverty over this period (ARA, 2020; Mikkonen, 2013; Statistics Finland, 2019).

However, there are also noteworthy differences in the role and design of welfare states and their impact *within* the liberal world. The configuration and more limited objectives of the relatively anemic US welfare state have rendered it a distinct and sustained outlier in the fight against poverty. It underinvests in supports for its children and their families (Rainwater & Smeeding, 2003; Wilson & Schieder, 2018). Without a universal healthcare system like those found in every other rich capitalist nation (and some developing ones), the crushing cost of healthcare and loss of income due to serious illness have made "medical bankruptcies" a large and ever-increasing share of all US bankruptcies (Dickman et al., 2017; Himmelstein et al., 2009, 2019). In the absence of a developed and coherent housing policy, the displacement of well-paid union jobs by low-wage service-sector jobs has left millions of Americans unable to meet their mortgage and rental payments – and evictions have become ubiquitous (Desmond, 2016; Desmond & Bell, 2015).

Welfare states might be dismissed as viable solutions because they have not eliminated poverty and homelessness or adequately addressed all of the conditions associated with them, in *any* nation. But this, at least in part, reflects a need to keep better pace with ongoing changes in society and sustain a stronger commitment to meeting them. Many nations with universal public healthcare have not always ensured that poor and homeless people can easily access it; when they have done so, homeless people are often returned to the streets to endure the same brutal conditions responsible for their poor health. Welfare states have been most successful tackling poverty in nations where the three pillars upon which they are built are broad and sturdy. Protective legislation, the third pillar, has received the least research attention, but it is an increasingly crucial consideration today. In the critical housing policy domain, for example, generous housing allowances and a greater emphasis on social housing can be undermined, and much less effective, if large multinational investors are allowed to buy up properties, houses, and apartment blocks and turn them into high-end units unaffordable to most families (Olsen, 2019b; United Nations, 2017). Some municipal governments in Barcelona, Berlin, Paris, and elsewhere have recently introduced a suite of financial penalties and fees, restrictions on rent hikes, and other laws to regulate the housing market and promote affordable housing.

The onset of severe economic downturns, major social upheavals, and health crises almost always impact the people at the bottom the hardest, casting into sharp relief the issues addressed throughout this book – the extreme vulnerabilities associated with poverty and the inadequacy of state responses, greatly amplified by decades of neoliberal austerity in the Anglo nations. When the coronavirus (COVID-19) emerged on the global stage, many people referred to it as the "great leveler" because no one was immune from it. From a medical perspective, this was true; it is a highly contagious disease that posed a threat to all. But from a socioeconomic perspective, poor and low-income families have faced a set of tightly interlocking and compounding conditions that have made them much more likely to contract the disease and to die from it. People living in poverty are already far more likely to be unhealthy, with a wide range of underlying chronic medical conditions and serious health problems that render them more vulnerable. Those employed and underemployed in the low-wage service sector as nursing home workers, grocery store workers, cleaning employees, and so on have no option but to continue to work and face contagion on a daily basis. Working at home from a computer and "social distancing" are privileges denied to most of them. These workers and their families are clustered together in close proximity in low-income neighborhoods. Homeless people cram into crowded shelters, seek refuge "couch surfing" with families and friends, or stay on the streets.

Not surprisingly, those that have disproportionately high infection and death rates are the very people facing the greatest deprivation in the three Anglo nations highlighted in earlier chapters – especially Indigenous people in Canada; Black people in the United States; and Black, Asian, and minority ethnic groups (BAME) in the United Kingdom. Other groups, including large numbers of recent immigrants who, for various reasons, do not qualify for emergency COVID-19-related benefits, are also much more vulnerable. In Canada and the UK, despite the existence of universal healthcare systems, these highly vulnerable groups have had difficulty easily accessing proper medical treatment. In the United States, the situation is notably worse. The poorest people are the most likely to be infected but the least likely to have health insurance and therefore the least likely to be tested and treated for the virus. Karl Marx's (1881/1963) late-nineteenth-century observation that the capitalist economy in the United States had "developed more rapidly and shamelessly there than in any other country" is painfully applicable to its handling of the pandemic under President

Trump (p. 129). The pandemic has also underscored the value of a universal basic income program that could allow more people to stay safe at home, enable them to care for one another, and provide relief to the self-employed and small businesses.

Basic income (BI) is a measure with a long history that is often proffered today as a means of fighting poverty in capitalist nations, and in the most direct way – by providing an income for everyone.[2] However, there are many different incarnations of BI advanced by its advocates across the political spectrum. The strongest model envisions it as an adequate, "no frills" income that is delivered at predetermined, regular intervals (e.g., weekly, monthly, or annually) and is provided (1) *universally* – as a right to every adult that is a legal resident (regardless of marital, family, or household status) and (2) *unconditionally* – without any behavioral qualifications, means tests, or conditions on how the money is spent. Like welfare state demogrants, a universal basic income avoids all of the problems associated with social assistance programs (which exclude people who are deemed undeserving, have high administrative and policing costs, and are stigmatizing) and social insurance schemes (which exclude people who are unemployed or underemployed and unable to contribute to them).[3]

BI addresses poverty by decommodifying and empowering people, even those who are not in the paid labor force. With a guaranteed annual income provided as a right, workers are not obliged to accept or remain in insecure, low-wage bad jobs. BI can also provide workers and unions with a supplemental "strike fund" that can increase their bargaining power vis-à-vis employers. It also enables women to exit situations of domestic abuse – one of the most common causes of homelessness for women – without falling into poverty. A basic income would also begin to address the undervaluing of unpaid care labor and domestic work still largely carried out by women. However, without other supplementary social services and legislation that directly challenge the gendered division of labor, BI might also serve to secure it (Calnitsky, 2017; McKay, 2013; Standing, 2017; Wright, 2004).

A BI is most effective when introduced as a central part of the welfare state's income pillar and as a complement to other welfare state provisions because they all furnish different forms of support and empowerment. The provision of a network of universal social services can ensure that all families can access high-quality healthcare, childcare, eldercare, education, and so on, but such a network leaves people dependent on the labor market and employers, without viable exit options from bad work situations and "wage slavery." On its own, BI reduces dependency on jobs and employers but leaves families vulnerable to markets and rising market prices because they have to purchase essential social services. The provision of both a dense network of universal income programs (including BI) *and* social services buttressed by a grid of rights and strictly enforced laws and entitlements can be a highly effective way of addressing poverty and its unequal burden across groups.

The tremendous amount of interest in basic income generated over the past decade was recently given a significant boost in the context of COVID-19, which exposed the limitations of existing unemployment insurance programs and other social supports and pressed governments to introduce additional measures – like the Canadian Emergency Response Benefit (CERB) for those employed and self-employed – to assist at least some desperate people and families directly affected by the pandemic. Temporary BI trials and pilot studies – most often implemented at the subnational level and on a small scale, providing short-term benefits to a particular group rather than universally – have been underway in dozens of nations across the globe and have generated some promising results, reducing rates of poverty and family stress and promoting greater health (Gilbert et al., 2018; Kangas et al., 2019). The Mincome program in place between 1974 and 1979 in the Canadian town of Dauphin in the province of Manitoba, for example, is one of the oldest, most faithful, and successful BI experiments. It improved population health in Dauphin and, as a universal provision, did not stigmatize its recipients (Calnitsky, 2016; Forget, 2011, 2020). Its positive impact supports the extensive body of research clearly demonstrating that more egalitarian nations are healthier (e.g., Kawachi & Kennedy, 2002; Marmot, 2004, 2015; Wilkinson, 1996, 2005; Wilkinson & Pickett, 2006, 2010, 2019). The Alaska Permanent Fund Dividend, a state-level BI program in place since 1982 and funded by state oil revenues, has been particularly successful in reducing poverty rates among the Indigenous peoples there (Berman, 2018).[4] Pragmatically, of course, as often pointed out, a radical, emancipatory form of BI – one that is not installed as an alternative to welfare state supports or as a means of enabling low-wage employers by topping up the low wages they offer – will be opposed by powerful elites and those who benefit most from the status quo. But this is true of any new, progressive policies and ideas, including more supportive welfare state measures.

Welfare states are most effective when they uphold people's rights and greatly limit their dependence upon markets for their well-being.[5] Nations with developed, comprehensive welfare states have gone furthest in "decommodifying" people and, in many respects, have created more egalitarian and humane societies. But they have not freed people from the obligation to sell their labor power. Moreover, the success and viability of comprehensive welfare states depend upon the support of large financial institutions and corporations and the small group of extremely wealthy people who own and control them. In varying ways and to different degrees, greater capital mobility and fiscal policies that favor corporations and the rich (and their use of tax havens) have promoted the erosion and unraveling of welfare states, which are particularly crucial to low-income families (Bernstein, 2017; Stanford, 2014; Stiglitz et al., 2020).

Social policy retrenchment and restructuring have occurred in virtually every capitalist nation through some blend of privatization, marketization (contracting out social services or requiring public sector services to adhere strictly to the logic and principles of the market), the introduction of user fees, the reduction of benefit levels, an increase in waiting periods and shortened duration periods for many benefits, a deterioration in the quality and availability of social services, a reluctance to address new social problems and areas adequately, cutbacks in social spending, the introduction of increasingly restrictive rules and eligibility requirements, and the elimination of some universal programs. These developments have been especially evident in the Anglo nations, but significant social policy retreat has occurred across Europe and elsewhere over the past few decades, often overseen by social democratic and labor parties that were once the welfare state's strongest advocates but have been swayed by neoliberalism. Even Sweden, a long-standing leader in social spending, poverty reduction, and other equality-promoting measures, has experienced marked setbacks over the past few decades. In the mid-1990s, its expenditure level was among the highest (32 percent of GDP); its overall poverty rate among the lowest (below 4 percent); and its middle class among the largest across the wealthy capitalist world (over 70 percent of its population). After more than three decades of restructuring, the Swedish welfare state remains highly developed compared to its liberal counterparts, but it is less of an international forerunner in some policy areas now (Banting & Myles, 2013; Blyth, 2013; Hills, 2015; O'Hara, 2015; Olsen, 2002, 2011, 2013).

The great effort that most nations, including the Anglo countries, have expended to address the pandemic and the considerable resources they were able to locate and deploy clearly indicate that we can do much better in addressing crises, including pre-pandemic crises such as poverty and homelessness. But the limitations of these measures have also been repeatedly demonstrated. Even amid the pandemic, economic and political elites routinely remind us that we will need to return to "normal" soon – a free-market economy and the class relations that have allowed for ever-greater concentrations of wealth and privilege while the numbers of the poor and homeless steadily increase, flooding pools of deprivation and marginalization across most nations.

BEYOND THE WELFARE STATE: FROM REDISTRIBUTION TO ECONOMIC DEMOCRACY

French socialist philosopher Andre Gorz's (1968) distinction between reforms that are only *reformist* and those that are more *transformative* is useful in assessing the potential of welfare states and related measures like BI.[6] "Reformist reforms" can improve the quality of life for people, or at least certain groups of them. But because they do not alter the nature of capitalism or the power structure associated with it, their impact on our well-being is always limited and often contradictory – both supportive and punitive. Moreover, these reforms are always precariously placed and easily pruned back or withdrawn. "Transformative reforms" are rights based. They render people less dependent on the market and reduce inequalities. They are also empowering and, most important, they challenge the status quo, opening the way for further, more far-reaching change. Depending upon their design, welfare state measures and BI fall somewhere between these two tendencies.

Contributory social insurance schemes, like unemployment insurance, sickness insurance, and pensions, have played an important role in keeping people out of poverty. But they are still commodifying, increasing dependence upon employment and labor markets, and they do not help those who are not employed or not making adequate contributions. Means-tested social assistance programs are considerably less supportive than insurance programs, and can do as much harm as good. They can be important to a family's survival and raise its members above the poverty line, but these programs are also demeaning and stigmatizing, constitute an intrusive invasion of privacy, and are often used to control their dependent and beholden recipients who, like their poor-relief ancestors centuries ago, must continually prove they are deserving of support. Increasingly tied to an obligation to work ("workfare"), these punitive supports reflect the long-standing and widespread view that poor people are largely responsible for their plight. A primary function of these measures is to discipline and regulate recipients, forcing them to change their outlook and behavior and become market-compliant actors. Failure to do so can lead to termination of support and even incarceration ("prisonfare"), a particularly familiar outcome among Black families in the United States and Indigenous families in Canada (Piven & Cloward, 1971; Soss et al., 2011; Schram, 2006; Wacquant, 2009).[7] A substantial amount of the policy DNA of most social/public assistance programs in the Anglo nations today is shared with eighteenth-century poor relief laws and the "culture of poverty" perspective examined earlier.

Demogrants and universal services, by definition, have a wider reach, including people who are not in the paid labor force as well as subpopulations typically overrepresented among the poor and homeless. They are also the most decommodifying. Public healthcare systems, for example, render parts of this policy area off-limits to capital, the profit motive, and inflated market prices. They also leave people less dependent upon their incomes, markets, and employer-based health insurance, and they promote greater equality of care. But many healthcare systems do not go far enough, excluding, or inadequately including, mental health, dental care, home care, or pharmaceuticals in their purview, making these products and services inaccessible for poor and low-income families. Public education is another good example of a universal service that is decommodifying. But even nations that provide primary, secondary, and tertiary education for everyone do not cover all of the costs associated with schooling, nor do they do enough to ensure that everyone who wants to attend college or university is well prepared and has other supports necessary to succeed – particularly people from poor and low-income families. These examples illustrate the urgent need to extend and improve social services and other provisions across the three welfare state pillars, not pare them back. Doing so entails a much broader conception of the goals, roles, and compass of welfare states, and a much greater emphasis upon preventive, proactive, and promotional measures across many areas. Public transportation, the environment, and climate change, for example, are intertwined policy areas that are crucial to our health and well-being but only rarely and weakly recognized as central welfare state considerations; acknowledging them would necessarily involve a more direct confrontation with capitalism (Gough, 2016; Hutter, 2017).

However, even highly developed, comprehensive welfare states are strictly limited. None of them has uprooted poverty, and, by omission or commission, virtually all of them have been subject to fairly steady erosion over the past three decades. More important, as indicated in the previous chapter, poverty and homelessness are systemically generated by the profit-driven, expansionist imperatives of capitalist systems and the exercise of power by a small group of economic elites, whose control over the economy has been greatly augmented through the ongoing extension of the rights of corporate personhood, and by the political elites with whom the economic elites are closely aligned. These two systemic forces impose uncompromising constraints on political democracy, removing the majority of the most impactful domains of activity – decisions concerning investment, employment, wages, resources, and the health of the environment – from democratic control and subjecting the most central domains of human activity and flourishing to market forces. The economic, social, and fiscal policies these elites have pursued have led to record-high levels of wealth and income inequality – both nationally and globally (e.g., Brown, 2017; Collins, 2018; Credit Suisse Research Institute, 2016; Dorling, 2018; Heisz, 2016; Jackson, 2020; Osberg, 2018; Oxfam, 2016, 2107; Piketty, 2014, 2015) – swelling the numbers of the poor and homeless. Redressing poverty and inequality by restoring or expanding social welfare state measures or introducing a progressive form of basic income is not on their agenda.

Under Thatcher and Reagan respectively, the UK and the US were among the first to fervently break with the postwar Keynesian consensus, the redistributive state, and the collective rights of citizens in favor of neoliberalism and the rights of taxpayers in the 1980s, but their ideas were soon adopted in Canada and across the globe (Fodor, 2014; Hall, 1988; Hay, 2010; Reich, 2020; Stiglitz et al., 2020). Deregulation, regressive fiscal policy, suicidal austerity measures, the spread of low wages, and the consequent dramatic growth of income and wealth inequality are commonly identified as among the most detrimental developments over the past few decades and as changes critical to the spread of poverty and homelessness. A recent study by the Institute on Taxation and Economic Policy indicated that sixty profitable Fortune 500 companies, including Amazon, International Business Machines (IBM), Netflix, Molson Coors, and General Motors, paid no federal taxes in the United States in 2018, and some of them even received tax rebates (Gardner et al., 2019). High profile economists in the United States, such as Nobel laureates Paul Krugman (2013) and Joseph Stiglitz (2013; Stiglitz et al., 2020) and public policy professor and former secretary of labor Robert Reich (2016, 2020), have recurrently called for measures that will make capitalism "work for everyone," such as salary limits on financial and corporate executives; transaction taxes on the financial sector; and more progressive fiscal policies, including raising tax rates for corporations and eliminating their ability to evade them, restoring wealth and estate taxes, and halting the legal and illegal use of tax havens. But how likely is this within the current power structure?

A large body of research accumulated over the past few decades clearly indicates that welfare states are most developed in nations with strong labor movements, and both are closely associated with lower rates of poverty (Brady, 2003b, 2009; Brady et al., 2016; Huber & Stephens, 2014; Korpi, 1980, 1983; Moller et al., 2003). But unionization rates are declining virtually everywhere, and the social policy options for parties on the left – when they can get elected – have been considerably more circumscribed in the context of globalization and easier capital mobility. Rebuilding welfare states, reinvigorating labor movements, and restoring more progressive fiscal and social policies will always be central to fighting poverty, but, however valuable, they do not directly or fully address the imperatives of capitalist systems or the power of elites. Moreover, even if we could restore capitalism to its earlier if still poverty-stricken "golden" days, how can we prevent similar developments from recurring? What other additional strategies and concerns are necessary?

Like welfare states, strategies for addressing poverty and inequality must start by firmly rejecting the idea that markets can fairly or effectively distribute society's resources. More far-reaching proposals call for democratizing the economy in varied but not mutually exclusive ways. While they cannot always be simply adopted holus-bolus across national or societal boundaries, they might be adapted to new locations and cultures. However, we are often deeply reluctant to consider alternatives to the status quo, particularly if they challenge capitalism as we know it. As the economist John Kenneth Galbraith (1971) famously quipped, "Faced with the choice between changing one's mind and proving that there is no need to do so, almost everyone gets busy on the proof" (p. 50). A full discussion of the democratization of the economy is beyond the scope of this volume, but it is useful to review briefly some of the most successful and promising approaches.[8]

Welfare states have had considerable success, to varying degrees, in reducing the levels and attenuating the impact of poverty, but its eradication requires *transformative* reforms that can gradually democratize the economy, prioritizing the needs of all citizens, their communities, and the environment over profits and the short-term interests and gains of a small elite. Public ownership of financial institutions and industries, employee ownership of companies, worker owned and controlled cooperative enterprises, and economic planning are among many measures that have been successful in the past. Many nations have created public corporations in key areas such as utilities (gas, electricity, water), transportation (airlines and railroads), and telecommunications and media (radio and television). In the post–WWII period, nationalization of industry accelerated in many countries, such as the United Kingdom and France, and even in the United States. Canada also introduced a range of publicly owned enterprises and "Crown corporations" providing commercial services at the federal, provincial, and municipal levels. Although some of them did not perform as well as expected – governments often nationalized industries that were unprofitable ("lemons") – many were highly successful in instituting policies and programs that have helped low-income families. Through its purchase of government bonds, the publicly owned Bank of Canada provided interest-free loans to Canadian governments to finance family allowances, old age pensions, hospitals and healthcare, universities, and infrastructure projects; Sweden's national Riksbank financed the construction of one million housing units between 1965 and 1974 (the "million program") to address a severe housing shortage in the nation. Governments have also used indicative planning and a range of incentives such as subsidies, grants, and tax breaks to encourage private enterprises to invest in regions in greatest need, as well as in essential goods and services (Carnoy & Shearer, 1980; Crisan & McKenzie, 2013; Hanna, 2018, 2019; Rhodes, 2018). However, conservative governments steadily privatized most public corporations and ended many of these planning practices during the neoliberal period.

Other solutions that deserve our attention include the creation of worker-owned and worker-managed cooperative enterprises. The highly successful Mondragon cooperative, a network of over one hundred individual cooperative enterprises across multiple industrial sectors in the Basque region of Spain, forms the backbone of the economy and is a central reason for the low levels of inequality and virtually nonexistent poverty and homelessness there; a recent study noted that "there are neither mansions in the hills nor poverty in the streets" (Kelly, 2017, p. 8; see also Flecha & Cruz, 2011; Gibson-Graham, 2003; Redondo et al., 2011). In Sweden, the "Meidner Plan" to create wage-earner funds that would gradually transfer ownership and control of the largest industries from employers to workers was another promising measure proposed in the 1970s to promote economic democracy (Meidner, 1978; Olsen, 1992).[9] Although none of these proposals or existing measures is a panacea, they all hold promise and provide inspiration and direction. Poverty, homelessness, and inequality cannot be eradicated with the same thinking, policies, and measures, or within the same system and market forces, that created and cultivated them. To paraphrase Irish poet, playwright, and socialist Oscar Wilde, we are all in the gutter; we must look to the stars.

NOTES

1 The term *welfare state* suggests that such states are always designed to eliminate poverty, or greatly reduce its magnitude, and secure our well-being. But this is not necessarily true or true to the same extent across all nations or in any one of them over time. In some instances,

social policy measures have been pernicious, vitiating the well-being of many people and especially that of some of the most vulnerable groups in society. The aggressive assimilation objectives associated with the establishment of Indian residential schools by the Canadian government, for example, culminated in physical, emotional, and sexual abuse; substandard living conditions; and the deaths of countless Indigenous children. Although commonly associated with Nazi Germany, eugenicist "health" policies and practices, such as the forced sterilization of people deemed physically or mentally unfit, were introduced in many rich, developed countries, often targeting marginalized groups, especially poor women.

2 Basic income is referred to by several different terms, such as a basic income grant (BIG), a universal basic income (UBI), an unconditional basic income, a citizenship income, and a citizen's dividend. It is a kind of "stand-alone" demogrant that can be distinguished from a minimum income guarantee, which tops up low income and requires a means test, or a negative income tax (NIT), which is a kind of fiscal support paid to low-income earners retrospectively, at the end of the tax year. With the last two measures, only certain people qualify for support; these measures are neither universally nor unconditionally provided (Standing, 2017).

3 Regressive models envision BI as an alternative to welfare state programs and/or as a de facto wage top-up. In these models, BI allows employers to continue to pay their workers low wages, particularly workers in unpleasant and unrewarding low-wage service-sector jobs.

4 Neoliberal and conservative governments have sometimes terminated BI experiments early (as in Manitoba and more recently Ontario) despite scant evidence for their claims that the additional income would discourage people from working and lead to inflation. Others have suggested as a less costly alternative a "negative income tax" (NIT), which, instead of providing an income to everyone, allows people whose income is below the poverty line to receive income rather than pay taxes (Wiederspan et al., 2015). However, it has many of the same drawbacks as other targeted programs.

5 Although outside of this book's purview, it is important to acknowledge that a large part of the wealth used to fund welfare states in the advanced capitalist nations and to reduce levels of poverty and inequality there was generated by exploiting nations in the developing world. A recent comprehensive study by experts and research institutions across the globe (Centre for Applied Research et al., 2015) notes that, using its broader definition of net resource transfers (NRT), "developing countries have effectively served as net creditors to the rest of the world, an ironic twist to the development narrative" (p. xi).

6 The distinction Gorz made is usually rendered as that between "reformist reforms" and "non-reformist reforms." This can be confusing since the term "non-reformist" might be interpreted as not reformist at all, rather than as transformative.

7 In the Anglo nations, particularly in the United States, poor and homeless people are more likely to be incarcerated than in nations with more developed welfare states. Prison populations per 100,000 people were notably different in 2013 in Canada (118), England and Wales (148), and, especially, the United States (716) than in nations with more developed social supports such as Denmark (73), Finland (58), Norway (72), and Sweden (67; Walmsley, 2013). Black people and Indigenous people have also been greatly overrepresented among incarcerated populations in Canada and the United States (Alexander, 2012; Statistics Canada, 2013; Western & Beckett, 1999; Western & Pettit, 2010).

8 For an overview of some of these proposals and strategies, see Carnoy and Shearer (1980), Swift (2014), and Wright (2010).

9 The powerful Swedish Employers Federation (SAF) ensured that the wage-earner fund (WEF) program was never implemented in its original form because it would have gradually transferred control over the nation's largest corporations from employers to workers. However, it still holds great promise as a strategy to foster economic democracy. On the character and fate of the wage-earner program (the "Meidner Plan") see Meidner (1978) and Olsen (1992).

FURTHER READINGS

Ackerman, B., Alstott, A., & van Parijs, P. (Eds.). (2006). *Resigning distribution: Basic income and stakeholder grants as cornerstones for an egalitarian capitalism.* Verso.

Calnitsky, D. (2017). Debating basic income. *Catalyst, 1*(3), 63–90.

Einstein, A. (2009). Why socialism? *Monthly Review: An Independent Socialist Magazine, 61*(1), 55–61. (Original work published 1949)

Felber, C. (2012). *Change everything: Creating an economy for the common good.* Zed Books.

Flecha, R., & Santa Cruz, I. (2011). Cooperation for economic success: The Mondragon case. *Analyse & Kritik, 33*(1), 157–170.

Gibson-Graham, J.K. (2003). Enabling ethical economies: Cooperativism and class. *Critical Sociology, 29*(2), 123–161.

Olsen, G.M. (1992). *The struggle for economic democracy in Sweden.* Avebury/ Ashgate.

Panitch, L., & Gindin, S. (2020). *The socialist challenge today.* Haymarket Books.

Ranis, P. (2016). *Cooperatives confront capitalism: Challenging the neoliberal economy.* Zed Books.

Redondo, G., Santa Cruz, I., & Maria Rotger, J. (2011). Why Mondragon? Analyzing what works in overcoming inequalities. *Qualitative Inquiry, 17*(3), 277–283.

Reich, R.B. (2016). *Saving capitalism for the many, not the few.* Vintage Books.

Stiglitz, J. (2013). *The price of inequality: How today's divided society endangers our future.* W.W. Norton and Company.

Stiglitz, J.E., Tucker, T.N., & Zucman, G. (2020). The starving state: Why capitalism's salvation depends on taxation. *Foreign Affairs, 99*(1), 30–37.

Swift, R. (2014). *S.O.S.: Alternatives to capitalism.* Between the Lines.

Wolff, R. (2012). *Democracy at work: A cure for capitalism.* Haymarket Books.

Wright, E.O. (2010). *Envisioning real utopias.* Verso.

References

Aalbers, M. (2016). Housing finance as harm. *Crime, Law, and Social Change,*
66(2), 115–129. https://doi.org/10.1007/s10611-016-9614-x

Abel-Smith, B. (1992). The Beveridge report: Its origins and outcomes.
International Social Security Review, 45(1–2), 5–16. https://doi.org/10.1111
/j.1468-246X.1992.tb00900.x

Abrahamson, P. (1999). The welfare modelling business. *Social Policy and*
Administration, 33(4), 394–415. https://doi.org/10.1111/1467-9515.00160

Abramovich, A., & Shelton, J. (Eds.). (2017). *Where am I going to go?*
Intersectional approaches to ending LGBTQ2S youth homelessness in Canada and
the U.S. Canadian Observatory on Homelessness.

Abramovitz, M. (1988). *Regulating the lives of women: Social welfare policy from*
colonial times to the present. South End Press.

Alber, J. (1995). A framework for the comparative study of social services.
Journal of European Social Services, 5(2), 131–149. https://doi.org/10.1177
/095892879500500204

Albert, M. (1993). *Capitalism against capitalism.* Whurr.

Alesina, A., & Angeletos, G.-M. (2005). Fairness and redistribution. *The*
American Economic Review, 95(4), 960–980. https://doi.org/10.1257
/0002828054825655

Alexander, M. (2012). *The new Jim Crow: Mass incarceration in the age of*
colorblindness. The New Press.

Alston, L.J., & Ferrie, J.P. (1999). *Southern paternalism and the American welfare*
state. Cambridge University Press.

American Association for Justice. (n.d.). *They knew and failed to … True stories of*
corporations that knew their products were dangerous, sometimes deadly. American
Association for Justice. https://www.howardlawpc.com/files/10-_they
_knew_and_failed.pdf

American Association for Justice. (2018). *Worst corporate conduct of 2018.* American Association for Justice. https://www.justice.org/resources /research/worst-corporate-conduct-of-2018

Amore, K., Baker, M., & Howden-Chapman, P. (2011). The ETHOS definition and classification of homelessness: An analysis. *European Journal of Homelessness, 5*(2), 19–37. https://www.feantsaresearch.org/download /article-1-33278065727831823087.pdf

Anderson, I., Baptista, I., Wolf, J., Edgar, B., Benjaminsen, L., Sapounakis, A., & Schoibl, H. (2006). *The changing role of service provision: Barriers of access to health services for homeless people.* FEANTSA.

ARA (The Housing Finance and Development Centre of Finland). (2020). *Homelessness in Finland 2019: Report 2020.* ARA.

Armitage, A. (2003). *Social welfare in Canada* (4th ed.). Oxford University Press.

Arnesen, E. (Ed.). (2007). *The Black worker: Race, labor, and civil rights since emancipation.* University of Illinois Press.

Arrow, K., Bowles, S., & Durlauf, S.N. (Eds.). (2000). *Meritocracy and economic inequality.* Princeton University Press.

Arts, W., & Gelissen, J. (2002). Three worlds of welfare capitalism or more. *Journal of European Social Policy, 12*(2), 137–158. https://doi.org/10.1177 /0952872002012002114

Atkinson, A.B. (2015). *Inequality: What can be done.?* Harvard University Press.

Bailey, M.J., & Danziger, S. (Eds.). (2013). *Legacies of the war on poverty.* Russell Sage Foundation.

Bakan, J. (2004). *The corporation: The pathological pursuit of profit and power.* Viking Canada.

Bakan, J. (2020). *The new corporation: How "good" corporations are bad for democracy.* Vintage.

Baldus, B. (2016). *Origins of inequality in human societies.* Routledge.

Baldwin, J. (1992). *Nobody knows my name.* Vintage Books. (Original work published 1961)

Ball, P. (2020, June 10). The gene delusion. *New Statesman.*

Bambra, C. (2004). Three worlds of welfare: Illusory and gender blind? *Social Policy and Society, 3*(3), 201–211. https://doi.org/10.1017 /S147474640400171X

Bambra, C. (2005). Cash versus services: "Worlds of welfare" and the decommodification of cash benefits and health services. *Journal of Social Policy, 34*(2), 195–213. https://doi.org/10.1017/S0047279404008542

Bane, M.J., & Ellwood, D.T. (1986). Slipping in and out of poverty: The dynamics of spells. *Journal of Human Resources, 21*(1), 1–23. https://doi.org /10.2307/145955

Banfield, E.C. (1974). *The unheavenly city revisited.* Littlefield.

Banting, K., & Myles, J. (Eds.). (2013). *Inequality and the fading of redistributive politics.* UBC Press.

Barak, G. (2017). *Unchecked corporate power: Why the crimes of multinational corporations are routinized away.* Routledge.

Barkan, J. (2013). Plutocrats at work: How big philanthropy undermines democracy. *Dissent, 80*(2), 635–653. https://www.jstor.org/stable/24385621

Barnard, H. (2014). *Tackling poverty across all ethnicities in the UK.* Joseph Rowntree Foundation.

Barr, N. (2020). *The economics of the welfare state.* Oxford University Press.

Bartels, L.M. (2008). *Unequal democracy: The political economy of the new gilded age.* Princeton University Press.

Bashford, A., & Levine, P. (Eds.). (2010). *The Oxford handbook of the history of eugenics.* Oxford University Press.

Battle, K., & Torjman, S. (2001). *The post-welfare state in Canada: Income-testing and inclusion.* Caledon Institute.

Baumberg, B. (2016). The stigma of claiming benefits: A quantitative study. *Journal of Social Policy, 45*(2), 181–199. https://doi.org/10.1017/S0047279415000525

Beatty, C., & Fothergill, S. (2018). Welfare reform in the United Kingdom 2010–16: Expectation, outcomes, and local impacts. *Social Policy and Administration, 52*(5), 950–968. https://doi.org/10.1111/spol.12353

Beatty, J. (2008). *The age of betrayal: The triumph of money in America, 1865–1900.* Vintage Books.

Beaudry, P., Green, D.A., & Sand, B.M. (2013). *The great reversal in the demand for skill and cognitive tasks* (NBER Working Paper No. 18901). National Bureau of Economic Research (NBER).

Béland, D., & Daignault, P.-M. (2015). *Welfare reform in Canada: Provincial social assistance in comparative perspective.* University of Toronto Press.

Belanger, Y.D., Awosoga, O., & Weasel Head, G. (2013). Homelessness, urban Aboriginal peoples, and the need for enumeration. *Aboriginal Policy Studies, 2*(2), 4–33. https://doi.org/10.5663/aps.v2i2.19006

Bendixsen, S., Bente Bringslid, M., & Halvard, V. (Eds.). (2018). *Egalitarianism in Scandinavia: Historical and contemporary perspectives.* Palgrave Macmillan.

Benjaminsen, L., & Dyb, E. (2008). The effectiveness of homeless policies: Variations among the Scandinavian countries. *European Journal of Homelessness, 2,* 45–67. https://www.feantsaresearch.org/download/article-24800881193787296954.pdf

Bergqvist, C., Borchost, A., Dorte-Christensen, A., Ramstedt-Silén, V., Raaum, N.C., & Styrkásdóttir, A. (Eds.). (1999). *Equal democracies? Gender and politics in the Nordic countries.* Scandinavian University Press.

Berman, M. (2018). Resource rents, universal basic income, and poverty among Alaska's Indigenous peoples. *World Development, 106,* 161–172. https://doi.org/10.1016/j.worlddev.2018.01.014

Bernstein, J. (2007). Is education the cure for poverty? *The American Prospect, 18*(5), 17–18. https://prospect.org/special-report/education-cure-poverty/

Bernstein, J. (2017). *Secrecy world: Inside the Panama papers investigation of illicit money networks and the global elite*. Henry Holt and Company.

Berthoud, R. (2002). *Poverty and prosperity among Britain's ethnic minorities*. Institute for Social and Economic Research (ISER).

Beveridge, W.H. (1942). *Social insurance and allied services*. HMSO.

Bevir, M. (2011). *The making of British socialism*. Princeton University Press.

Biegert, T. (2017). Welfare benefits and unemployment in affluent democracies: The moderating role of the institutional insider/outsider divide. *American Sociological Review, 82*(5), 1037–1064. https://doi.org/10.1177/0003122417727095

Bishop-Stall, S. (2005). *Down to this: Squalor and splendor in a big-city shantytown*. Vintage Books.

Björn, L. (1979). Labour parties, economic growth, and the redistribution of income in five capitalist democracies. In R.F. Tomasson (Ed.), *Comparative social research: An annual publication: Vol. 2* (pp. 93–128). JAI Press.

Blackmon, D.A. (2009). *Slavery by another name: The re-enslavement of black people in America from the Civil War to World War II*. Anchor Books/Random House.

Blake, W. (1970). *Songs of innocence and of experience*. Oxford University Press. (Original work published 1789 and 1794)

Blanden, J., & Gibbons, S. (2006). *The persistence of poverty across generations: A view from two British cohorts*. Policy Press/Joseph Rowntree Foundation.

Blanden, J., Gregg, P., & Machin, S. (2005). Intergenerational mobility in Europe and North America. Centre for Economic Performance (London School of Economics).

Blekesaune, M., & Quadagno, J. (2003). Public attitudes toward welfare state policies. *European Sociological Review, 19*(5), 415–427. https://doi.org/10.1093/esr/19.5.415

Blundell, R., Joyce, R., Norris Keiller, A., & Ziliak, J.P. (2018). Income inequality and the labour market in Britain and the US. *Journal of Public Economics, 162*, 48–62. https://doi.org/10.1016/j.jpubeco.2018.04.001

Blyth, M. (2013). *Austerity: The history of an idea*. Oxford University Press.

Bonoli, G. (2000). Public attitudes to social protection and political economy traditions in Western Europe. *European Societies, 2*(4), 431–452. https://doi.org/10.1080/713767005

Booth, C. (1897). *Life and labour of the people in London*. Macmillan.

Borchorst, A. (1994). The Scandinavian welfare states: Patriarchal, gender neutral or woman-friendly? *International Journal of Contemporary Sociology, 31*(1), 45–67.

Bourguignon, F. (2015). *The globalization of inequality*. Princeton University Press.

Boyer, G.R. (2019). *The winding road to the welfare state: Economic insecurity and welfare policy in Britain*. Princeton University Press.

Bradley, D., Huber, E., Moller, S., Nielsen, F., & Stephens, J.D. (2003). Distribution and redistribution in postindustrial democracies. *World Politics, 55*(2), 193–228. https://doi.org/10.1353/wp.2003.0009

Bradshaw, E.A. (2018). Pipelines, presidents and people power: Resisting state-corporate environmental crime. In S. Bittle, L. Snider, S. Tombs, & D. Whyte (Eds.), *Revisiting crimes of the powerful: Marxism, crime and deviance* (pp. 157–173). Routledge.

Brady, D. (2003a). Rethinking the sociological measurement of poverty. *Social Forces, 81*(3), 715–752. https://doi.org/10.1353/sof.2003.0025

Brady, D. (2003b). The politics of poverty: Left political institutions, the welfare state, and poverty. *Social Forces, 82*(2), 557–588. https://doi.org/10.1353/sof.2004.0004

Brady, D. (2005). The welfare state and poverty in rich western democracies, 1967–1997. *Social Forces, 83*(4), 1329–1364. https://doi.org/10.1353/sof.2005.0056

Brady, D. (2009). *Rich democracies, poor people: How politics explain poverty.* Oxford University Press.

Brady, D. (2019). Theories of the causes of poverty. *American Review of Sociology, 45*, 155–175. https://doi.org/10.1146/annurev-soc-073018-022550

Brady, D., Blome, A., & Kleider, H. (2016). How politics and institutions shape poverty and inequality. In D. Brady & L.M. Burton (Eds.), *The Oxford handbook of the social science of poverty* (pp. 117–140). Oxford University Press.

Brady, D., & Bostic, A. (2015). Paradoxes of social policy: Welfare transfers, relative poverty, and redistribution preferences. *American Sociological Review, 80*(2), 268–298. https://doi.org/10.1177/0003122415573049

Brady, D., Finnigan, R.M., & Hübgen, S. (2017). Rethinking the risks of poverty: A framework for analyzing prevalences and penalties. *American Journal of Sociology, 123*(3), 740–786. https://doi.org/10.1086/693678

Brady, D., & Kall, D. (2008). Nearly universal, but somewhat distinct: The feminization of poverty in affluent Western democracies, 1969–2000. *Social Science Research, 37*(3), 976–1007. https://doi.org/10.1016/j.ssresearch.2007.07.001

Bretherton, J. (2017). Reconsidering gender in homelessness. *European Journal of Homelessness, 11*(1), 13–33. https://www.feantsaresearch.org/download/feantsa-ejh-11-1_a1-v04591394126960449255.pdf

Briggs, A. (1961). The welfare state in historical perspective. *European Journal of Sociology*, 221–258. https://doi.org/10.1017/S0003975600000412

Brittain, M., & Blackstock, C. (2015). *First Nations child poverty: A literature review and analysis.* First Nations Children's Action Research and Education Service.

Broadbent Institute. (2014). *Haves and have-nots: Deep and persistent wealth inequality in Canada.* Broadbent Institute.

Broadway, R., & Cuff, K. (2014). The recent evolution of tax-transfer policies in Canada. In K. Banting & J. Myles (Eds.), *Inequality and the fading of redistributive politics* (pp. 335–380). UBC Press.

Broberg, G., & Rolls-Hansen, N. (2005). *Eugenics and the welfare state: Sterilization policy in Norway, Sweden, Denmark, and Finland.* Michigan State University Press.

Brooks, A. (2019). *Clothing poverty: The hidden world of fashion and second-hand clothes.* Zed Books.

Brown, R. (2017). *The inequality crisis: The facts and what we can do about it.* Polity Press.

Brynin, M., & Longhi, S. (2015). *The effect of occupation on poverty among ethnic minority groups.* Joseph Rowntree Foundation.

Burt, M., Aron, L.Y., & Lee, E., with Valente, J. (2001). *Helping America's homeless: Emergency shelter or affordable housing?* Urban Institute Press.

Burt, M., & Cohen, B.E. (1989). *America's homeless.* Urban Institute.

Calnitsky, D. (2016). "More normal than welfare": The Mincome experiment, stigma, and community experience. *Canadian Review of Sociology, 53*(1), 26–71. https://doi.org/10.1111/cars.12091

Calnitsky, D. (2017). Debating basic income. *Catalyst, 1*(3), 63–90. https://catalyst-journal.com/vol1/no3/debating-basic-income

Canadian Council on Social Development. (2001). *Defining and re-defining poverty: A CCSD perspective.* Canadian Council on Social Development.

Canadian Human Rights Commission. (2013). *Report on equality of rights of Aboriginal people.* Canadian Human Rights Commission.

Canadian Observatory on Homelessness. (2012). *Canadian definition of homelessness.* Canadian Observatory on Homelessness Press. www.homelesshub.ca/homelessdefinition

Cancian, M., & Danziger, S. (2009). *Changing poverty, changing policies.* Russell Sage Foundation.

Caplovitz, D. (1963). *The poor pay more.* The Free Press.

Card, D., & Freeman, R.B. (Eds.). (2009). *Small differences that matter: Labor markets and income maintenance in Canada and the United States.* University of Chicago Press. (Original work published 1993)

Carmichael, S., & Hamilton, C.V. (1967). *Black power: The politics of liberation in America.* Vintage Books.

Carnoy, M., & Shearer, D. (1980). *Economic democracy: The challenge of the 1980s.* M.E. Sharpe.

Carroll, W. (2010). *Corporate power in a globalizing world.* Oxford University Press.

Carroll, W.K., & Sapinski, J.P. (2018). *Organizing the 1%: How corporate power works.* Fernwood.

Caskey, J.P. (1996). *Fringe banking: Check-cashing outlets, pawn shops, and the poor.* Russell Sage Foundation.

Castles, F.G. (1985). *The working class and welfare: Reflections on the political development of the welfare state in Australia and New Zealand 1890–1980.* Allen and Unwin.

Castles, F.G. (Ed.). (1993). *Families of nations: Patterns of public policy in Western democracies.* Dartmouth.

Castles, F.G., Leibfried, S., Lewis, J., Obinger, H., & Pierson, C. (Eds.). (2010). *The Oxford handbook of the welfare state.* Oxford University Press.

Centre for Applied Research (Norwegian School of Economics), Global Financial Integrity, Jawaharlal Nehru University, Instituto Socioeconômicos, & Nigerian Institute of Social and Economic Research. (2015). *Financial flows and tax havens: Combining to limit the lives of billions of people*. https://www.gfintegrity.org/wp-content/uploads/2016/12/Financial_Flows-final.pdf

Centre for Social Justice. (2007a). *Breakthrough Britain – Ending the costs of social breakdown: Vol. 1. Family breakdown*. Social Justice Policy Group.

Centre for Social Justice. (2007b). *Breakthrough Britain – Ending the costs of social breakdown: Vol. 2. Economic dependency and worklessness*. Social Justice Policy Group.

Cerri, L. (2018). Birth of the modern corporation: From servant of the state to semi-sovereign state power. *The Journal of Economics and Sociology, 77*(2), 239–277. https://doi.org/10.1111/ajes.12212

Chandy, L. (Ed.). (2016). *The future of work in the developing world*. Brookings Institution.

Charles, J.M. (2009). "America's lost cause": The unconstitutionality of criminalizing our country's homeless population. *Public Interest Law Journal, 18*(2), 315–348. https://www.bu.edu/pilj/files/2015/09/18-2CharlesNote.pdf

Checkland, S.G., & Checkland, E.O.A. (Eds.). (1974). *The poor law report of 1834*. Penguin.

Chernomas, R., & Hudson, I. (2013). *To live and die in America: Class, power, health and healthcare*. Pluto Press.

Chomsky, N. (2011). *Media control: The spectacular achievements of propaganda*. Seven Stories Press.

Chung, H., Taylor-Gooby, P., & Leruth, B. (2018). Political legitimacy and welfare state futures: Introduction. *Social Policy and Administration, 52*(4), 835–846. https://doi.org/10.1111/spol.12400

Clairmont, D.H.J., & McGill, D. (1974). *Africville: The life and death of a Canadian Black community*. McClelland & Stewart.

Clawson, R.A., & Trice, R. (2000). Poverty as we know it: Media portrayals of the poor. *The Public Opinion Quarterly, 64*(1), 53–64. https://doi.org/10.1086/316759

Clement, W. (1977). The corporate elite, the capitalist class, and the Canadian state. In L.V. Panitch (Ed.), *The Canadian state: Political economy and political power* (pp. 225–248). Toronto University Press.

CMCRP (Canadian Media Concentration Research Project). (2019). Media and internet concentration in Canada, 1984–2018 [Research report]. School of Journalism and Communication, Carleton University.

Cody, C. (2014, January 13). Majority in Congress are millionaires. *NPR: It's All Politics*. https://www.npr.org/sections/itsallpolitics/2014/01/10/261398205/majority-in-congress-are-millionaires

Cole, M. (2016). *Racism: A critical analysis*. Pluto Press.

Collin, C., & Jensen, H. (2009). *A statistical profile of poverty in Canada* (PRB 09-17E). Parliamentary Information and Research Service of the Library of Parliament.

Collins, C. (2016, April 5). The Panama papers expose the hidden wealth of the world's super-rich. *The Nation*.

Collins, C. (2018). *Is inequality in America irreversible?* Polity Press.

Collins, C., & Hoxie, J. (2017). *Billionaire bonanza: The* Forbes *400 and the rest of us*. Institute for Policy Studies.

Condon, S. (2012, March 27). Why is Congress a millionaire's club? *CBS News*. https://www.cbsnews.com/news/why-is-congress-a-millionaires-club/

Congressional Research Service. (2018). *Homelessness: Targeted federal programs*. Congressional Research Service.

Cooper, A. (2007). Acts of resistance: Black men and women engage slavery in Upper Canada, 1793–1803. *Ontario History, 99*(1), 5–17. https://doi.org/10.7202/1065793ar

Coughlin, R.M. (1979). Social policy and ideology: Public opinion in eight rich nations. In R.F. Tomasson (Ed.), *Comparative social research: An annual publication: Vol. 2.* (pp. 3–40). JAI Press.

Credit Suisse Research Institute. (2016). *Global wealth report 2015*. Credit Suisse AG Research Institute.

Crisan, D., & McKenzie, K.J. (2013). Government-owned enterprises in Canada. *SPP Research Paper, 6*(8). https://www.policyschool.ca/wp-content/uploads/2016/03/government-owned-enterprises-final.pdf

CSDH (Commission on Social Determinants of Health). (2008). *Closing the gap in a generation: Health equity through action on the social determinants of health*. World Health Organization.

d'Addio, A.C. (2007). *Intergenerational transmission of disadvantage: Mobility or immobility across generations? A review of evidence from OECD countries* [OECD Social, Employment and Migration Working Papers]. OECD. https://www.oecd.org/els/38335410.pdf

Daguerre, A. (2008). The second phase of US welfare reform, 2000–2006: Blaming the poor again? *Social Policy Administration, 42*(4), 362–378. https://doi.org/10.1111/j.1467-9515.2008.00609.x

Daly, G. (1996). *Homeless: Policies, strategies and lives on the street*. Routledge.

Daly, M. (1999). Regimes of social policy in Europe and the patterning of homelessness. In D. Avramov (Ed.), *Coping with homelessness: Issues to be tackled and best practices in Europe* (pp. 309–322). Ashgate.

Darwin, C. (1958). *The origin of species* (6th ed.). New American Library. (Original work published 1872)

Daschuk, J. (2019). *Clearing the plains: Disease, politics of starvation, and the loss of Indigenous life* (2nd ed.). University of Regina Press.

Daun, Å. (1991). Individualism and collectivity among Swedes. *Ethnos, 56*(3/4), 165–172. https://doi.org/10.1080/00141844.1991.9981433

Davidson, L. (2012). *Cultural genocide*. Rutgers University Press.

Davies, J.B., Sandström, S., Shorrocks, A.F., & Wolff, E.N. (2008). *The world distribution of household wealth* (Discussion Paper No. 2008/03). United Nations University, World Institute for Economic Development Economics Research.

de Coninck-Smith, N., Sandin, B., & Schrumpf, E. (Eds.). (1997). *Industrious children: Work and childhood in the Nordic countries, 1850–1990*. Odense University Press.

de Schweinitz, K. (1943). *England's road to social security: From the Statute of Labourers in 1349 to the Beveridge Report of 1942*. University of Pennsylvania Press.

Denice, P., & Rosenfeld, J. (2018). Unions and nonunion pay in the United States, 1977–2015. *Sociological Science, 5*, 541–561. http://dx.doi.org/10.15195/v5.a23

Department for Communities and Local Government. (2014). *Homelessness prevention and relief: England 2013/2014*. Department for Communities and Local Government.

Department for Work and Pensions. (2011). *Households below average income: An analysis of the income distribution 1994/1995–2009/2010*. Department for Work and Pensions.

Department for Work and Pensions. (2014). *Households below average income: An analysis of the income distribution 1994/1995–2012/2013*. Department for Work and Pensions.

Department for Work and Pensions. (2019a). *Households below average income: An analysis of the UK income distribution, 1994/95–2017/18*. Department for Work and Pensions.

Department for Work and Pensions. (2019b). *Households below average income: 1994/95 to 2017/18* [Data tables]. Department for Work and Pensions.

Department for Work and Pensions. (2020). *Households below average income, 1994/95–2018/19* (14th ed.). UK Data Service. http://doi.org/10.5255/UKDA-SN-5828-12

Desmond, M. (2016). *Evicted: Poverty and profit in the American city*. Broadway Books.

Desmond, M., & Bell, M. (2015). Housing, poverty, and the law. *Annual Review of Law and Social Science, 11*(1), 15–35. https://doi.org/10.1146/annurev-lawsocsci-120814-121623

Devinatz, V.G. (2019). Left-wing SPA-led and SPUSA-led unions and worker organizations as the vanguard of US social democracy's left-wing, circa 1935–1950. *Labor Studies Journal, 44*(1), 60–78. https://doi.org/10.1177/0160449X19828471

Devlin, B., Fienberg, S.E., Resnick, D.P., & Roeder, K. (1997). *Intelligence, genes, and success: Scientists respond to the bell curve*. Springer-Verlag.

Dickens, C. (1995). *Hard times*. Wordsworth Editions. (Original work published 1854)

Dickens, C. (2010). *Night walks*. Penguin Books. (Original work published 1860)

Dickman, S.L., Himmelstein, D.U., & Woolhandler, S. (2017). Inequality and the health-care system in the USA. *The Lancet, 389*(100077). https://doi.org/10.1016/S0140-6736(17)30900-5

Dill, B.T. (1998). A better life for me and my children: Low-income mothers struggle for self-sufficiency in the rural South. *Journal of Comparative Family Studies, 29*(2), 419–428. https://doi.org/10.3138/jcfs.29.2.419

Dimick, M. (2019). Counterfeit liberty. *Catalyst: A Journal of Theory and Strategy, 3*(1), 47–88. https://catalyst-journal.com/vol3/no1/counterfeit-liberty

Domhoff, G.W. (1990). *The power elite and the state: How policy is made in America.* Aldine De Gruyter.

Domhoff, G.W. (2014). *Who rules America: The triumph of the corporate rich.* McGraw-Hill.

Dorling, D. (2014). *Inequality and the 1%.* Verso.

Dorling, D. (2015). *Injustice: Why inequality persists.* Policy Press.

Dorling, D. (2017). *The equality effect: Improving life for everyone.* New Internationalist.

Dorling, D. (2018). *Do we need economic inequality.* Polity Press.

Dowie, M. (1977, September/October). Pinto madness. *Mother Jones.* https://www.motherjones.com/politics/1977/09/pinto-madness/

Doyle, G. (2002). *Media ownership: The economics and politics of convergence and concentration in the UK and European media.* Sage.

Dryzek, J. (1978). Politics, economics and inequality: A cross-national analysis. *European Journal of Political Research, 6*, 399–410. https://doi.org/10.1111/j.1475-6765.1978.tb00803.x

Du Bois, W.E.B. (1933). Marxism and the Negro problem. *The Crisis, 40*(5), 103–104, 118.

Duncan, G.J., & Brooks-Gunn, J. (Eds.). (2009). *Consequences of growing up poor.* Russell Sage Foundation.

Duncan, G.J., Magnuson, K., Kalil, A., & Ziol-Guest, K. (2012). The importance of early childhood development. *Social Indicators Research, 108*(1), 87–98. https://doi.org/10.1007/s11205-011-9867-9

Economic Policy Institute. (2019). *State of Working America Data Library: Poverty-level wages* [Data source website]. https://www.epi.org/data/#?subject=povwage

Edelman, P. (2012). *So rich, so poor: Why it's so hard to end poverty in America.* The New Press.

Edgar, B., & Meert, H. (2006). *Fifth review of statistics on homeless in Europe: Developing an operational definition of homelessness.* FEANTSA.

Edgar, B., Meert, H., & Doherty, J. (2004). *Third review of statistics on homeless in Europe: Developing an operational definition of homelessness.* FEANTSA.

Edwards, M.E., Plotnick, R., & Klawitter, M. (2001). Do attitudes and personality characteristics affect socioeconomic outcomes? The case of welfare use by young women. *Social Science Quarterly, 82*(4), 827–843. https://doi.org/10.1111/0038-4941.00062

Egleton, M., Marcus Banigo, D., McLeod, B.A., & Halaevalu, F.O. (2016). Homelessness among formerly incarcerated African men: Contributors and consequences. *Contemporary Social Science, 11*(4), 403–414. https://doi.org /10.1080/21582041.2016.1258590

Eidlin, B. (2018). *Labour and the class idea in the United States and Canada.* Cambridge University Press.

Eighner, L. (1993). *Travels with Lizbeth: Three years on the road and on the streets.* St. Martin's Press.

Einhorn, E.S., & Logue, J. (1989). *Modern welfare states: Politics and policies in social democratic Scandinavia.* Praeger.

Einstein, A. (2009). Why socialism? *Monthly Review: An Independent Socialist Magazine, 61*(1), 55–61. https://doi.org/10.14452/MR-061-01-2009-05_7 (Original work published 1949)

Ellison, N. (2006). *The transformation of welfare states?* Routledge.

Elton, G.R. (1953). An early Tudor poor law. *The Economic History Review, 6*(1), 55–67. https://doi.org/10.2307/2591021

Employment and Social Development Canada. (2018). *Opportunity for all: Canada's first poverty reduction strategy.* Employment and Social Development Canada.

Engels, F. (2009). *The condition of the working class in England.* Oxford University. (Original work published 1845)

Engle, P.L., & Black, M.M. (2008). The effect of poverty on child development and educational outcomes. *Annals of the New York Academy of Sciences, 1136*(June), 243–256. https://doi.org/10.1196/annals.1425.023

Erasmus, G., & Dussault, R. (1996). *Report of the Royal Commission on Aboriginal Peoples, Volume 3: Gathering strength.* The Commission.

Erikson, R. (1993). Descriptions of inequality: The Swedish approach to welfare research. In M. Nussbaum & A. Sen (Eds.), *The quality of life* (pp. 67–83). Clarendon Press.

Esping-Andersen, G. (1985a). Power and distributional regimes. *Politics and Society, 14*(2), 223–256. https://doi.org/10.1177/003232928501400204

Esping-Andersen, G. (1985b). *Politics against markets: The social democratic road to power.* Princeton University Press.

Esping-Andersen, G. (1990). *The three worlds of welfare capitalism.* Princeton University Press.

Esping-Andersen, G. (1992). The making of a social democratic state. In K. Misgeld, K. Molin, & K. Åmark (Eds.), *Creating social democracy: A century of the Social Democratic Labor Party in Sweden.* Pennsylvania State University Press.

Esping-Andersen, G. (2015). Welfare regimes and social stratification. *Journal of European Social Policy, 25*(1), 124–134. https://doi.org/10.1177 /0958928714556976

Esping-Andersen, G., Friedland, R., & Olin Wright, E. (1976). Modes of class struggle and the capitalist state. *Kapitalistate, 4/5,* 186–220.

Esping-Andersen, G., & Myles, J. (2009). Economic inequality and the welfare state. In W. Salverda, B. Nolan, & T.M. Smeeding (Eds.), *The Oxford handbook of economic inequality* (pp. 639–664). Oxford University Press.

Evans, G.W. (2004). The environment of childhood poverty. *The American Psychologist, 59*(2), 77–92. https://doi.org/10.1037/0003-066X.59.2.77

Evans, P. (2010). Women's poverty in Canada: Cross-currents in an ebbing tide. In G. Schaffner Goldberg (Ed.), *Poor women in rich countries: The feminization of poverty over the life course* (pp. 151–173). Oxford University Press.

Evans, R., Pegg, D., Lawrence, F., & Barr, C. (2019, November 29). The US donors who gave generously to rightwing UK groups. *The Guardian.* https://www.theguardian.com/politics/2019/nov/29/the-us-donors-who-gave-generously-to-rightwing-uk-groups

Evers-Hillstrom, K. (2020). *Majority of lawmakers in 116th Congress are millionaires.* Center for Responsive Politics. https://www.opensecrets.org/news/2020/04/majority-of-lawmakers-millionaires/

Facundo, A., Chancel, L., Piketty, T., Saez, E., & Zucman, G. (Eds.). (2018). *World inequality report.* Harvard University Press.

Fanelli, C., & Shields, J. (Eds.). (2015). Precarious work and the struggle for living wages. *Alternate Routes: A Journal of Critical Social Research, 27.* http://www.alternateroutes.ca/index.php/ar/article/view/22415

Fantasia, R., & Voss, K. (2004). *Hard work: Remaking the American labor movement.* University of California Press.

Farnsworth, K. (2012). *Social versus corporate welfare: Competing needs and interests within the welfare state.* Palgrave Macmillan.

Fellegi, I.P. (1997). *On poverty and low income.* Statistics Canada.

Finkel, A. (2006). *Social policy and practice in Canada: A history.* Wilfrid Laurier University Press.

Finkel, A. (2019). *Compassion: A global history of social policy.* Red Globe Press.

Fischer, C.S., Hout, M., Sanchez Jankowski, M., Lucas, S.R., Swidler, A., & Voss, K. (Eds.). (1996). *Inequality by design: Cracking the bell curve myth.* Princeton University Press.

Fishback, P.V. (2020). Social insurance and public assistance in the twentieth-century United States. *Journal of Economic History, 80*(2), 311–335. https://doi.org/10.1017/S0022050720000200

Fisher, G. (1992). The development and history of the poverty thresholds. *Social Security Bulletin, 5*(4), 3–14. PMID: 1300640.

Fitzpatrick, S., Pawson, H., Bramley, G., Wilcox, S., & Watts, B. (2012). *The homelessness monitor: Scotland 2012.* Crisis.

Fitzpatrick, S., Pawson, H., Bramley, G., Wilcox, S., & Watts, B. (2013). *The homelessness monitor: Wales 2012.* Crisis.

Fitzpatrick, S., Pawson, H., Bramley, G., Wilcox, S., & Watts, B. (2014). *The homelessness monitor: Northern Ireland 2013.* Crisis.

Fitzpatrick, S., Pawson, H., Bramley, G., Wilcox, S., & Watts, B. (2015). *The homelessness monitor: England 2015.* Crisis.

Flecha, R., & Santa Cruz, I. (2011). Cooperation for economic success: The Mondragon case. *Analyse & Kritik, 33*(1), 157–170. https://doi.org/10.1515/auk-2011-0113

Fleras, A. (2017). *Unequal relations: A critical introduction to race, ethnic, and Aboriginal dynamics in Canada* (8th ed.). Pearson.

Fleury, D., & Fortin, M. (2006). *When working is not enough to escape poverty: An analysis of Canada's working poor.* Policy Research Group, Human Resources and Social Development Canada.

Fodor, M. (2014). Taxation and the neo-liberal counter revolution: The Canadian case. In A. Himelfarb & J. Himelfarb (Eds.), *Tax is not a four-letter word: A different take on taxes in Canada* (pp. 101–117). Wilfrid Laurier University Press.

Foner, E. (1984). Why is there no socialism in the United States? *History Workshop, 17,* 57–84. https://doi.org/10.1093/hwj/17.1.57

Foner, E. (2005). *Forever free: The story of emancipation and reconstruction.* Vintage Books.

Food Banks Canada. (2014). *Hungercount 2014: A comprehensive report on hunger and food bank use in Canada, and recommendations for change.* Food Banks Canada.

Forbes. (2018, October 31). The *Forbes* 400 [Special issue]. *Forbes.*

Forget, E.L. (2011). The town with no poverty: The health effects of a Canadian guaranteed annual income field experiment. *Canadian Public Policy, 37*(3), 283–305. https://doi.org/10.3138/cpp.37.3.283

Forget, E.L. (2020). *Basic income for Canadians: From the COVID-19 emergency to financial security for all.* James Lorimer and Company.

Forsberg, M. (1986). *The evolution of social welfare policy in Sweden.* Swedish Institute.

Fortin, P. (2010). Quebec is fairer: There is less poverty and less inequality in Quebec. *Inroads, 26*(Winter), 58–65.

Foster, J.B. (1998). Malthus' essay on population at age 200. *Monthly Review, 50*(7). https://monthlyreview.org/1998/12/01/malthus-essay-on-population-at-age-200/

Foster, J.B. (2008). Peak oil and energy imperialism. *Monthly Review, 60*(3), 12–33. https://doi.org/10.14452/MR-060-03-2008-07_2

Francis-Devine, B. (2020). *Poverty in the UK: Statistics* (Briefing Paper Number 7096). House of Commons Library.

Frank, T. (2012). *Pity the billionaire: The hard-times swindle and the unlikely comeback of the right.* Picador.

Frankish, C.J., Wang, S.W., & Quantz, D. (2005). Homelessness and health in Canada. *Canadian Journal of Public Health, 96*(Supplement 2), 23–29. https://doi.org/10.1007/BF03403700

Fraser, D. (2009). *The evolution of the British welfare state* (4th ed.). Palgrave Macmillan.

Fraser, N. (1989). Women, welfare and the politics of need interpretation. In P. Lassman (Ed.), *Politics and social theory* (pp. 104–122). Routledge.

Fraser, S. (Ed.). (1995). *The bell curve wars: Race, intelligence, and the future of America*. Basic Books.

Freeland, C. (2012). *Plutocrats: The rise of the new super rich and the fall of everyone else*. Doubleday Canada.

Frege, C.M., & Kelly, J. (2003). Union revitalization strategies in comparative perspective. *European Journal of Industrial Relations, 9*(1), 7–24. https://doi. org/10.1177/095968010391002

Freitag, P.J. (1975). The cabinet and big business: A study of interlocks. *Social Problems, 23*(2), 137–152. https://doi.org/10.2307/799652

Frideres, J. (2016). *First Nations people in Canada*. Oxford University Press.

Friedman, H.H., & Hertz, S. (2015). *Is the United States still the best country in the world? Think again*. Social Science Research Network (SSRN). http:// dx.doi.org/10.2139/ssrn.2622722

Friedman, Z. (2018, June 13). Student loan debt statistics in 2018: A $1.5 trillion crisis. *Forbes*. https://www.forbes.com/sites/zackfriedman/2018/06/13 /student-loan-debt-statistics-2018/#72a8997b7310

Fryer, P. (2018). *Staying power: The history of Black people in Britain*. Pluto Press.

Fuller, C. (2011, October 27). Homeless shelter systems and what they don't tell you. *Huffpost*. https://www.huffpost.com/entry/homeless -shelter-parents_b_1035952

Furniss, N., & Tilton, T. (1979). *The case for the welfare state: From social security to social equality*. Indiana University Press.

Gaetz, S. (2013). The criminalization of homelessness: A Canadian perspective. *European Journal of Homelessness, 7*(2), 357–362. https://www. feantsa.org/download/sg_response7772916537698278481.pdf

Gaetz, S. (2020). Making the prevention of homelessness a priority: The role of social innovation. *American Journal of Economics and Sociology, 79*(2), 353–381. https://doi.org/10.1111/ajes.12328

Gaetz, S., Dej, E., Richter, T., & Redman, M. (2016). *The state of homelessness in Canada 2016*. The Homeless Hub Press.

Gaetz, S., Gulliver, T., & Richter, T. (2014). *The state of homelessness in Canada 2014*. The Homeless Hub Press.

Galbraith, J.K. (1971). *A contemporary guide to economics, peace, and laughter*. Houghton Mifflin.

Galbraith, J.K. (1976). *The affluent society*. Houghton Mifflin. (Original work published in 1958)

Gangl, M. (2005). Income inequality, permanent incomes, and income dynamics: Comparing Europe to the United States. *Work and Occupations, 32*(2), 140–162. https://doi.org/10.1177/0730888404274354

Gans, H.J. (1962). The positive functions of poverty. *American Journal of Sociology, 78*(2), 275–289. https://doi.org/10.1086/225324

Gans, H.J. (1995). *The war against the poor: The underclass and anti-poverty policy*. Basic Books.

Gans, H.J. (1996). The so-called underclass and the future of antipoverty policy. In B. Lykes, A. Banuazizi, R. Liem, & M. Morris (Eds.), *Myths about the powerless: Contesting social inequalities* (pp. 87–104). Temple University Press.

Gans, H.J. (2012). The benefits of poverty. *Challenge, 55*(1), 114–125. https://doi.org/10.2753/0577-5132550106

Gardner, H. (1983). *Frames of mind: The theory of multiple intelligences.* Basic Books.

Gardner, H. (1999). *Intelligence reframed: Multiple intelligences for the 21st century.* Basic Books.

Gardner, M., Wamhoff, S., Martellotta, M., & Rocque, L. (2019). *Corporate tax avoidance remains rampant under new tax law: 60 profitable companies avoided all federal taxes in 2018.* Institute on Taxation and Economic Policy. https://itep.sfo2.digitaloceanspaces.com/04119-Corporate-Tax-Avoidance-Remains-Rampant-Under-New-Tax-Law_ITEP.pdf

Garfinkel, I., Rainwater, L., & Smeeding, T. (2010). *Wealth and welfare states: Is America a laggard or leader.* Oxford University Press.

Garland, D. (2016). *The welfare state: A very short introduction.* Oxford University Press.

Gaskell, E. (2010). *Mary Barton.* Wordsworth Editions. (Original work published 1848)

Gautie, J., & Schmitt, J. (2010). *Low-wage work in the wealthy world.* Russell Sage Foundation.

Gebelhoff, R. (2018, January 22). Projections for student loan deficits are terrifying. It's time to act. *The Washington Post.* https://www.washingtonpost.com/blogs/post-partisan/wp/2018/01/22/projections-for-student-loan-defaults-are-terrifying-its-time-to-act/

Gelissen, J. (2002). *Worlds of welfare, worlds of consent: Public opinion on the welfare state.* Brill Academic Publishing.

Geremek, B. (1997). *Poverty: A history.* Blackwell Books.

Gerull, S. (2014). Evictions due to rent arrears: A comparative analysis of evictions in fourteen countries. *European Journal of Homelessness, 8*(2), 137–155. https://www.feantsaresearch.org/download/feantsa-ejh-8-2-web9013629343468406009.pdf

Gibson-Graham, J.K. (2003). Enabling ethical economies: Cooperativism and class. *Critical Sociology, 29*(2), 123–161. https://doi.org/10.1163/156916303769155788

Gilbert, R., Murphy, N.A., Stepka, A., Barrett, M., & Worku, D. (2018). Would a basic income guarantee reduce the motivation to work? An analysis of labor responses in 16 trial programs. *Basic Income Studies, 13*(2), 1–12. https://doi.org/10.1515/bis-2018-0011

Gilder, G. (1981). *Wealth and poverty.* Bantam Books.

Gilens, M. (1999). *Why Americans hate welfare: Race, media, and the politics of antipoverty policy.* University of Chicago Press.

Gill, T.M. (2018). The persistence of the power elite: Presidential cabinets and corporate interlocks, 1968–2018. *Social Currents, 5*(6), 501–511. https://doi.org/10.1177/2329496518797857

Gillie, A. (1996). The origin of the poverty line. *Economic History Review, 49*(4), 715–730. https://doi.org/10.2307/2597970

Ginsburg, N. (1992). *Divisions of welfare: A critical introduction to comparative social policy*. Sage.

Giroux, H.A. (2013). *America's educational deficit and the war on youth*. Monthly Review Press.

Glasbeek, H. (2002). *Wealth by stealth: Corporate crime, corporate law, and the perversion of democracy*. Between the Lines.

Glasbeek, H. (2017). *Class privilege: How law shelters shareholders and coddles capitalism*. Between the Lines.

Glasbeek, H. (2018a). Coerced and unfree in the private sector. *Critical Criminology, 26*(4), 579–593. https://doi.org/10.1007/s10612-018-9419-6

Glasbeek, H. (2018b). Law: Ideological whitewashing and positive enabling of coercion. In S. Bittle, L. Snider, S. Tombs, & D. Whyte (Eds.), *Revisiting crimes of the powerful: Marxism, crime and deviance* (pp. 20–31). Routledge.

Goldberg, G.S. (2010a). Feminization of poverty in the US: Any surprises? In G. Schaffner Goldberg (Ed.), *Poor women in rich countries: The feminization of poverty over the life course* (pp. 235–267). Oxford University Press.

Goldberg, G.S. (Ed.). (2010b). *Poor women in rich countries: The feminization of poverty over the life course*. Oxford University Press.

Goldberg, G.S., & Kremen, E. (Eds.). (1990). *The feminization of poverty: Only in America?* Praeger.

Goldfield, M. (1989). *The decline of organized labor in the United States*. University of Chicago Press.

Goldfield, M. (1997). *The color of politics: Race and the mainsprings of American politics*. New Press.

Gomez, R., & Tzioumis, K. (2006). *What do unions do to CEO compensation?* (CEP Discussion Paper No. 720). Centre for Economic Performance, London School of Economics and Political Science.

Gordon, D.M., Reich, M., & Edwards, R. (1982). *Segmented work, divided workers: The historical transformation of labor in the United States*. Cambridge University Press.

Gordon, L. (1988). What does welfare regulate. *Social Research, 55*, 609–630. https://doi.org/10.1017/S0022029900033409

Gordon, L. (Ed.). (1990). *The new feminist scholarship on the welfare state*. University of Wisconsin Press.

Gordon, L. (1994). *Pitied but not entitled: Single mothers and the history of welfare*. Free Press.

Gorski, P. (2008). The myth of the culture of poverty. *Educational Leadership, 65*(7), 32–36. http://www.ascd.org/publications/educational-leadership/apr08/vol65/num07/The-Myth-of-the-Culture-of-Poverty.aspx

Gorz, A. (1968). Reform and revolution. *Socialist Register, 5*, 111–143. https://socialistregister.com/index.php/srv/article/view/5272/2173

Gough, I. (2016). Welfare states and environmental states: A comparative analysis. *Environmental Politics, 25*(1), 24–47. https://doi.org/10.1080/0964 4016.2015.1074382

Gould, A. (1993). *Capitalist welfare systems: A comparison of Japan, Britain and Sweden.* Longman.

Gould, E., Davis, A., & Kimball, W. (2015). *Broad-based wage growth is a key tool in the fight against poverty* (EPI Briefing Paper #399). Economic Policy Institute.

Gould, S.J. (1994, November 28). Curveball. *The New Yorker, 70*(39), 139–149. https://www.newyorker.com/magazine/1994/11/28

Government Statistical Service. (2019). *Harmonisation of definitions of homelessness for UK official statistics: A feasibility report.* Government Statistical Service.

Graubard, S.R. (1986). *Norden – Passion for equality.* Norwegian University Press.

Greenbaum, S. (2015). *Blaming the poor: The long shadow of the Moynihan report on cruel images of poverty.* Rutgers University Press.

Greene, J.A., & Riggs, K.R. (2015). Why is there no generic insulin? Historical origins of a modern problem. *New England Journal of Medicine, 372*(12), 1171–1175. https://doi.org/10.1056/NEJMms1411398

Grenier, A., Barken, R., Sussman, T., Rothwell, D., Bourgeois-Guérin, V., & Lavoie, J.-P. (2016). A literature review of homelessness and aging: Suggestions for a policy and practice-relevant research agenda. *Canadian Journal on Aging, 35*(1), 28–41. https://doi.org/10.1017 /S0714980815000616

Greve, B. (Ed.). (2019). *Routledge handbook of the welfare state* (2nd ed.). Routledge.

Griffin, L., Wallace, M.E., & Rubin, B.A. (1986). Capitalist resistance to the organization of labor before the New Deal. *American Sociological Review, 51*(2), 147–167. https://doi.org/10.2307/2095513

Guest, D. (1997). *The emergence of social security in Canada.* UBC Press.

Gupta, R.P.-S., de Wit, M.L., & McKeown, D. (2007). The impact of poverty on the current and future health status of children. *Paediatrics and Child Health, 12*(8), 667–672. https://doi.org/10.1093/pch/12.8.667

Gustafsson, B., & Lindblom, M. (1993). Poverty lines in seven European countries: Australia, Canada and the USA. *Journal of European Social Policy, 3*(1), 21–38. https://doi.org/10.1177/095892879300300102

Haber, H. (2015). Regulation as social policy: Home evictions and repossession in the UK and Sweden. *Public Administration, 93*(3), 806–821. https://doi.org/10.1111/padm.12171

Hacker, A. (1995). Caste, crime, and precocity. In S. Fraser (Ed.), *The bell curve wars: Race, intelligence, and the future of America* (pp. 97–108). Basic Books.

Hacker, J.S. (2008). *The great risk shift: The new economic insecurity and the decline of the America dream.* Oxford University Press.

Haddow, R. (2014). Power resources and the Canadian state: Unions, partisanship and interprovincial differences in inequality and poverty reduction. *Canadian Journal of Sociology, 47*(4), 717–739. https://doi .org/10.1017/S0008423914001036

Haddow, R. (2015). *Comparing Quebec and Ontario: Political economy and public policy at the turn of the century.* University of Toronto Press.

Haddow, R., & Klassen, T. (2006). *Partnership, globalization, and Canadian labour market policy: Four provinces in comparative perspective.* University of Toronto Press.

Hadler, M. (2009). Why do people accept different income ratios? *Acta Sociologica, 48*(2), 131–154. https://doi.org/10.1177/0001699305053768

Hagenaars, A.M. (1986). *The perception of poverty.* North Holland.

Hall, P.A., & Soskice, D. (Eds.). (2001). *Varieties of capitalism: The institutional foundation of comparative advantage.* Oxford University Press.

Hall, S. (1977). Rethinking the base and superstructure metaphor. In J. Bloomfield (Ed.), *Class, hegemony and party* (pp. 43–72). Lawrence and Wishart.

Hall, S. (1988). *The hard road to renewal: Thatcherism and the crisis of the left.* Verso.

Halleröd, B. (1995). The truly poor: Direct and indirect measurement of consensual poverty in Sweden. *European Journal of Social Policy, 5*(2), 111–129. https://doi.org/10.1177/095892879500500203

Hanna, T.M. (2018). *Our common wealth: The return of public ownership in the United States.* Manchester University Press.

Hanna, T. (2019). *A history of nationalization in the United States, 1917–2009.* The Democracy Collaborative. https://thenextsystem.org/history -of-nationalization-in-the-us

Hansen, R., & King, D. (2013). *Sterilized by the state: Eugenics, race and the population scare in North America.* Cambridge University Press.

Harles, J. (2017). *Seeking equality: The political economy of the common good in the United States and Canada.* University of Toronto Press.

Harrington, M. (1981). *The other America: Poverty in the United States.* Penguin Books. (Original work published 1962)

Harrington, M. (1984). *The new American poverty.* Holt, Rinehart and Winston.

Harrison, B., & Sum, A. (1979). The theory of "dual" or segmented labor markets. *Journal of Economic Issues, 13*(3), 687–706. https://doi.org/10.1080 /00213624.1979.11503671

Harriss-White, B. (2006). Poverty and capitalism. *Economic and Political Weekly, 41*(13), 1241–1246. https://www.epw.in/journal/2006/13/perspectives /poverty-and-capitalism.html

Hartlep, N.D., Eckrich, L.L.T., & Hensley, B.O. (Eds.). (2017). *The neoliberal agenda and the student debt crisis in U.S. higher education.* Routledge.

Hartman, P. (2013, December 3). Why do some homeless people shun shelters. *House the Homeless* [blog]. https://housethehomeless.org/2013 /12/why-do-some-homeless-people-shun-shelters/

Hartmann, T. (2002). *Unequal protection: The rise of corporate dominance and the theft of human rights.* Berrett-Koehler Publishers.

Hartz, L. (1955). *The liberal tradition in America: An interpretation of American political thought since the revolution.* Harcourt Brace.

Hartz, L. (1964). *The founding of new societies.* Harcourt, Brace & World.

Harvey, D.L., & Reed, M.H. (1996). The culture of poverty: An ideological analysis. *Sociological Perspectives, 39*(4), 465–496. https://doi.org/10.2307/1389418

Hasen, R.L. (2016). *Plutocrats united: Campaign money, the Supreme Court, and the distortion of American elections.* Yale University Press.

Haveman, R.H. (1987). The war on poverty, and the poor and non-poor. *Political Science Quarterly, 102*(1), 65–78. https://doi.org/10.2307/2151485

Hawke, W., Davis, M., Erlenbusch, B., Angeles, L., & Coalition to End Hunger and Homelessness. (2007). *Dying without dignity: Homeless deaths in Los Angeles County: 2000–2007.* Los Angeles Coalition to End Hunger and Homelessness.

Hay, C. (2010). Chronicles of a death foretold: The winter of discontent and construction of the crisis of British Keynesianism. *Parliamentary Affairs, 65*(3), 446–470. https://doi.org/10.1093/pa/gsp056

Heclo, H. (1974). *Modern social politics in Britain and Sweden: From relief to income maintenance.* Yale University Press.

Heisz, A. (2016). Trends in income inequality in Canada and elsewhere. In D. Green, C. Riddell, & F. St.-Hillaire (Eds.), *Income inequality: The Canadian story* (pp. 78–102). Institute for Research on Public Policy.

Hennock, E.P. (1987). The measurement of urban poverty: From the metropolis to the nation, 1880–1920. *Economic History Review, 40*(2), 208–227. https://doi.org/10.1111/j.1468-0289.1987.tb00426.x

Hernes, H.M. (1987). *Welfare state and woman power: Essays in state feminism.* Norwegian University Press.

Herring, C. (2014). The new logics of homeless seclusion: Homeless encampments in America's West Coast cities. *City and Community, 13*(4), 285–309. https://doi.org/10.1111/cico.12086

Herring, C. (2015). Tent City, America. *Places Journal,* 12–14. https://doi.org/10.22269/151214

Herrnstein, R.J. (1971). I.Q. *Atlantic Monthly, 238*(3), 43–64. https://www.gwern.net/docs/iq/1971-herrnstein.pdf

Herrnstein, R.J., & Murray, C. (1994). *The bell curve: Intelligence and class structure in American life.* The Free Press.

Hertzman, C. (2010). Framework for the social determinants of early child development. In R.E. Tremblay, M. Boivin, & R.D. Peters (Eds.), *Encyclopedia of early childhood development* (pp. 1–9). Centre of Excellence for Early Childhood Development and Strategic Knowledge Cluster on Early Child Development.

Hewitt, C. (1977). The effect of political democracy and social democracy on equality in industrialized societies: A cross-national comparison. *American Sociological Review, 42*, 450–464. https://doi.org/10.2307/2094750

Hicks, A. (1991). Unions, social democracy, welfare and growth. *Research in Political Sociology, 5*, 209–234.

Hicks, A. (1999). *Social democracy and welfare capitalism: A century of income security politics.* Cornell University Press.

Hicks, A., & Swank, D. (1984). On the political economy of welfare expansion: A comparative analysis of 18 advanced capitalist democracies. *Comparative Political Studies, 17*(1), 81–119. https://doi.org/10.1177/001041408401700 1003

Hills, J. (2015). *Good times, bad times: The welfare myth of them and us.* Policy Press.

Hills, J., Ditch, J., & Glennerster, H. (Eds.). (2001). *Beveridge and social security: An international retrospective.* Clarendon Press.

Himelfarb, A., & Himelfarb, J. (Eds.). (2014). *Tax is not a four letter word: A different take on taxes in Canada.* Wilfrid Laurier University Press.

Himmelfarb, G. (1985). *The idea of poverty.* Vintage Books.

Himmelstein, D.U., Lawless, R.M., Thorne, D., Foohey, P., & Woolhandler, S. (2019). Medical bankruptcy: Still common despite the Affordable Care Act. *American Journal of Public Health, 109*(3), 431–433. https://doi.org/10.2105/AJPH.2018.304901

Himmelstein, D.U., Thorne, D., Warren, E., & Woolhandler, S. (2009). Medical bankruptcy in the United States, 2007: Results of a national study. *The American Journal of Medicine, 122*, 741–746. https://doi.org/10.1016/j.amjmed.2009.04.012

Hindman, H.D. (2002). *Child labor: An American history.* M.E. Sharpe.

Hirsch, D. (2013). *Addressing the poverty premium: Approaches to regulation.* Consumer Futures.

Hirschler, B. (2015, October 13). How the U.S. pays 3 times more for drugs: In Britain the world's top-selling medicines are three times cheaper than in the U.S. *Scientific American.* https://www.scientificamerican.com/article/how-the-u-s-pays-3-times-more-for-drugs/

Hofstadter, R. (1955). *Social Darwinism in American thought.* Beacon Press.

Hofstede, G. (2001). *Culture's consequences: Comparing values, behaviors, institutions, and organizations across nations.* Sage Publications.

Hofstede, G., Jan Hofstede, G., & Minkov, M. (2010). *Cultures and organizations: Software of the mind.* McGraw-Hill.

Hofstede Insights. (n.d.). *Home.* Hofstede Insights. https://www.hofstede-insights.com

Hollingsworth, J.R., & Boyer, R. (Eds.). (1999). *Contemporary capitalism: The embeddedness of institutions.* Cambridge University Press.

Holmes, I. (2018, April 25). What happens when geneticists talk sloppily about race. *The Atlantic.* http://www.theatlantic.com

Homelessadvice.com. (2018, July 3). *Why do homeless people avoid shelters?* http://homelessadvice.com/

Hope, J.G. (2016). Why is there no socialism in the United States? Law and the racial divide in the American working class, 1676–1964. *Texas Law Review, 94*(7), 1555–1590. https://texaslawreview.org/wp-content/uploads/2016/09/Pope.pdf

Horowitz, G. (1968). *Canadian labour in politics.* University of Toronto Press.

Hotten, R. (2015, December 10). Volkswagen: The scandal explained. *BBC News.* https://www.bbc.com/news/business-34324772

Huang, Q., Jiang, F., Lie, E., & Que, T. (2017). The effect of labor unions on CEO compensation. *Journal of Financial and Quantitative Analysis, 52*(2), 553–582. https://doi.org/10.1017/S0022109017000072

Huber, E., Huo, J., & Stephens, J.D. (2017). Power, policy, and top income shares. *Socio-Economic Review, 17*(2), 231–253. https://doi.org/10.1093/ser/mwx027

Huber, E., & Stephens, J.D. (2001). *Development and crisis of the welfare state: Parties and policies in global markets.* University of Chicago Press.

Huber, E., & Stephens, J.D. (2014). Income inequality and redistribution in post-industrial democracies: Demographic, economic and political determinants. *Socio-Economic Review, 12*(2), 245–267. https://doi.org/10.1093/ser/mwu001

Hudson, M. (1996a). Cashing in on poverty. *The Nation, 262*(20), 11–14.

Hudson, M. (Ed.). (1996b). *Merchants of misery: How corporate America profits from poverty.* Common Courage Press.

Hugo, V. (2001). *Les misérables.* Penguin. (Original work published 1862)

Hunter, J., Linden-Retek, P., Shebaya, S., and Halpert, S. (Eds.). (2014). *Welcome home: The rise of tent cities in the United States.* National Law Center on Homelessness and Poverty/Allard K. Lowenstein International Human Rights Clinic, Yale University.

Huston, A.C. (Ed.). (1994). *Children in poverty.* Cambridge University Press.

Huston, A.C., McLoyd, V.C., & Garcia Coll, C. (1994). Children and poverty: Issues in contemporary research. *Child Development, 65*(2), 275–282. https://doi.org/10.1111/j.1467-8624.1994.tb00750.x

Hutter, B. (Ed.). (2017). *Risk, resilience, and environmental law.* Edward Elgar Publishing.

Huyser, K.R., Takei, I., and Sakamoto, A. (2014). Demographic factors associated with poverty among American Indians and Alaska Natives. *Race and Social Problems, 6*(2), 120–134. https://doi.org/10.1007/s12552-013-9110-1

Huzel, J.P. (2006). *The popularization of Malthus in early nineteenth-century England: Martineau, Cobbett, and the pauper press.* Ashgate Publishing.

Hvid, H., & Falkum, E. (Eds.). (2018). *Work and wellbeing in the Nordic countries: A critical perspective on the world's best working lives.* Routledge.

Hwang, S.W. (2001). Homelessness and health. *Canadian Medical Association Journal, 164*(2), 229–233. https://www.cmaj.ca/content/164/2/229

Iceland, J. (2013). *Poverty in America: A handbook* (3rd ed.). University of California Press.

ILO (International Labour Organization). (2017). *Global estimates of child labour: Results and trends*. ILO.

ILO (International Labour Organization). (2019). *Work for a brighter future: Global Commission on the Future of Work*. ILO.

International Trade Union Confederation (ITUC). (2020). *2020 ITUC global rights index: The ten worst countries for workers*. ITUC.

Inter-Parliamentary Union. (2019). *Women in national parliaments*. http://archive.ipu.org/wmn-e/classif.htm (accessed June 2020)

Iversen, R.R., & Farber, N.R.B. (1996). Transmission of family values, work, and welfare among poor urban Black women. *Work and Occupations, 23*(4), 437–460. https://doi.org/10.1177/0730888496023004006

Jackson, A. (2020). *The case for a wealth tax in Canada*. Broadbent Institute.

Jackson, B., & Saunders, R. (Eds.). (2012). *Making Thatcher's Britain*. Cambridge University Press.

Jacobson, M.F. (1998). *Whiteness of a different color: European immigrants and the alchemy of race*. Harvard University Press.

Jacoby, R., & Glauberman, N. (Eds.). (1995). *The bell curve debate: History, documents, opinions*. Random House.

Jacoby, S.M. (Ed.). (1991). *Masters to managers: Historical and comparative perspectives on American employers*. Columbia University Press.

Jacques, O., & Noël, A. (2018). The case for welfare state universalism, or the lasting relevance of the paradox of redistribution. *Journal of European Social Policy, 28*(1), 70–85. https://doi.org/10.1177/0958928717700564

Jæger, M.M. (2006). Welfare regimes and attitudes towards redistribution: The regime hypothesis revisited. *European Sociological Review, 22*(2), 157–170. https://doi.org/10.1093/esr/jci049

Janoski, T., Oliver, C., & Luke, D. (2014). *The causes of structural unemployment: Four factors keeping people from the jobs they deserve*. Polity Press.

Jäntti, M. (2009). Mobility in the United States in comparative perspective. In M. Cancian & S. Danziger (Eds.), *Changing poverty, changing policies* (pp. 180–200). Russell Sage Foundation.

Jäntti, M., & Danziger, S. (2000). Income poverty in advanced countries. In A. Atkinson & F. Bourguignon (Eds.), *Handbook of income distribution* (pp. 309–378). North Holland.

Jay, M. (1973). *The dialectical imagination: A history of the Frankfurt school and the Institute for Social Research, 1923–1950*. Little Brown.

Jeffries, S. (2016). *Grand hotel abyss: The lives of the Frankfurt school*. Verso.

Jencks, C. (1992). *Rethinking social policy: Race, poverty, and the underclass*. Harper.

Jenkins, S.P. (2011). *Changing fortunes: Income mobility and poverty dynamics in Britain*. Oxford University Press.

Jensen, A. (1969). How much can we boost IQ and scholastic achievement? *Harvard Educational Review, 39*(1), 1–123. https://doi.org/10.17763/haer.39.1.l3u15956627424k7

Jensen, A. (1995). Psychological research on race differences. *American Psychologist, 50*(1), 41–42. https://doi.org/10.1037/0003-066X.50.1.41

Johnson, D.S., & Smeeding, T.M. (2012). A consumer's guide to interpreting U.S. poverty measures. *Fast Focus, 14*, 1–7. https://www.irp.wisc.edu/publications/fastfocus/pdfs/FF14-2012.pdf

Johnson, G., Ribar, D.C., & Zhu, A. (2017). *Women's homelessness: International evidence on causes, consequences, coping and policies.* IZA Institute of Labor Economics.

Johnson, R. (2010). African Americans and homelessness: Moving through history. *Journal of Black Studies, 40*(4), 583–605. https://doi.org/10.1177/0021934708315487

Johnson, S. (2013) *Delphi complete works of Samuel Johnson.* Delphi Classics. (Original work published 1750)

Jones, M.M. (2016). Does race matter in addressing homelessness? A review of the literature. *World Medical and Health Policy, 8*(2), 139–156. https://doi.org/10.1002/wmh3.189

Josephson, M. (1962). *The robber barons.* Harcourt, Brace Jovanovich.

Jütte, R. (1994). *Poverty and deviance in early modern Europe.* Cambridge University Press.

Kahl, S. (2005). The religious roots of poverty policy: Catholic, Lutheran, and reformed Protestant traditions compared. *European Journal of Sociology, 46*(1), 91–126. https://doi.org/10.1017/S0003975605000044

Kalleberg, A.L. (2009). Precarious work, insecure workers: Employment relations in transition. *American Sociological Review, 74*(1)1–22. https://doi.org/10.1177/000312240907400101

Kalleberg, A.L. (2011). *Good jobs, bad jobs: The rise of polarized and precarious employment systems in the United States, 1970s–2000s.* Russell Sage Foundation.

Kalleberg, A.L. (2018). *Precarious lives: Job insecurity and well-being in rich democracies.* Polity Press.

Kalleberg, A.L., Wallace, M., & Althauser, R.P. (1981). Economic segmentation, worker power, and income inequality. *American Journal of Sociology, 87*(3), 651–683. https://doi.org/10.1086/227499

Kananen, J. (2016). *The Nordic welfare state in three eras: From emancipation to discipline.* Routledge.

Kangas, O. (1991). *The politics of social rights: Studies on the dimensions of sickness insurance in OECD countries.* Swedish Institute for Social Research, Stockholm University.

Kangas, O., Jauhiainen, S., Simanainen, M., & Yikännö, M. (2019). *The basic income experiment 2017–2018 in Finland: Preliminary results.* Ministry of Social Affairs and Health.

Kangas, O., & Palme, J. (Eds.). (2005). *Social policy and economic development in the Nordic countries.* Palgrave Macmillan.

Karim, N. (2020, March 9). Bangladesh urged to stop worker abuse in garment industry. *Reuters.* https://ca.reuters.com/article/idUSKBN20W25O

Karp, B. (2011). *The girl's guide to homelessness: A memoir.* Harlequin Enterprises.

Katz, M.B. (1986). *In the shadow of the poorhouse: A social history of welfare in America.* Basic Books.

Katz, M.B. (2013). *The undeserving poor: America's enduring confrontation with poverty* (2nd ed.). Oxford University Press.

Kautto, M., Fritzell, J., Hvinden, B., Kvist, J., & Uusitalo, H. (Eds.). (2001). *Nordic welfare states in the European context.* Routledge.

Kawachi, I., & Kennedy, B.P. (2002). *The health of nations: Why inequality is harmful to your health.* The New Press.

Kealey, G. (Ed). (1973). *Canada investigates industrialism.* University of Toronto Press.

Keller, H. (1913). *Out of the dark: Essays, letters and addresses on physical and social vision.* Doubleday.

Kelly, G. (Ed.). (2017). *The Mondragón report.* Praxis Peace Institute. https://www.praxispeace.org/assets/pdf/THE-MONDRAGON-REPORT.pdf

Kelso, W.A. (1994). *Poverty and the underclass: Changing perceptions of the poor in America.* New York University Press.

Kendi, I.X. (2016). *Stamped from the beginning: The definitive history of racist ideas in America.* Bold Type Books.

Kennedy, D. (1996). The decline of the Socialist Party of America, 1901–1919. *Socialist History, 9,* 8–22.

Kenway, P., & Palmer, G. (2007). *Poverty among ethnic groups: How and why does it differ?* New Policy Institute/Joseph Rowntree Foundation.

Kenworthy, L. (2007). *Measuring poverty and material deprivation.* Unpublished report prepared for Statistics Canada.

Kenworthy, L. (2008). *Jobs with equality.* Oxford University Press.

Kenworthy, L. (2011). *Progress for the poor.* Oxford University Press.

Kenworthy, L. (2020). *Social democratic capitalism.* Oxford University Press.

King Jr., M.L. (2015). The world house. In *The Radical King* (pp. 75–96). Beacon Press. (Original work published 1967)

King, S., & Stewart, J. (Eds.). (2007). *Welfare peripheries: The development of welfare states in nineteenth and twentieth century Europe.* Peter Lang.

Kjeldstad, R. (2001). Gender policies and gender equality. In M. Kautto, J. Fritzell, B. Hvinden, J. Kvist, & H. Uusitalo (Eds.), *Nordic welfare states in the European context* (pp. 66–97). Routledge.

Klare, M.T. (2004). *Blood and oil: The dangers and consequences of America's growing petroleum dependency.* Metropolitan Books.

Klein, E. (2018, March 27). Sam Harris, Charles Murray, and the allure of race science. *Vox.* https://www.vox.com/policy-and-politics/2018/3/27/15695060/sam-harris-charles-murray-race-iq-forbidden-knowledge-podcast-bell-curve

Koblik, S. (1975). *Sweden's development from poverty to affluence, 1750–1979.* University of Minnesota Press.

Korpi, W. (1980). Approaches to the study of poverty in the United States: Critical notes from a European perspective. In V.T. Covello (Ed.), *Poverty and public policy: An evaluation of social science research* (pp. 287–314). Schenkman.

Korpi, W. (1983). *The democratic class struggle.* Routledge and Kegan Paul.

Korpi, W., & Palme, J. (1998). The paradox of redistribution and strategies of equality: Welfare state institutions, inequality, and poverty in Western countries. *American Sociological Review, 63,* 661–687. https://doi .org/10.2307/2657333

Kouri, E.I. (1997). Health care and poor relief in Sweden and Finland. In O. Peter Grell & A. Cunningham (Eds.), *Health care and poor relief in Protestant Europe, 1500–1700* (pp. 167–203). Routledge.

Kristal, T. (2010). Good times, bad times: Postwar labor's share of national income in capitalist democracies. *American Sociological Review, 75*(5), 729–763. https://doi.org/10.1177/0003122410382640

Krugman, P. (2013). *End this depression now.* W.W. Norton & Company.

Kusmer, K.L. (2002). *Down and out and on the road: The homeless in American history.* Oxford University Press.

Kvist, J., Fritzell, J., Hvinden, B., & Kangas, O. (Eds.). (2012). *Changing social equality: The Nordic welfare model in the 21st century.* Policy Press.

Ladd-Taylor, M. (2020). *Fixing the poor: Eugenic sterilization and child welfare in the twentieth century.* Johns Hopkins University Press.

Ladner, J. (1971). *Tomorrow's tomorrow: The Black woman.* Doubleday.

Lansley, S. (2006). *Rich Britain: The rise and rise of the new super-wealthy.* Politicos.

Lansley, S. (2012). *The cost of inequality: Three decades of the super-rich and the economy.* Gibson Square Books.

Lansley, S., & Mack, J. (2015). *Breadline Britain: The rise of mass poverty.* Oneworld Publications.

Larsen, C.A. (2006). *The institutional logic of welfare states: How welfare regimes influence public support.* Ashgate.

Larsen, C.A. (2008). The institutional logic of welfare attitudes: How welfare regime attitudes influence public support. *Comparative Political Studies, 41*(2), 146–168. https://doi.org/10.1177/0010414006295234

Larsen, C.A. (2013). *The rise and fall of social cohesion: The construction and deconstruction of social trust in the US, UK, Sweden, and Denmark.* Oxford University Press.

Larsen, C.A., & Engel Dejgaard, T. (2013). The institutional logic of images of poor welfare recipients: A comparative study of British, Swedish, and Danish Newspapers. *Journal of European Social Policy, 23*(3), 287–299. https://doi.org/10.1177/0958928713480068

Laslett, J.H.M., & Martin Lipset, S. (Eds.). (1984). *Failure of a dream?: Essays in the history of American socialism.* University of California Press.

Lave, J. (1988). *Cognition in practice: Mind, mathematics, and culture in everyday life.* Cambridge University Press.

Leichter, H.M. (1979). *A comparative approach to policy analysis: Health care policy in four nations.* Cambridge University Press.

Leiman, M. (2010). *The political economy of racism.* Haymarket Books.

Lepianka, D., van Oorschot, W., & Gelissen, J. (2009). Popular explanations of poverty: A critical discussion of empirical research. *Journal of Social Policy, 38*(8), 421–438. https://doi.org/10.1017/S0047279409003092

Lester, H.E. (2001). Barriers to primary healthcare for the homeless: The general practitioner's perspective. *European Journal of General Practice, 7*(1), 6–12. https://doi.org/10.3109/13814780109048777

Lewis, H. (1967). *Culture, class, and poverty.* Cross-Tell Publishing Co.

Lewis, J. (1992). Gender and the development of welfare regimes. *Journal of European Social Policy, 2*(3), 159–173. https://doi.org/10.1177/095892879200200301

Lewis, O. (1959). *Five families: Mexican case studies in the culture of poverty.* Basic Books.

Lewis, O. (1966a). *La vida: A Puerto Rican family in the culture of poverty – San Juan and New York.* Random House.

Lewis, O. (1966b). The culture of poverty. *Scientific American, 215*(4), 19–25. https://doi.org/10.1038/scientificamerican1066-19

Lewis, O. (1968). The culture of poverty. In D.P. Moynihan (Ed.), *On understanding poverty: Perspectives from the social sciences* (pp. 187–200). Basic Books.

Lexier, R., Bangarth, S., & Weier, J. (Eds.). (2018). *Party of conscience: The CCF, NDP, and social democracy in Canada.* Between the Lines.

Lichter, D.T., & Crowley, M.L. (2002). Poverty in America: Beyond welfare reform. *Population Bulletin, 57*, 1–36. https://www.prb.org/povertyinamericabeyondwelfarereformpdf106mb/

Lieberman, R.C. (1998). *Shifting the color line: Race and the American welfare state.* Harvard University Press.

Liebow, E. (1967). *Tally's corner: A study of Negro street corner men.* Little, Brown and Company.

Lightman, E. (2003). *Social policy in Canada.* Oxford University Press.

Lindio-McGovern, L., & Wallimann, I. (Eds.). (2016). *Globalization and third world women: Exploitation, coping, and resistance.* Routledge.

Lindqvist, A., Björklund, F., & Bäckström, M. (2017). The perception of the poor: Capturing stereotype content with different measures. *Nordic Psychology, 69*(4), 231–247. https://doi.org/10.1080/19012276.2016.1270774

Lipina, S., & Posner, M.I. (2012). The impact of poverty on the development of brain networks. *Frontiers in Human Neuroscience, 6*, 1–12. https://doi.org/10.3389/fnhum.2012.00238

Lipset, S.M. (1986). Historical traditions and national characteristics: A comparative analysis of Canada and the United States. *Canadian Journal of Sociology, 11*(2), 113–155. https://doi.org/10.2307/3340795

Lipset, S.M. (1990). *Continental divide: The values and institutions of the United States and Canada.* Routledge.

Lipset, S.M. (1996). *American exceptionalism: A double-edged sword.* W.W. Norton & Company.

Lipset, S.M., & Marks, G. (2000). *It didn't happen here: Why socialism failed in the United States.* W.W. Norton & Company.

Lis, C., & Soly, H. (1979). *Poverty and capitalism in pre-industrial Europe.* Humanities Press.

LIS Cross-National Data Center. (2021). *Inequality and poverty key figures.* https://www.lisdatacenter.org/lis-ikf-webapp/app/search-ikf-figures

Lister, R. (2004). *Key concepts: Poverty.* Polity Press.

Little, K. (1971). *West African urbanization: A study of voluntary associations in social change.* Cambridge University Press. (Original work published 1965)

Loiacono, G. (2013). Poor laws and construction of race in the early republican Providence, Rhode Island. *The Journal of Policy History, 25*(2), 264–287. https://doi.org/10.1017/S0898030613000067

London, J. (2001). *The people of the abyss.* Pluto Press. (Original work published 1903)

Luby, J., Belden, A., Botteron, K., Marrus, N., Harms, M.P., Babb, C., Nishino, T., & Barch, D. (2013). The effects of poverty on brain development: The mediating effect of caregiving and stressful life events. *Journal of the American Medical Association Pediatrics, 167*(12), 1135–1142. https://doi.org/10.1001/jamapediatrics.2013.3139

Lynn, R. (2015). *Race differences in intelligence: An evolutionary analysis.* Washington Summit Publishers.

Lynn, R., & Becker, D. (2019). *The intelligence of nations.* Ulster Institute for Social Research.

Macdonald, D., & Wilson, D. (2013). *Poverty or prosperity: Indigenous children in Canada.* Canadian Centre for Policy Alternatives.

MacInnes, T., Aldridge, H., Bushe, S., Tinson, A., & Barry Born, T. (2014). *Monitoring Poverty and Social Exclusion 2014.* New Policy Institute/Joseph Rowntree Foundation.

Mack, J., & Lansley, S. (1985). *Poor Britain.* George Allen and Unwin.

Mackie, P., Johnsen, S., & Wood, J. (2017). *Ending rough sleeping: What works? – An international evidence review.* Crisis.

Macnicol, J. (2017). Reconstructing the underclass. *Social Policy & Society, 16*(1), 99–108. https://doi.org/10.1017/S1474746416000403

Magdoff, F., & Foster, J.B. (2011). *What every environmentalist needs to know about capitalism: A citizen's guide to capitalism and the environment.* Monthly Review Press.

Magnet, M. (1987, May 11). America's underclass: What to do? *Fortune,* pp. 130–150.

Magnet, M. (1993). *The dream and the nightmare: The sixties' legacy to the underclass.* William Morrow.

Mahon, R. (2008). Varieties of liberalism: Canadian social policy from the "Golden Age" to the present. *Social Policy and Administration, 42*(4), 342–361. https://doi.org/10.1111/j.1467-9515.2008.00608.x

Malthus, T.R. (1890). *An essay on the principle of population; or, a view of its past and present effects on human happiness; with an inquiry into our prospects respecting the future removal or mitigation of the evils which it occasions.* Ward, Lock and Co. (Original edition published 1803)

Malthus, T.R. (2008). *An essay on the principle of population as it affects the future improvement of society, with remarks on the speculations of Mr. Godwin, M. Condorcet, and other writers.* Oxford University Press. (Original work published 1798)

Mandel, M. (1986). Marxism and the rule of law. *UNB Law Journal, 35,* 7–34. https://digitalcommons.osgoode.yorku.ca/cgi/viewcontent.cgi?article=2389&context=scholarly_works

Mandela, N. (2005). *Address by Nelson Mandela for the "Make Poverty History" campaign, London – United Kingdom.* Nelson Mandela Foundation. http://www.mandela.gov.za/mandela_speeches/2005/050203_poverty.htm

Mani, A., Mullainathan, S., Shafir, E., & Zhao, J. (2013). Poverty impedes cognitive function. *Science, 341*(6149), 976–980. https://doi.org/10.1126/science.1238041

Markkola, P. (2007). Changing patterns of welfare: Finland in the nineteenth and early twentieth centuries. In S. King & J. Stewart (Eds.), *Welfare peripheries: The development of welfare states in nineteenth and twentieth century Europe* (pp. 207–230). Peter Lang.

Marmot, M. (2004). *The status syndrome: How social standing affects our health and longevity.* Owl Books.

Marmot, M. (2015). *The health gap: The challenge of an unequal world.* Bloomsbury.

Marsh, J. (2011). *Class dismissed: Why we cannot teach or learn our way out of inequality.* Monthly Review Press.

Marsh, L. (1975). *Report on social security for Canada.* University of Toronto Press. (Original work published 1943)

Marsland, D. (Ed.). (1995). *Self reliance: Reforming welfare in advanced societies.* Transaction Publishers.

Marwaha, S. (2016, November 7). This is why Canada has the second-highest medications costs in the world. *National Post.* https://nationalpost.com/news/canada/this-is-why-canada-has-the-second-highest-medication-costs-in-the-world

Marx, I., Nolan, B., & Olivera, J. (2015). The welfare state and antipoverty policy in rich countries. In A.B. Atkinson & F. Bourguignon (Eds.), *Handbook of income distribution* (pp. 2063–2139). Elsevier.

Marx, K. (1963). Letter to Friedrich Sorge (June 30, 1881). In K. Marx & F. Engels (Eds.), *Letters to Americans, 1848–1895*. International Publishers. (Original work published 1881)

Marx, K. (1969). *Theories of surplus value, Part 2*. Lawrence and Whishart.

Marx, K. (1970). *A contribution to the critique of political economy*. International Publishers. (Original work published 1859)

Marx, K. (1973). *Grundrisse*. Vintage Books. (Original work published 1845–1846)

Marx, K. (1977). *Capital, Volume 1*. Vintage Books. (Original work published 1867)

Marx, K., & Engels, F. (1967). *The communist manifesto*. Penguin Books. (Reprint of edition published 1888)

Maslow, A.H. (1943). A theory of human motivation. *Psychological Review, 50*, 370–396. https://doi.org/10.1037/h0054346

Maslow, A.H. (1970). *Motivation and Personality*. Harper and Row.

Masson, N., & Lester, H. (2003). The attitudes of medical students toward the homeless: Does medical school make a difference? *Medical Education, 37*(1), 869–872. https://doi.org/10.1046/j.1365-2923.2003.01625.x

McCartin, J.A. (2011). *Collision course: Ronald Reagan, the air traffic controllers, and the strike that changed America*. Oxford University Press.

McChesney, R.W. (1997). *Corporate media and the threat to democracy*. Seven Stories Press.

McChesney, R.W. (1998). *Rich media, poor democracy: Communication politics in dubious times*. University of Illinois Press.

McChesney, R.W. (2008). *The political economy of the media: Enduring issues, emerging dilemmas*. Monthly Review Press.

McFadden, R. (2014, July 4). Richard Mellon Scaife, influential US conservative, dies at 82. *New York Times*. https://www.nytimes.com/2014/07/05/us/richard-mellon-scaife-influential-us-conservative-dies-at-82.html

McGarry, K. (2013). The safety net for the elderly. In M.J. Bailey & S. Danziger (Eds.), *Legacies of the war on poverty* (pp. 179–199). Russell Sage Foundation.

McKay, A. (2013). Crisis, cuts, citizenship, and a basic income: A wicked solution to a wicked problem. *Basic Income Studies, 8*(1), 93–104. https://doi.org/10.1515/bis-2012-0011

McKay, I. (2005). *Rebels, reds, radicals: Rethinking Canada's left history*. Between the Lines.

McKibbon, R. (1984). Why was there no Marxism in Great Britain? *English Historical Review, 99*(391), 299–331. https://doi.org/10.1093/ehr/XCIX.CCCXCI.297

McLanahan, S.S. (2009). Fragile families and the reproduction of poverty. *Annals of the American Academy of Political and Social Science, 621,* 111–131. https://doi.org/10.1177/0002716208324862

McNaught, K. (1988). *The Penguin history of Canada.* Penguin Books.

Mead, L. (1986). *Beyond entitlement: The social obligation of citizenship.* Free Press.

Mead, L. (1992). *The new politics of poverty: The non-working poor in America.* Basic Books.

Media Reform Coalition. (2019). *Who owns the media?* Media Reform Coalition.

Meidner, R. (1978). *Employee investment funds: An approach to collective capital formation.* George Allen and Unwin.

Melville, H. (1997). *The complete shorter fiction.* Alfred A. Knopf. (Work published 1854)

Meyer, B.D., & Sullivan, J.X. (2012). Identifying the disadvantaged: Official poverty, consumption poverty, and the new supplemental poverty measure. *Journal of Economic Perspectives, 26*(3), 111–136. https://doi.org/10.1257/jep.26.3.111

Meyer, B.D., & Wu, D. (2018). The poverty reduction of social security and means-tested transfers. *ILR Review, 71*(5), 1106–1153. https://doi.org/10.1177/0019793918790220

Mikkonen, J. (2013). The politics of poverty in Finland. *Social Alternatives, 32*(1), 24–30. https://search.informit.org/doi/10.3316/informit.338682702194909

Miliband, R. (1974). Politics and poverty. In D. Wedderburn (Ed.), *Poverty, inequality and class structure* (pp. 183–195). Cambridge University Press.

Miliband, R. (1977). *Marxism and politics.* Oxford University Press.

Millar, J. (2010). The United Kingdom: The feminization of poverty? In G. Schaffner Goldberg (Ed.), *Poor women in rich countries: The feminization of poverty over the life course* (pp. 121–150). Oxford University Press.

Milne, S. (2014). *The enemy within: The secret war against the miners.* Verso.

Mishel, L., Bivens, J., Gould, E., & Heidi, S. (2012). *The state of working America.* (12th ed.). Economic Policy Institute/ILR Press.

Mishel, L., & Davis, A. (2014). *CEO pay continues to rise as typical workers are paid less* [Issue brief]. Economic Policy Institute.

Mishra, R. (1977). *Society and social policy: Theoretical perspectives on welfare.* Macmillan.

Mishra, R. (1990). *The welfare state in capitalist society: Policies of retrenchment and maintenance in Europe, North America, and Australia.* University of Toronto Press.

Mitchell, A., & Shillington, R. (2008). *Are Statistics Canada's low-income cutoffs an absolute or relative poverty measure?* Canadian Social Research Network.

Mitchnick, M., & Etherington, B. (2006). *Labour arbitration in Canada.* Lancaster House.

Mollat, M. (1986). *The poor in the Middle Ages: An essay in social history.* Yale University Press.

Moller, S., Bradley, D., Huber, E., & Stephens, J.D. (2003). Determinants of relative poverty in advanced capitalist democracies. *American Sociological Review, 68*(1), 22–51. https://doi.org/10.2307/3088901

Monday Morning. (2012). *The Nordic model: Local government, global competitiveness in Denmark, Finland and Sweden.* Mondag Morgan.

Montalban, P.Z. (2017). *Paradise papers: Offshore investments of the rich and powerful.* Createspace Independent Publishing Platform.

Moody, K. (1988). *An injury to all: The decline of American unionism.* Verso.

Moynihan, D.P. (1965). *The negro family: The case for national action.* Office of Planning and Research, US Department of Labor.

Murali, V., & Oyebode, F. (2004). Poverty, social inequality, and mental health. *Advances in Psychiatric Treatment, 10*(3), 216–224. https://doi.org/10.1192/apt.10.3.216

Murphy, B., Zhang, X., & Dionne, C. (2012). *Low income in Canada: A multi-line and multi-index perspective.* Statistics Canada.

Murray, C. (1984). *Losing ground: American social policy, 1950–1980.* Basic Books.

Murray, C. (2006). *In our hands: A plan to replace the welfare state.* American Enterprise Institute.

Murray, C. (2012). *Coming apart: The state of white America, 1960–2010.* Crown Forum.

Murray, C. (2020). *Human diversity: The biology of gender, race, and class.* Grand Central Publishing/Twelve.

Myers, G. (1936). *History of the great American fortunes.* The Modern Library.

Myles, J. (1998). How to design a "liberal" welfare state: A comparison of Canada and the United States. *Social Policy & Administration, 32*(4), 341–364. https://doi.org/10.1111/1467-9515.00120

Myles, J. (2000). The maturation of Canada's retirement income system: Income levels, income inequality, and low income among older persons. *Canadian Journal on Aging, 19*(3), 287–316. https://doi.org/10.1017/S0714980800015014

Myles, J. (2013). Income security for seniors: System maintenance and policy drift. In K. Banting & J. Myles (Eds.), *Inequality and the fading of redistributive politics* (pp. 312–334). UBC Press.

Myles, J. (2015). Canadian Sociological Outstanding Contribution Lecture: The fading of redistributive politics in Canada. *Canadian Review of Sociology, 52*(1), 1–21. https://doi.org/10.1111/cars.12058

Nace, T. (2003). *Gangs of America: The rise of corporate power and the disabling of democracy.* Berrett-Koehler.

National Alliance to End Homelessness. (2014). *The state of homelessness in America 2014: An examination of homelessness, economic, housing, and demographic trends at the national and state levels.* National Alliance to End Homelessness.

National Center for Homeless Education. (2014). *Education for homeless children and youth.* National Center for Homeless Education.

National Center for Homeless Education. (2017). *Identifying children and youth in homeless situations.* https://files.eric.ed.gov/fulltext/ED594620.pdf

National Center for Infants, Toddlers, and Families. (2014). *Zero to three: Early experiences matter.* National Center for Infants, Toddlers, and Families.

National Center on Family Homelessness. (2011). *State report card on child homelessness: America's youngest outcasts, 2010.* National Center on Family Homelessness.

National Center on Family Homelessness. (2014). *America's youngest outcasts: A report card on child homelessness.* The National Center on Family Homelessness at American Institutes for Research.

National Coalition for the Homeless. (2010). *Winter homeless services: Bringing our neighbours in from the cold.* National Coalition for the Homeless.

National Congress of American Indians. (2020). *Demographics: Indian country demographics.* http://www.ncai.org/about-tribes/demographics

National Council of Welfare. (2009). *Poverty profile 2007.* National Council of Welfare.

National Law Center on Homelessness and Poverty. (2017). *Don't count on it: How the HUD point-in-time count underestimates the homelessness crisis in America.* National Law Center on Homelessness and Poverty.

Naylor, J. (2016). *The fate of labour socialism: The Co-operative Commonwealth Federation and the dream of a working-class future.* University of Toronto Press.

Nelson, B. (1990). The origins of the two-channel welfare state: Workmen's Compensation and Mother's Aid. In L. Gordon (Ed.), *Women, the state, and welfare* (pp. 123–151). University of Wisconsin Press.

Nelson, J. (2009). *Razing Africa: A geography of racism.* University of Toronto Press.

Neubeck, K.J., & Cazenave, N.A. (2001). *Welfare racism: Playing the race card against America's poor.* Routledge.

Newman, K.S., & O'Brien, R.L. (2011). *Taxing the poor: Doing damage to the truly disadvantaged.* University of California Press.

Nichols, J., & McChesney, R.W. (2013). *Dollarocracy: How the money and media election complex is destroying America.* Bold Types Books.

Noam, E.M. (2015). *Who owns the media? Media concentration and ownership around the world.* Oxford University Press.

Nordic Statistical Committee. (2017). *Social protection in Nordic countries, 2015/2016: Scope, Expenditure, and Financing.* Nordic Statistical Committee.

Nussbaum, M. (1997). Capabilities and human rights. *Fordham Law Review, 66,* 273–300. https://ir.lawnet.fordham.edu/flr/vol66/iss2/2

Nussbaum, M. (2000). *Women and human development: The capabilities approach.* Cambridge University Press.

Nussbaum, M., & Sen, A. (1993). *The quality of life.* Clarendon Press.

Obermeyer, B., & Obermaier, F. (2017a, November 5). How we reported the Paradise Papers. *Süddeutsche Zeitung.* https://projekte.sueddeutsche.de

/paradisepapers/wirtschaft/answers-to-pressing-questions-about -the-leak-e574659/.

Obermeyer, B., & Obermaier, F. (2017b). *The Panama Papers: Breaking the story of how the rich and powerful hide their money.* Oneworld Publications.

O'Connor, A. (2001). *Poverty knowledge: Social science, social policy, and the poor in twentieth century US history.* Princeton University Press.

O'Connor, J. (1973). *The fiscal crisis of the state.* St. Martin's Press.

O'Connor, J. (1998). *Natural causes: Essays in ecological Marxism.* Guilford Press.

O'Connor, J.S., & Olsen, G.M. (Eds.). (1998). *Power resources and the welfare state: A critical approach.* University of Toronto Press.

O'Connor, J.S., Orloff, A.S., & Sheila, S. (1999). *States, markets, families: Gender, liberalism and social policy in Australia, Canada, Great Britain and the United States.* Cambridge University Press.

OECD. (2013). *Pensions at a glance 2013: OECD and G20 indicators.* OECD Publishing.

OECD. (2015). *In it together: Why less inequality benefits all.* OECD Publishing.

OECD. (2020a). *OECD Income Distribution Database (IDD): Gini, poverty, income.* https://www.oecd.org/social/income-distribution-database.htm (accessed July 7, 2020)

OECD. (2020b). *Social Expenditure Database (SOCX).* https://www.oecd.org/social/expenditure.htm (accessed July 7, 2020)

OECD. (2021a). *Poverty gap.* https://doi.org/10.1787/7f420b4b-en (accessed January 5, 2021).

OECD. (2021b). *Poverty rate.* https://doi.org/10.1787/7f420b4b-en (accessed January 5, 2021)

Offe, C. (1972). Advanced capitalism and the welfare state. *Politics and Society, 2*(4), 479–488. https://doi.org/10.1177/003232927200200406

Offe, C. (1985). *Contradictions of the welfare state.* MIT Press.

Ogbu, J.U. (1992). Understanding cultural diversity and learning. *Educational Researcher, 21*(8), 5–14, 24. https://doi.org/10.3102/0013189X021008005

O'Hara, M. (2015). *Austerity bites: A journey to the sharp end of the cuts in the UK.* Policy Press.

Olsen, G.M. (1992). *The struggle for economic democracy in Sweden.* Avebury /Gower.

Olsen, G.M. (1994). Locating the Canadian welfare state: Family policy and health care in Canada, Sweden and the United States. *The Canadian Journal of Sociology, 19*(1), 1–20. https://doi.org/10.2307/3341235

Olsen, G.M. (2002). *The politics of the welfare state: Canada, Sweden and the United States.* Oxford University Press.

Olsen, G.M. (2007). Toward global welfare state convergence?: Family policy and health care in Sweden, Canada and the United States. *Journal of Sociology and Social Welfare, 34*(2), 143–164. https://scholarworks.wmich.edu/jssw/vol34/iss2/10

Olsen, G.M. (2008). Labour market policy in the United States, Canada and Sweden: Addressing the issue of convergence. *Social Policy & Administration, 42*(4), 323–341. https://doi.org/10.1111/j.1467-9515.2008.00607.x

Olsen, G.M. (2011). *Power and inequality: A comparative introduction.* Oxford University Press.

Olsen, G.M. (2013). What's "left" in the garden of Sweden. *International Journal of Health Services, 43*(1), 7–30. https://doi.org/10.2190/HS.43.1.b

Olsen, G.M. (2019a). Housing policy, the welfare state and social inequality. In B. Greve (Ed.), *The Routledge handbook of the welfare state* (pp. 378–392). Routledge.

Olsen, G.M. (2019b). Protective legislation: The "third pillar" of the welfare state. *Social Policy & Administration, 53*(3), 478–492. https://doi. org/10.1111/spol.12471

Olsen, G.M., & Benjaminsen, L. (2019). Homelessness and social policy. In B. Greve (Ed.), *The Routledge handbook of the welfare state* (pp. 393–406). Routledge.

Oorschot, W.J.H., & Halman, L. (2000). Blame or fate, individual or social? An international comparison of popular explanations of poverty. *European Societies, 2*(1), 1–28. https://doi.org/10.1080/146166900360701

Orloff, A.S. (1993). Gender and the social rights of citizenship: The comparative analysis of state policies and gender relations. *American Sociological Review, 58*(3), 303–328. https://doi.org/10.2307/2095903

Orwell, G. (1958) *The road to Wigan Pier.* Houghton, Mifflin Harcourt. (Original work published 1937)

Orwell, G. (1961). *Down and out in Paris and London.* Harcourt, Brace Jovanovich. (Original work published 1933)

Osberg, L. (2018). *The age of increasing inequality: The astonishing rise of Canada's 1%.* Lorimer.

Osberg, L., & Smeeding, T. (2006). "Fair" inequality? Attitudes toward pay differentials: The United States in comparative perspective. *American Sociological Review, 71*(3), 450–473. https://doi.org/10.1177/000312240607100305

Oshinsky, D.M. (1997). *Worse than slavery: Parchman farm and the ordeal of Jim Crow justice.* Free Press.

O'Sullivan, E. (2012). Varieties of punitiveness in Europe: Homelessness and urban marginality. *European Journal of Homelessness, 6*(2), 69–97. https:// www.feantsa.org/download/ejh6_2_article34473401968653742230.pdf

Oxfam. (2016). *An economy for the 1%.* Oxfam GB.

Oxfam. (2017). *An economy for the 99%.* Oxfam GB.

Packard, V. (1960). *The waste makers.* Pocket Books.

Pagani, L. (2007). How does poverty beget poverty? *Paediatrics and Child Health, 12*(8), 693–697. https://doi.org/10.1093/pch/12.8.693

Palme, J. (1990). *Pension rights in welfare capitalism: The development of old age pensions in 18 OECD countries, 1930–1985.* Swedish Institute for Social Research, Stockholm University.

Palme, J. (1999). *The Nordic model and the modernization of social protection in Europe.* The Nordic Council of Ministers.

Panitch, L., & Swartz, D. (1984). Toward permanent exceptionalism: Coercion and consent in Canadian industrial relations. *Labour/Le Travail, 13*(Spring), 133–158. https://doi.org/10.2307/25140404

Pantazis, C. (2016). Policies and discourses of poverty during a time of recession and austerity. *Critical Social Policy, 36*(1), 3–20. https://doi.org/10.1177/0261018315620377

Parekh, A., MacInnes, T., & Kenway, P. (2010). *Monitoring poverty and social exclusion.* New Policy Institute/Joseph Rowntree Foundation.

Parenti, M. (1995). *Democracy for the few* (6th ed.). St. Martin's Press.

Parish, P.J. (1989). *Slavery: History and historians.* Westview Press.

Parr, J. (1980). *Labouring children: British immigrant apprentices in Canada.* University of Toronto Press.

Parr, J. (Ed.). (1982). *Children and family in Canadian history.* McClelland and Stewart.

Pearce, D. (1978). The feminization of poverty: Women, work, and welfare. *Urban and Social Change Review, 11*(1–2), 28–36. https://eric.ed.gov/?id=EJ182487

Peck, J., & Theodore, N. (2007). Variegated capitalism. *Progress in Human Geography, 31*(6), 731–772. https://doi.org/10.1177/0309132507083505

Peet, R. (1975). Inequality and poverty: A Marxist-geographic theory. *Annals of the Association of American Geographers, 64*(4), 564–571. https://doi.org/10.1111/j.1467-8306.1975.tb01063.x

Pelling, H. (1991). *A short history of the Labour Party.* Palgrave Macmillan.

Pemberton, S., Fahmy, E., Sutton, E., & Bell, K. (2016). Navigating the stigmatized identities of poverty in austere times: Resisting and responding to narratives of personal failure. *Critical Social Policy, 36*(1), 21–37. https://doi.org/10.1177/0261018315601799

Peters, E.J., & Christensen, J. (Eds.). (2016). *Indigenous homelessness: Perspectives from Canada, Australia, and New Zealand.* University of Manitoba Press.

Petersen, J.H., & Petersen, K. (2007). Shake, rattle and roll! From charity to social rights in the Danish welfare state, 1890–1933. In S. King & J. Stewart (Eds.), *Welfare peripheries: The development of welfare states in nineteenth and twentieth century Europe* (pp. 149–179). Peter Lang.

Petersen, P.E. (Ed.). (1985). *The new urban reality.* Brookings Institution.

Peterson-Withorn, C. (2017, July 5). The 4.3 billion dollar cabinet: See what each top Trump advisor is worth. *Forbes.*

Phillips, P. (2018). *Giants: The global power elite.* Seven Stories Press.

Pierson, C. (1990). The "exceptional" United States: First new nation or last welfare state? *Social Policy & Administration, 24*(3), 186–198. https://doi.org/10.1111/j.1467-9515.1990.tb00338.x

Pierson, C. (2006). *Beyond the welfare state: The new political economy of welfare* (3rd ed.). Polity Press.

Pierson, P. (2004). *Politics in time: History, institutions and social analysis.* Princeton University Press.

Pike, E.R. (Ed.). (1966). *Hard times: Human documents of the Industrial Revolution.* Praeger.

Piketty, T. (2014). *Capital in the twenty-first century.* Harvard University Press.

Piketty, T. (2015). *The economics of inequality.* Harvard University Press.

Piven, F.F., & Cloward, R. (1971). *Regulating the poor: The functions of public welfare.* Pantheon Books.

Piven, F.F., & Cloward, R. (1979). *Poor people's movements: Why they succeed and how they fail.* Vintage Books.

Piven, F.F., & Minnite, L.C. (2016). Poor people's politics. In D. Brady & L.M. Burton (Eds.), *The Oxford handbook of the social science of poverty* (pp. 751–753). Oxford University Press.

Platt, L. (2007). *Poverty and ethnicity in the UK.* Policy Press.

Plotnick, R.D. (1992). Changes in poverty, income inequality and the standard of living during the Reagan years. *Journal of Sociology & Social Welfare, 19*(1), 29–44. https://scholarworks.wmich.edu/jssw/vol19/iss1/4

Polanyi, K. (2001). *The great transformation: The political and economic origins of our time.* Beacon Press. (Original work published 1944)

Pomeranz, K., & Topik, S. (2012). *The world that trade created: Culture and the world economy, 1400 to the present* (3rd ed.). Routledge.

Pope, J.G. (2016). Why is there no socialism in the United States? Law and the racial class divide in the American working class, 1676–1964. *Texas Law Review, 94*(7), 1555–1590. https://texaslawreview.org/wp-content/uploads/2016/09/Pope.pdf

Porter, A. (2012). Neo-conservatism, neo-liberalism and Canadian social policy: Challenges for feminism. *Canadian Woman Studies, 29*(3), 19–31. https://cws.journals.yorku.ca/index.php/cws/article/view/36010/32694

Powell, M., & Barrientos, A. (2011). An audit of the welfare modelling business. *Social Policy & Administration, 45*(1), 69–84. https://doi.org/10.1111/j.1467-9515.2010.00754.x

Powell, M., & Miller, R. (2016). Seventy years of privatizing the British National Health Services? *Social Policy & Administration, 50*(1), 99–118. https://doi.org/10.1111/spol.12161

Pressman, S. (2011). How poor are America's poor? *Challenge, 54*(2), 109–121. https://doi.org/10.2753/0577-5132540205

Pressman, S., & Scott, R. (2009). Consumer debt and the measurement of poverty and inequality in the US. *Review of Social Economy, 67*(2), 127–148. https://doi.org/10.1080/00346760802578890

Quadagno, J. (1994). *The color of welfare: How racism undermined the war on poverty.* Oxford University Press.

Quigley, W.P. (1996/1997). Five hundred years of English poor laws, 1349–1834: Regulating the working and non-working poor. *Akron Law Review, 30*(1), 73–128. https://ssrn.com/abstract=3506885

Rainwater, L., & Smeeding, T.M. (2003). *Poor kids in a rich country: America's children in comparative perspective*. Russell Sage Foundation.

Ramdin, R. (2017). *The making of the Black working class in Britain*. Verso.

Ramsey, S., Blough, D., Kirchoff, A., Kreizenbeck, K., Federenko, C., Snell, K., Newcomb, P., Hollingworth, W., & Overstreet, K. (2013). Washington State cancer patients found to be at greater risk for bankruptcy than people without a cancer diagnosis. *Health Affairs, 32*(6), 1143–1152. https://doi.org/10.1377/hlthaff.2012.1263

Rank, M.R. (1994). *Living on the edge: The realities of welfare in America*. Columbia University Press.

Rank, M.R. (2005). *One nation, underprivileged: Why American poverty affects us all*. Oxford University Press.

Rank, M.R. (2011). Rethinking American poverty. *Contexts, 10*, 16–21. https://doi.org/10.1177/1536504211408794

Raphael, D. (2011). *Poverty in Canada* (2nd ed.). Canadian Scholar's Press.

Raphael, D. (Ed.). (2013). *Social determinants of health: Canadian perspectives* (3rd ed.). Canadian Scholars' Press.

Rattansi, A. (2007). *Racism: A very short introduction*. Oxford University Press.

Rauch, D. (2007). Is there really a Scandinavian social service model? A comparison of childcare and elderlycare in six European countries. *Acta Sociologica, 50*(3), 249–269. https://doi.org/10.1177/0001699307080931

Rector, R., & Sheffield, R. (2011). *Air conditioning, cable TV, and an Xbox: What is poverty in the United States today?* The Heritage Foundation. https://www.heritage.org/poverty-and-inequality/report/air-conditioning-cable-tv-and-xbox-what-poverty-the-united-states

Redondo, G., Santa Cruz, I., & Maria Rotger, J. (2011). Why Mondragon? Analyzing what works in overcoming inequalities. *Qualitative Inquiry, 17*(3), 277–283. https://doi.org/10.1177/1077800410397806

Reich, D. (2018a, March 23). How genetics is changing our understanding of "race." *New York Times*. https://nyti.ms/2u95sc4

Reich, D. (2018b, March 30). How to talk about "race" and genetics. *New York Times*. https://nyti.ms/2GmRY2n

Reich, D. (2019). *Who we are and how we got here: Ancient DNA and the new science of the human past*. Vintage Books.

Reich, R.B. (2012). *Beyond outrage: What has gone wrong with our economy and how to fix it*. Vintage Books.

Reich, R.B. (2016). *Saving capitalism for the many, not the few*. Vintage Books.

Reich, R.B. (2020). *The system: Who rigged it and how we fix it*. Alfred A. Knopf.

Reid, A.G. (1946). The first poor relief system of Canada. *Canadian Historical Review, 27*(4), 424–431. https://doi.org/10.3138/CHR-027-04-07

Reiss, E. (1997). *Marx: A clear guide*. Pluto Press.

Reiss, S. (2018). *The female face of poverty: Examining the cause and consequences of economic deprivation for women*. Women's Budge Group.

Rhodes, C., Booth, L., Brown, J., Butcher, L., Harari, D., Keep, M., Mor, F., & Edward, P. (2018). *Public ownership of industries and services* [Briefing Paper No. CBP8325]. House of Commons Library.

Richards, J. (2010). *Reducing lone-parent poverty: A Canadian success story.* CD Howe Institute.

Ridge, T. (2009). *Living with poverty: A review of the literature on children's and families' experiences of poverty* [Department for Work and Pensions, Research Report No. 594]. Department for Work and Pensions.

Riley, A.J., Harding, G., Underwood, M.R., & Carter, Y. (2003). Homelessness: A problem for primary care? *British Journal of General Practice, 53*(491), 473–479. https://bjgp.org/content/53/491/473

Rimawi, B.H., Mirdamadi, M., & John, J.F., Jr. (2014). Infections and homelessness: Risks of increased infectious diseases in displaced women. *World Medical & Health Policy, 6*(2), 118–132. https://doi.org/10.1002/wmh3.95

Rimlinger, G.V. (1966). Welfare policy and economic development: A comparative historical perspective. *Journal of Economic History, 26*(4), 556–571. https://doi.org/10.1017/S002205070007755X

Rimlinger, G.V. (1971). *Welfare policy and industrialization in Europe, America, and Russia.* John Wiley & Sons.

Ringen, S. (1988). Direct and indirect measures of poverty. *Journal of Social Policy, 17*(3), 351–365. https://doi.org/10.1017/S0047279400016858

Robbins, R. (1999). *Global problems and the culture of capitalism.* Allyn and Bacon.

Robinson, N.J. (2017, July 17). Why is Charles Murray odious? *Current Affairs: A Magazine of Politics and Culture.* https://www.currentaffairs.org/2017/07/why-is-charles-murray-odious

Robinson, N.J. (2020, October 26). Wendell Potter on how the health insurance industry manipulated public opinion. *Current Affairs.* https://www.currentaffairs.org/2020/10/interview-wendell-potter-on-how-the-health-insurance-industry-manipulates-public-opinion

Roex, K., Huijts, T., & Sieben, I. (2019). Attitudes toward income inequality: "Winners" versus "losers" of the perceived meritocracy. *Acta Sociologica, 62*(1), 47–63. https://doi.org/10.1177/0001699317748340

Roosma, F., Gelissen, J., & van Oorschot, W. (2012). The multidimensionality of welfare state attitudes: A European cross-national study. *Social Indicators Research, 113*(1), 235–255. https://doi.org/10.1007/s11205-012-0099-4

Rosenberg, L.B. (1969). The "failure" of the Socialist Party of America. *Review of Politics, 31*(3), 329–352. https://doi.org/10.1017/S0034670500010366

Rosenfeld, J., & Denice, P. (2019). What do government unions do? Public sector unions and nonunion wages, 1977–2015. *Social Science Research, 78*(February), 41–56. https://doi.org/10.1016/j.ssresearch.2018.10.011

Rosenfeld, J., & Laird, J. (2016). Unions and poverty. In D. Brady & L.M. Burton (Eds.), *The Oxford handbook of the social science of poverty* (pp. 800–819). Oxford University Press.

Ross, D.P., Scott, K.J., & Smith, P. J. (2000). *The Canadian fact book on poverty*. The Canadian Council on Social Development.

Ross, M., & Bateman, N. (2019). *Meet the low-wage workforce*. Brookings Institution.

Rothkopf, D. (2008). *Super class: The global power elite and the world they are making*. Farrar, Straus, and Giroux.

Rothwell, D.W., & McEwen, A. (2017). Comparing child poverty risks by family structure during the 2008 recession. *Journal of Marriage and Family, 79*(5), 1224–1240. https://doi.org/10.1111/jomf.12421

Round, M.A. (2013). *Grounded: Reagan and the PATCO strike*. Routledge.

Rowntree, B.S. (1901). *Poverty: A study of town life*. Macmillan.

Royce, E. (2009). *Poverty and power: The problem of structural inequality*. Rowman and Littlefield.

Ruggie, M. (1996). *Realignments in the welfare state: Health policy in the United states, Britain, and Canada*. Columbia University Press.

Ruggles, P. (1990). *Drawing the line: Alternative poverty measures and their implications for public policy*. The Urban Institute.

Rushton, J.P. (1995). *Race, evolution, and behavior: A life history perspective*. Transaction Books.

Rushton, J.P., & Jensen, A.R. (2005). Thirty years of research on race differences in cognitive ability. *Psychology, Public Policy, and Law, 11*(2), 235–294. https://doi.org/10.1037/1076-8971.11.2.235

Russell, J.W. (2009). *Class and race formation in North America*. University of Toronto Press.

Rustin, M. (2016). The neoliberal university and its alternatives. *Soundings, 63*(July), 147–176. https://doi.org/10.3898/136266216819377057

Saez, E., & Veall, M.R. (2007). The evolution of high incomes in Canada, 1920–2000. In A.B. Atkinson & T. Piketty (Eds.), *Top incomes over the twentieth century: A contrast between continental and English-speaking countries* (pp. 226–308). Oxford University Press.

Saez, E., & Zucman, G. (2014). *Wealth inequality in the United States since 1913: Evidence from capitalized income tax data* [Working Paper 20625]. National Bureau of Economic Research.

Sahlin, I. (2012). The logos of ETHOS. *European Journal of Homelessness, 6*(2), 227–234. https://www.feantsa.org/download/ejh6_2_resp _ethosdef21202296260998435422.pdf

Samuelsson, K. (1975). The philosophy of Swedish welfare policies. In S. Koblik (Ed.), *Sweden's development from poverty to affluence, 1750–1970* (pp. 335–353). University of Minnesota Press.

Sandoval, D., Rank, M.R., & Hirschl, T.A. (2009). The increasing risk of poverty across the American life course. *Demography, 46*(4), 717–737. https://doi.org/10.1353/dem.0.0082

Sandoval, E., Eisinger, D.W., & Smith, G.B. (2016, March 14). NYC homeless would rather risk the street than hellish shelter system. *New York Times*.

Sarche, M., & Spicer, P. (2008). Poverty and health disparities for American Indian and Alaska Native children: Current knowledge and future prospects. *Annals of the New York Academy of Sciences, 1136*(1), 126–136. https://doi.org/10.1196/annals.1425.017

Sarlo, C.A. (1992). *Poverty in Canada.* The Fraser Institute.

Sarlo, C.A. (2019). *The causes of poverty.* The Fraser Institute.

Saunders, K.M., & Levine, L. (2004). Better, faster, cheaper – later: What happens when technologies are suppressed. *Michigan Telecommunications and Technology Law Review, 11*(23), 25–69. https://repository.law.umich.edu/mttlr/vol11/iss1/2

Saville, J. (1988). *The labour movement in Britain.* Faber and Faber.

Sawhill, I.V. (2003). The behavioral aspects of poverty. *Public Interest, 153*(Fall), 79–93

Saxonberg, S. (2013). From defamilialization to degenderization: Toward a new gender typology. *Social Policy & Administration, 47*(1), 26–49. https://doi.org/10.1111/j.1467-9515.2012.00836.x

Sayer, A. (2015). *Why we can't afford the rich.* Policy Press.

Schmitter, P.C., & Lembruch, G. (Eds.). (1980). *Trends toward corporatist intermediation.* Sage.

Schneider, B.R., & Soskice, D. (2009). Inequality in developed countries and Latin America. *Economy and Society, 38*(1), 17–52. https://doi.org/10.1080/03085140802560496

Schram, S.F. (2006). *Welfare discipline: Discourse, governance and globalization.* Temple University Press.

Scott, F.D. (1988). *Sweden: The nation's history.* Southern Illinois University Press.

Scott, H. (1984). *Working your way to the bottom.* Pandora Press.

Scott, R.H., & Pressman, S. (2013). Debt-poor kids. *Journal of Poverty, 17*(3), 356–373. https://doi.org/10.1080/10875549.2013.804478

Scott, S. (2007). *All our sisters: Stories of homeless women in Canada.* University of Toronto Press.

Scruggs, L., & Allan, J.P. (2006). The material consequences of welfare states: Benefit generosity and absolute poverty in 16 OECD countries. *Comparative Political Studies, 39*(7), 880–904. https://doi.org/10.1177/0010414005281935

Seccombe, K. (1999). *So you think I drive a Cadillac?: Welfare recipients' perspectives on the system and its reform.* Allyn & Bacon.

Seip, A.Å. (2007). Poor relief and welfare legislation in Norway, 1814–1920. In S. King & J. Stewart (Eds.), *Welfare peripheries: The development of welfare states in nineteenth and twentieth century Europe* (pp. 97–124). Peter Lang.

Sen, A. (1984). *Resources, values, and development.* Harvard University Press.

Sen, A. (1992). *Inequality re-examined.* Clarendon.

Sen, A. (2006). Conceptualizing and measuring poverty. In D.B. Grusky & R. Kanbur (Eds.), *Poverty and inequality* (pp. 30–46). Stanford University Press.

Serafina, P., & Tonkin, R. (2014). *Intergenerational transmission of disadvantage in the UK and EU.* Office for National Statistics.

Shaefer, H.L., & Edin, K. (2013). Rising extreme poverty in the United States and the response of federal means-tested transfer programs. *Social Service Review, 87*(2), 250–268. https://doi.org/10.1086/671012

Shalev, M., & Korpi, W. (1980). Working class mobilization and American exceptionalism. *Economic and Industrial Democracy, 1*(1), 31–31. https://doi.org/10.1177/0143831X8000100104

Shelter, Support and Housing Administration. (2018). *Street needs assessment 2018: Results report.* City of Toronto.

Shepherd, A. (2020, January 28). Charles Murray is never going away. *New Republic.*

Shewell, H. (2004). *Enough to keep them alive: Indian welfare in Canada, 1873–1965.* University of Toronto Press.

Shildrick, T. (2012). *Poverty and insecurity life in low-pay, no-pay Britain.* Policy Press.

Shildrick, T. (2018). *Poverty propaganda: Exploring the myths.* Bristol University Press.

Shillington, R., & Stapleton, J. (2010). Cutting through the fog: Why is it so hard to make sense of poverty measures? Metcalf Foundation.

Shinn, M. (2010). Homelessness, poverty and social exclusion in the United States and Europe. *European Journal of Homelessness, 4*(December), 19–44. https://www.feantsa.org/download/feantsa_ejh_v4_12-2010115869180704920086.pdf

Shiva, V. (2008). *Soil not oil: Environmental justice in an age of climate crisis.* South End Books.

Sicard, G. (2015). *The origins of the corporation: The mills of Toulouse in the Middle Ages.* Yale University Press.

Silver, J. (2014). *About Canada: Poverty.* Fernwood Publishing.

Simon, C. (2017). Why Norwegians don't have their pigs in the forest: Illuminating Nordic "co-operation." *Behavior and Social Issues, 26*(1), 172–186. https://doi.org/10.5210/bsi.v26i0.7317

Sinclair, U. (1951). *The jungle.* Harper and Row. (Original work published 1906)

Singletary, M. (2018, October 3). US student loan debt reaches a staggering $1.53 trillion. *Washington Post.* https://www.washingtonpost.com/business/2018/10/04/us-student-loan-debt-reaches-staggering-trillion/

Sipilä, J. (1998). *Social care services: The key to the Scandinavian model.* Ashgate.

Skoglund, A.-M. (1992). *Fattigvården på den svenska landsbygden år 1829* [Unpublished doctoral dissertation]. University of Stockholm.

Slade, G. (2006). *Made to break: Technology and obsolescence in America.* Harvard University Press.

Smeeding, T.M. (2006a). Government programs and social outcomes: Comparison of the United States with other rich nations. In A.J. Auerbach,

D. Card, & J.M. Quigley (Eds.), *Public policy and the income distribution* (pp. 149–218). Russell Sage Foundation.

Smeeding, T.M. (2006b). Poor people in rich nations: The United States in comparative perspective. *The Journal of Economic Perspectives, 20*(1), 69–90. https://doi.org/10.1257/089533006776526094

Smith, A. (2003). *An inquiry into the nature and causes of the wealth of nations.* Bantam Dell. (Original work published 1776)

Snider, L. (1993). *Bad business: Corporate crime in Canada.* Nelson.

Soderberg, S. (2018). Debtfarism, predatory lending and imaginary social orders: The case of the U.S. payday lending industry. In S. Bittle, L. Snider, S. Tombs, & D. Whyte (Eds.), *Revisiting crimes of the powerful: Marxism, crime, and deviance* (pp. 257–269). Routledge.

Solidarity Center. (2006). *The struggle for worker rights in Columbia.* Solidarity Center.

Soss, J., Fording, R.C., & Schram, S.F. (2011). *Disciplining the poor: Neoliberal paternalism and the persistent power of race.* University of Chicago Press.

Spencer, H. (1929). *The study of sociology.* Appleton and Company. (Original work published 1873)

Spencer, H. (1969) *Social statics.* Augustus M. Kelley. (Original work published 1851)

Spicker, P. (1984). *Stigma and social welfare.* Croom Helm.

SPLC (Southern Poverty Law Center). (n.d.). *Extremist info: Charles Murray.* https://www.splcenter.org/fighting-hate/extremist-files/individual/charles-murray (accessed March 21, 2021)

Stack, C. (1997). *All our kin: Strategies for survival in a Black community.* Basic Books. (Original work published 1974)

Standing, G. (2011). *The precariat: The new dangerous class.* Bloomsbury Academic.

Standing, G. (2017). *Basic income: And how we can make it happen.* Penguin Books.

Stanford, J. (2014). The economic consequences of taxing (and spending). In A. Himelfarb & J. Himelfarb (Eds.), *Tax is not a four letter word: A different take on taxes in Canada* (pp. 17–38). Wilfrid Laurier University Press.

Statistics Canada. (2010). *Low income lines, 2008–2009.* Statistics Canada.

Statistics Canada. (2013). *Backgrounder: Aboriginal offenders – a critical situation.* Statistics Canada.

Statistics Finland. (2019). *Statistics on living conditions, 2018.* Statistics Finland.

Steinberg, S. (1985). Human capital: A critique. *Review of Black Political Economy, 14*(1), 67–74. https://doi.org/10.1007/BF02902610

Steinberg, S. (1997). Science and politics in the work of William Julius Wilson. *New Politics, 6*(2). https://archive.newpol.org/issue22/steinb22.htm

Steinberg, S. (2007). *Race relations: A critique.* Stanford University Press.

Steinberg, S. (2011, January 13). Poor reason: Culture still doesn't explain poverty. *Boston Review.*

Steinberg, S. (2015, June 24). The Moynihan Report at fifty: The long reach of intellectual racism. *Boston Review*.

Stephens, J.D. (1980). *The transition from capitalism to socialism*. Humanities Press.

Sternberg, R.J. (1985). *Beyond IQ: A triarchic theory of intelligence*. Cambridge University Press.

Steven, P. (2004). *The no-nonsense guide to global media*. Verso.

Stevens, A.H. (1999). Climbing out of poverty, falling back in: Measuring the persistence of poverty over multiple spells. *Journal of Human Resources, 34*(3), 557–588. https://doi.org/10.2307/146380

Stiglitz, J.E. (2010). Lessons from the global financial crisis of 2008. *Seoul Journal of Economics, 23*(3), 321–339. https://www8.gsb.columbia.edu /faculty/jstiglitz/sites/jstiglitz/files/2010_Lessons_Global_Financial_Crisis _Seoul.pdf

Stiglitz, J.E. (2013). *The price of inequality: How today's divided society endangers our future*. W.W. Norton and Company.

Stiglitz, J.E., Tucker, T.N., & Zucman, G. (2020). The starving state: Why capitalism's salvation depends on taxation. *Foreign Affairs, 99*(1), 30–37. https://www.foreignaffairs.com/articles/united-states/2019-12-10 /starving-state

Stoesz, D., & Karger, H.J. (1993). Deconstructing welfare: The Reagan legacy and the welfare state. *Social Work, 38*(5), 619–628. https://doi.org/10.1093 /sw/38.5.619

Street Health. (2007). *The Street Health report, 2007*. Street Health.

Streib, J., Verma, S.J., Welsh, W., & Burton, L.M. (2016). Life, death, and resurrections: The culture of poverty perspective. In D. Brady & L.M. Burton (Eds.), *The Oxford handbook of the social science of poverty* (pp. 247–269). Oxford University Press.

Stringer, L. (1999). *Grand Central winter: Stories from the street*. Pocket Books.

Stromwell, L.K., Brzuzy, S., Sharp, P., & Andersen, C. (1998). The implications of welfare reform for American Indian families and communities. *Journal of Poverty, 2*(4), 1–15. https://doi.org/10.1300/J134v02n04_01

Sullivan, A. (2018, March 30). Denying genetics isn't shutting down racism, it's fueling it. *Intelligencer*. https://nymag.com/intelligencer/2018/03 /denying-genetics-isnt-shutting-down-racism-its-fueling-it.html

Sumner, W.G. (1963). *Social Darwinism: Selected essays of William Graham Sumner*. Prentice-Hall.

Sumner, W.G. (1974). *What social classes owe to each other*. The Caxton Printers. (Original work published 1883)

Svallfors, S. (1991). The politics of welfare policy in Sweden: Structural determinants and attitudinal cleavages. *British Journal of Sociology, 42*(4), 609–634. https://doi.org/10.2307/591450

Svallfors, S. (1997). Worlds of welfare and attitudes to redistribution: A comparison of eight Western nations. *European Sociological Review, 13*(3), 283–304. https://doi.org/10.1093/oxfordjournals.esr.a018219

Svallfors, S. (2003). Welfare regimes and welfare opinions: A comparison of eight Western countries. *Social Indicators Research, 69*(3), 495–520. https://doi.org/10.1023/A:1025931414917

Svallfors, S. (2010). Public attitudes. In F. Castles, S. Leibfried, J. Lewis, H. Obinger, & C. Pierson, *The Oxford handbook of the welfare state* (pp. 241–51). Oxford University Press.

Svallfors, S. (2011). A bedrock of support? Trends in welfare state attitudes in Sweden, 1981–2010. *Social Policy & Administration, 45*(7), 806–825. https://doi.org/10.1111/j.1467-9515.2011.00796.x

Svallfors, S. (2012). *Contested welfare states: Welfare attitudes in Europe and beyond.* Stanford University Press.

Swank, D. (2002). *Global capital, political institutions, and policy change in developed welfare states.* Cambridge University Press.

Swank, E. (1998). Clinton's domestic policy makers: Big business, think tanks, and welfare reform. *Journal of Poverty, 2*(1), 55–78. https://doi.org/10.1300/J134v02n01_03

Swanson, J. (2001). *Poor-bashing: The politics of exclusion.* Between the Lines.

Swift, R. (2014). *Alternatives to capitalism.* Between the Lines.

Tanner, M., & Hughes, C. (2013). *The work versus welfare trade-off, 2013: An analysis of the total level of welfare benefits by state.* Cato Institute.

Tarasuk, V., Mitchell, A., & Dachner, N. (2012). *Household food insecurity, 2012.* Research to Identify Policy Options to Reduce Food Insecurity (PROOF).

Taylor-Gooby, P., & Leruth, B. (Eds.). (2018). *Attitudes, aspiration and welfare: Social policy directions in uncertain times.* Palgrave Macmillan.

Teixeira, L., & Cartwright, J. (Eds.). (2020). *Using evidence to end homelessness.* Policy Press.

Thane, P. (1978). Women and the poor law in Victorian and Edwardian England. *History Workshop: A Journal of Socialist Historians, 6*(Autumn), 9–51. https://doi.org/10.1093/hwj/6.1.29

Thane, P. (1996). *Foundations of the welfare state.* Routledge.

The Week Staff. (2019, November 29). Foreign influence: How US donors are funding UK right-wing groups. *The Week.* https://www.theweek.co.uk/104630/foreign-influence-how-us-donors-are-funding-uk-right-wing-groups

Thistle, J. (2019). From the ashes: My story of being Métis, homeless, and finding my way. Simon and Schuster.

Thomas, M. (2009). *Belching out the devil: Global adventures with Coca Cola.* Ebury Press.

Thompson, E.P. (1968). *The making of the English working class.* Penguin Books.

Titmuss, R.M. (1974). *Social policy: An introduction.* Allen & Unwin.

Torjman, S. (2010). *Poverty reduction in Québec: The first five years.* Caledon Institute of Social Policy.

Toro, P.A., Tompsett, C.J., Lombardo, S., Philippot, P., Nachtergael, H., Galand, B., Schlienz, N., Stammel, N., Yabar, Y., Blume, M., MacKay, L.,

& Harvey, K. (2007). Homelessness in Europe and the United States: A comparison of prevalence and public opinion. *Journal of Social Issues, 63*(3), 505–524. https://doi.org/10.1111/j.1540-4560.2007.00521.x

Townsend, I. (2004). *Poverty: Measures and targets* [Research Paper 04/23]. House of Commons Library.

Townsend, P. (1979). *Poverty in the United Kingdom: A survey of household resources and standards of living.* Penguin Books.

Townson, M. (2000). *A report card on women and poverty.* Canadian Centre for Policy Alternatives.

Trägårdh, L. (1990). Swedish model or Swedish culture? *Critical Review, 4*(4), 569–590. https://doi.org/10.1080/08913819008459622

Trattner, W.I. (1999). *From poor law to welfare state: A history of social welfare in America* (3rd ed.). The Free Press.

Tressell, R. (2008). *The ragged-trousered philanthropists.* Oxford University Press. (Original work published 1914)

Trudel, M. (2013). *Canada's forgotten slaves: Two hundred years of bondage.* Véhicule Press.

Truth and Reconciliation Commission of Canada. (2015). *Final report of the Truth and Reconciliation Commission of Canada: Volume 1 – Summary.* James Lorimer and Company.

Trydegård, G.-B. (2000). From poorhouse overseer to production manager: One hundred years of old-age care in Sweden reflected in the development of an occupation. *Aging and Society, 20*(5), 571–597. https://doi.org/10.1017/S0144686X99007928

Tucker, W.H. (2002). *The funding of scientific racism: Wickliffe Draper and the Pioneer Fund.* University of Illinois Press.

Turkheimer, E., Paige Harden, K., & Nisbett, R.E. (2017, May 18). Charles Murray is once again peddling junk science about race and IQ. *Vox.* https://www.vox.com/the-big-idea/2017/5/18/15655638/charles -murray-race-iq-sam-harris-science-free-speech

Twain, M., & Warner, C.D. (2006). *The gilded age.* The Modern Library. (Original work published 1873)

UN HRC (United Nations Human Rights Council). (2009). *Report of the special rapporteur on adequate housing as a component of the right to an adequate standard of living, and on the right to non-discrimination in this context.* United Nations.

UN HRC (United Nations Human Rights Council). (2014). *Report of the special rapporteur on the rights of Indigenous peoples: The situation of Indigenous peoples in Canada.* United Nations.

UN HRC (United Nations Human Rights Council). (2017). *Report of the working group of experts on people of African descent on its mission to Canada.* United Nations.

UN HRC (United Nations Human Rights Council). (2019). *Report of the special rapporteur on extreme poverty and human rights on his visit to the United Kingdom of Great Britain and Northern Ireland.* United Nations.

UNDP (United Nations Human Development Program). (1997). *Human development report 1997*. Oxford University Press.

United Nations. (2017). *Report of the special rapporteur on adequate housing as a component of the right to an adequate standard of living, and on the right to non-discrimination in this context*. United Nations.

United Nations High Commissioner for Human Rights. (2016). *Improving accountability and access to remedy for victims of business-related human rights abuse*. United Nations.

Urban Institute. (2000). *Millions still face homelessness in a booming economy*. Urban Institute.

Urban Matters, & BC Non-Profit Housing Association. (2018). *Vancouver homeless count 2018*. City of Vancouver.

US Census Bureau. (2012). *The emergency and transitional shelter population: 2010 Special Census reports*. Government Printing Office.

US Census Bureau. (2013). *Income, poverty, and health insurance coverage in the United States: 2012*. US Government Printing Office.

US Census Bureau. (2014). *Income and poverty in the United States: 2013*. US Government Printing Office.

US Census Bureau. (2019a). *Income and poverty in the United States: 2018*. US Government Printing Office.

US Census Bureau. (2019b). *The supplemental poverty measure: 2018*. US Government Printing Office.

US Conference of Mayors. (2007). *Hunger and homelessness survey: A status report on hunger and homelessness in America's cities – A 23-city survey*. US Conference of Mayors.

US Department of Housing and Urban Development (HUD). (2013). *The 2013 annual homeless assessment report (AHAR) to Congress: Part 1, Point-in-time estimates of homelessness*. US Department of Housing and Urban Development.

US Department of Housing and Urban Development (HUD). (2017). *The 2017 annual homeless assessment report (AHAR) to Congress: Part 1, Point-in-time estimates of homelessness*. US Department of Housing and Urban Development.

US Department of Labor. (2019). *Bureau of Labor statistics*. https://www.bls.gov/

Useem, M. (1986). *The inner circle: Large corporations and the rise of business political activity in the US and the UK*. Oxford University Press.

Valencia, A.S. (2018). *The future of work: Super exploitation and social precariousness in the 21st century*. Haymarket Books.

Valentine, C. (1968). *Culture and poverty: A critique and counterproposal*. University of Chicago Press.

van den Berg, A., Plante, C., Raïq, H., Proulx, C., & Faustmann, S. (2017). *Combatting poverty: Quebec's pursuit of a distinctive welfare state*. University of Toronto Press.

Van Kersbergen, K., & Vis, B. (2014). *Comparative welfare state politics: Development, opportunities, and reform.* Cambridge University Press.

van Praag, B.M.S., Hagenaars, A.J.M., & van Weeren, H. (1982). Poverty in Europe. *Review of Income and Wealth, 28*(3), 345–359. https://doi.org /10.1111/j.1475-4991.1982.tb00621.x

Veall, M.R. (2012). Top income shares in Canada: Recent trends and policy implications. *Canadian Journal of Economics, 45*(4), 1247–1272. https://doi. org/10.1111/j.1540-5982.2012.01744.x

Veit-Wilson, J.H. (1986). Paradigms of poverty: A rehabilitation of B.S. Rowntree. *Journal of Social Policy, 15*(1), 69–99. https://doi.org/10.1017 /S0047279400023114

Verbruggen, R. (2020, February 5). What science can tell us about race, gender, and class differences. *National Review.* https://www.nationalreview.com /magazine/2020/02/24/what-science-can-tell-us-about-race-gender -and-class-differences/

Vinton, K. (2016). These 15 billionaires own America's news media companies. *Forbes.* https://www.forbes.com/sites/katevinton/2016/06 /01/these-15-billionaires-own-americas-news-media-companies /#470ed47a660a

Vlachantoni, A., Feng, Z., Evandrou, M., & Falkingham, J. (2017). Ethnic elders and pension protection in the United Kingdom. *Aging & Society, 37*(5), 1025–1049. https://doi.org/10.1017/S0144686X16000143

Vlachantoni, A., Shaw, R.J., Evandrou, M., & Falkingham, J. (2015). The determinants of receiving social care in later life in England. *Aging & Society, 35*(2), 321–345. https://doi.org/10.1017/S0144686X1300072X

Volscho, T.W., & Kelley, N.J. (2012). The rise of the super-rich: Power resources, taxes, financial markets, and the dynamics of the top 1 percent, 1949 to 2008. *American Sociological Review, 77*(5), 679–699. https://doi. org/10.1177/0003122412458508

Vosko, L.F., & Closing the Enforcement Gap Research Group. (2020). *Closing the enforcement gap: Improving employment standards protections for people in precarious jobs.* University of Toronto Press.

Voss, K. (1993). *The making of American exceptionalism: The Knights of Labor and class formation in the nineteenth century.* Cornell University Press.

Wacquant, L. (2009). *Punishing the poor: The neoliberal government of social insecurity.* Duke University Press.

Wacquant, L., & Wilson, W.J. (1989). The cost of racial and class exclusion in the inner city. *Annals of the American Academy of Political and Social Science, 501*(1), 8–25. https://doi.org/10.1177/0002716289501001001

Wade, N. (2015). *A troublesome inheritance: Genes, race, and human history.* Penguin.

Wagner, D. (2005). *The poorhouse: America's forgotten institution.* Rowman and Littlefield.

Waldfogel, J. (2010). *Britain's war on poverty.* Russell Sage Foundation.

Waldfogel, J. (2013). The safety net for families with children. In M.J. Bailey & S. Danziger (Eds.), *Legacies of the war on poverty* (pp. 153–178). Russell Sage Foundation.

Waldron, J. (1997). Homelessness and the issue of freedom. In R.E. Goodin & P.P. Pettit (Eds.), *Contemporary political philosophy: An anthology* (pp. 446–462). Blackwell.

Waller, R., Ingram, N., & Ward, M.R.M. (Eds.). (2018). *Higher education and social inequalities.* Routledge.

Walmsley, R. (2013). *World prison population* (10th ed.). International Centre for Prison Studies, King's College London.

Webb, S., & Webb, B. (1927). *English local government: English poor law history – Part 1, The old poor law.* Longmans, Green and Co.

Weekes-Bernard, D. (2017). *Poverty and ethnicity in the labour market.* Joseph Rowntree Foundation.

Welshman, J. (2002). The cycle of deprivation and the concept of an underclass. *Benefits, 10*(3), 199–205. https://eprints.lancs.ac.uk/id/eprint/13623

Welshman, J. (2006). *Underclass: A history of the excluded.* Hamilton Continuum.

West, D. (2014). *Billionaires: Reflections on the upper crust.* Brookings Institution.

Western, B., & Beckett, K. (1999). How unregulated is the US labor market? The penal system as a labor market institution. *American Journal of Sociology, 104*(4), 1030–1060). https://doi.org/10.1086/210135

Western, B., & Pettit, B. (2010). Incarceration and social inequality. *Daedalus, 139*(3), 8–19. https://doi.org/10.1162/DAED_a_00019

White, J. (1979). Andrew Carnegie and Herbert Spencer: A special relationship. *Journal of American Studies, 13*(1), 57–71. https://doi.org/10.1017/S002187580000709X

White, L. (2017). Which ideas, whose norms? Comparing the relative influence of international organizations on paid maternity and parental leave policies in liberal welfare states. *Social Politics, 24*(1), 55–80. https://doi.org/10.1093/sp/jxw010

Whitely, R. (1999). *Divergent capitalisms: The social structure and change of business systems.* Oxford University Press.

WHO (World Health Organization). (1995). *The world health report 1995: Bridging the gaps.* World Health Organization.

Whyte, D. (2020). *Ecocide: Kill the corporation before it kills us.* Manchester University Press.

Wiederspan, J., Rhodes, E., & Shaefer, H.L. (2105). Expanding the discourse on antipoverty policy: Reconsidering a negative income tax. *Journal of Poverty, 19*(2), 218–238. https://doi.org/10.1080/10875549.2014.991889

Wilensky, H.L. (1975). *The welfare state and equality.* University of California Press.

Wilensky, H.L., & Lebeaux, C.N. (1965). *Industrial society and social welfare.* The Free Press.

Wilkerson, I. (2020). *Caste: The origins of our discontents*. Random House.

Wilkinson, R.G. (1996). *Unhealthy societies: The afflictions of inequality*. Routledge.

Wilkinson, R.G. (2005). *The impact of inequality: How to make sick societies healthier*. The New Press.

Wilkinson, R.G., & Pickett, K.E. (2006). Income inequality and population health: A review and explanation of the evidence. *Social Science and Medicine, 62*(7), 1768–1784. https://doi.org/10.1016/j.socscimed.2005.08.036

Wilkinson, R.G., & Pickett, K.E. (2010). *The spirit level: Why equality is better for everyone*. Penguin Books.

Wilkinson, R.G., & Pickett, K.E. (2019). *The inner level: How more equal societies reduce stress, restore sanity, and improve everyone's well-being*. Penguin Press.

Williams, F. (1977). *Why the poor pay more*. Macmillan.

Williams, H.V. (1944). Benjamin Franklin and the poor laws. *Social Service Review, 18*(1), 77–91. https://doi.org/10.1086/634737

Williams, R. (1973). Base and superstructure in Marxist cultural theory. *New Left Review, 82*(November/December), 3–16.

Willie, C.V. (1978). The inclining significance of race. *Society, 125*(5), 10, 12–15. https://doi.org/10.1007/BF02701608

Wilson, D. (1979). *The welfare state in Sweden: A study in comparative social administration*. Heinemann.

Wilson, D., & Macdonald, D. (2010). *The income gap between Aboriginal peoples and the rest of Canada*. Canadian Centre for Policy Alternatives.

Wilson, V., & Schieder, J. (2018). *Countries investing more in social programs have less child poverty*. Economic Policy Institute. https://www.epi.org/publication/countries-investing-more-in-social-programs-have-less-child-poverty/

Wilson, W.J. (1978). *The declining significance of race*. University of Chicago Press.

Wilson, W.J. (1987). *The truly disadvantaged: The inner city, the underclass, and public policy*. Chicago University Press.

Wilson, W.J. (1996). *When work disappears*. Alfred A. Knopf.

Wilson, W.J. (2010). Why both social structure and culture matter in a holistic analysis of inner-city poverty. *Annals of the American Academy of Political and Social Science, 629*(1), 200–219.

Wimer, C., Collyer, S., & Jaravel, X. (2019). *The cost of being poor: Inflation inequality leads to three million more people in poverty*. The Groundwork Collaborative, Center on Poverty and Social Policy, Columbia University. https://groundworkcollaborative.org/wp-content/uploads/2019/11/The-Costs-of-Being-Poor-Groundwork-Collaborative.pdf

Winkler, A. (2018a, March 5). "Corporations are people" is built on an incredible 19th-century lie. *The Atlantic*.

Winkler, A. (2018b). *We the corporations: How American businesses won their civil rights*. W.W. Norton & Company.

Winks, R.W. (1997). *The Blacks in Canada: A history.* McGill-Queen's University Press.

Witoszek, N., & Midttun, A. (Eds.). (2018). *Sustainable modernity: The Nordic model and beyond.* Routledge.

Wolff, E.N. (2017). *A century of wealth in America.* Harvard University Press.

Wolff, R. (2012). *Occupy the economy: Challenging capitalism.* City Lights Publishing.

Woloch, I. (1994). *The new regime: Transformations of the French civic order, 1789–1820s.* W.W. Norton & Company.

Woodbury, S.A. (1993). Culture and human capital theory: Theory and evidence or theory versus evidence. In W. Darity Jr. (Ed.), *Labor economics: Problems in analyzing labor markets* (pp. 269–294). Kluwer.

Woodward, D. (2010). *How poor is poor? Towards a rights-based poverty line.* New Economics Foundation.

World Bank (2008). *2008 World development indicators – Poverty data: A supplement to world development indicators 2008.* World Bank.

Wright, E.O. (1994). *Interrogating inequality: Essays on class analysis, socialism, and Marxism.* Verso.

Wright, E.O. (1995). The class analysis of poverty. *International Journal of Health Services, 25*(1), 85–100. https://doi.org/10.2190/WYRM-630N-8M6V-7851

Wright, E.O. (2000). Working-class power, capitalist class interests and class compromise. *American Journal of Sociology, 105*(4), 957–1002. https://doi.org/10.1086/210397

Wright, E.O. (2004). Basic income, stakeholder grants and class analysis. *Politics and Society, 32*(1), 79–87. https://doi.org/10.1177/0032329203261099

Wright, E.O. (2010). *Envisioning real utopias.* Verso.

Wright, E.O. (2019). *How to be an anti-capitalist in the 21st century.* Verso.

Wright, E.O., & Rogers, J. (2015). *American society: How it really works.* W.W. Norton & Company.

Yalnizyan, A. (2010). *The rise of Canada's richest 1%.* Canadian Centre for Policy Alternatives.

Zinn, H. (2003). *A people's history of the United States.* Harper Perennial.

Zuberi, D. (2006). *Differences that matter: Social policy and the working poor in the United States and Canada.* ILR Press.

Zumoff, J.A. (2020). The left in the United States and the decline of the Socialist Party of America, 1934–1935. *Labour/Le Travail, 85*(Spring), 165–198. https://doi.org/10.1353/llt.2020.0006

Index

incarceration, 219, 225n7
inclusive poverty, 20–21
inclusive studies, *vs.* comparative
    contrasts, 10–11
income
    in Anglo nations, 62
    basic income (BI), 215–16, 224n2,
        224n4
    as indicator of poverty, 21
    inequalities in Anglo nations, 92,
        93, 128, 130, 200
    in measures in Canada, 38–39
    in measures in UK, 84
    and poverty in US, 64–65
    in relative poverty measures, 34, 84
    spending on measures, 116
    transfers in welfare states, 111–117
income poverty, in UK, 36
income supports pillar of welfare
        states, 110, 111–117
Indigenous peoples in Canada
    as homeless, 83
    living conditions, 80
    poverty rates, 75, 76, 79–80
    as term, 97n14
    treatment in Canada, 75–76
    See also Native Americans
"individualistic" cultures and values,
        162–163
individuals
    in explanation of poverty,
        141–143, 171
    historical roots of individualistic
        poverty, 143–147
    See also "culture of poverty"; poor
        people
inequalities
    in Anglo nations, 3, 6, 93, 200
    and capitalism, 7–8, 220
    in income, 92, 93, 128, 130, 200
    increase, 3, 6, 199–200
    reasons for, 3–4
    solutions, 200
    in US, 3, 193–194

insecure housing (homelessness),
        42, 43, 44
Institute on Taxation and Economic
        Policy, 221
intelligence and IQ, 148–150
intelligence tests, 148, 149, 166n15
involuntary minorities, 67–70, 75

Jenkins, Stephen, 88
Jensen, Arthur, 148
Johnson, Lyndon, 102

labor and labor market
    and basic income (BI), 215–216
    in capitalism, 174–75, 177, 180
    and globalization, 180, 182–183
    and poor relief, 122, 123, 124
    and power, 196–197, 198
    and protective legislation,
        119–120
    segmentation of market, 173
    in US, 66–67, 183
    See also unions and unionization
land occupation, 76
Lansley, Stewart, 28
leftist parties, 192, 193,
        205–206n25
"legal welfare," 110, 119–121, 213
Lewis, Hylan, 155–156
Lewis, Oscar, 152–53
LGBTQ2S people, 48
liberalism, in neoliberalism, 8
liberal regimes. *See* Anglo nations
liberal welfare states, 103, 104–107,
        112–113, 118–119
Liebow, Elliot, 155–156
long-term poverty, 57, 71
"low income," as euphemism, 75
Low Income Cut-Offs (LICOs),
        38–39, 40, 75, 78, 81, 97n13
Low Income Measure (LIM), 38, 80,
        97–98n16
low-income neighborhoods and
        communities, 60–62